VOL. 27
VIZ Media Edition

Story and Art by
RUMIKO TAKAHASHI

English Adaptation by Gerard Jones

Translation/Mari Morimoto
Touch-Up Art & Lettering/Bill Schuch
Cover and Interior Graphic Design/Yuki Ameda
Editor/Ian Robertson

Managing Editor/Annette Roman
Editorial Director/Elizabeth Kawasaki
Editor in Chief/Alvin Lu
Sr. Director of Acquisitions/Rika Inouye
Sr. VP of Marketing/Liza Coppola
Exec. VP of Sales & Marketing/John Easum
Publisher/Hyoe Narita

Printed in the U.S.A.

Published by VIZ Media, LLC
P.O. Box 77010
San Francisco, CA 94107

VIZ Media Edition
10 9 8 7 6 5 4 3 2 1
First printing, October 2006

www.viz.com store.viz.com

INUYASHA

™

VOL. 27

VIZ Media Edition

STORY AND ART BY
RUMIKO TAKAHASHI

CONTENTS

Long ago, in the "Warring States" era of Japan's Muromachi period (*Sengoku-jidai*, approximately 1467-1568 CE), a legendary dog-like half-demon called "Inuyasha" attempted to steal the Shikon Jewel—or "Jewel of Four Souls"—from a village, but was stopped by the enchanted arrow of the village priestess, Kikyo. Inuyasha fell into a deep sleep, pinned to a tree by Kikyo's arrow, while the mortally wounded Kikyo took the Shikon Jewel with her into the fires of her funeral pyre. Years passed.

Fast-forward to the present day. Kagome, a Japanese high school girl, is pulled into a well one day by a mysterious centipede monster and finds herself transported into the past—only to come face to face with the trapped Inuyasha. She frees him, and Inuyasha easily defeats the centipede monster.

The residents of the village, now 50 years older, readily accept Kagome as the reincarnation of their deceased priestess Kikyo, a claim supported by the fact that the Shikon Jewel emerges from a cut on Kagome's body. Unfortunately, the jewel's rediscovery means that the village is soon under attack by a variety of demons in search of this treasure. Then, the jewel is accidentally shattered into many shards, each of which may have the fearsome power of the entire jewel.

Although Inuyasha says he hates Kagome because of her resemblance to Kikyo, the woman who "killed" him, he is forced to team up with her when Kaede, the village leader, binds him to Kagome with a powerful spell. Now the two grudging companions must fight to reclaim and reassemble the shattered shards of the Shikon Jewel before they fall into the wrong hands...

THIS VOLUME Inuyasha and comrades are in the battle of their lives as they fend off the vicious attacks of the undead assassins known as the Band of Seven. But Inuyasha gains some unlikely comrades in his fight when his brother Sesshōmaru and feral rival Koga get entangled in the skirmish. As the Band of Seven's numbers dwindle, their increasingly desperate attacks push Inuyasha's new allies to their limits. All comes to a fiery climax as another of Naraku's malevolent plots is revealed!

INUYASHA
Half-demon hybrid, son of a human mother and demon father. His necklace is enchanted, allowing Kagome to control him with a word.

KAGOME
Modern-day Japanese schoolgirl who can travel back and forth between the past and present through an enchanted well.

MIROKU
Lecherous Buddhist priest cursed with a mystical "hellhole" in his hand that's slowly killing him.

NARAKU
Enigmatic demon-mastermind behind the miseries of nearly everyone in the story.

SANGO
"Demon Exterminator" or slayer from the village where the Shikon Jewel was first born.

KOGA
Leader of the Wolf Clan, Koga is himself a Wolf Demon and, because of several Shikon shards in his legs, possesses super speed. Enamored of Kagome, he quarrels with Inuyasha frequently.

BAND OF SEVEN
A group of undead killers brought back to life by Naraku through the powers of the Shikon Jewel Shards.

SCROLL ONE

EXPLOSION!

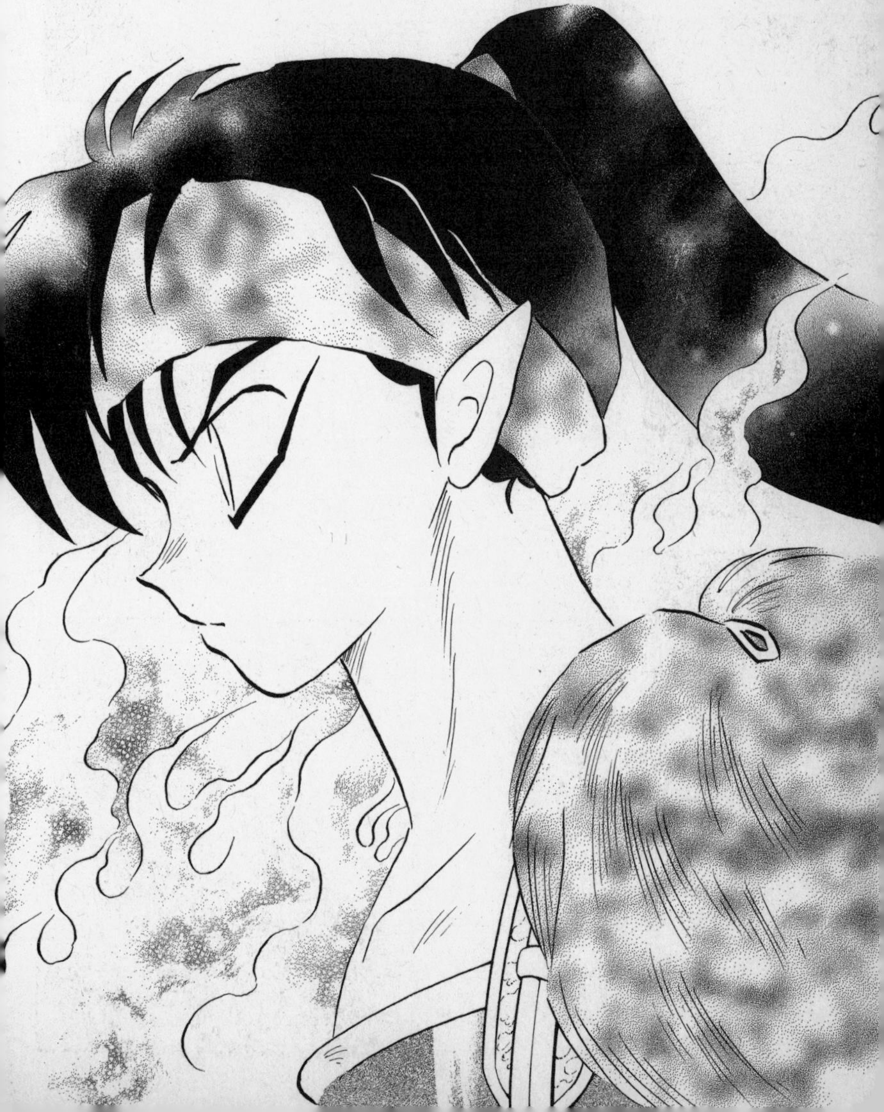

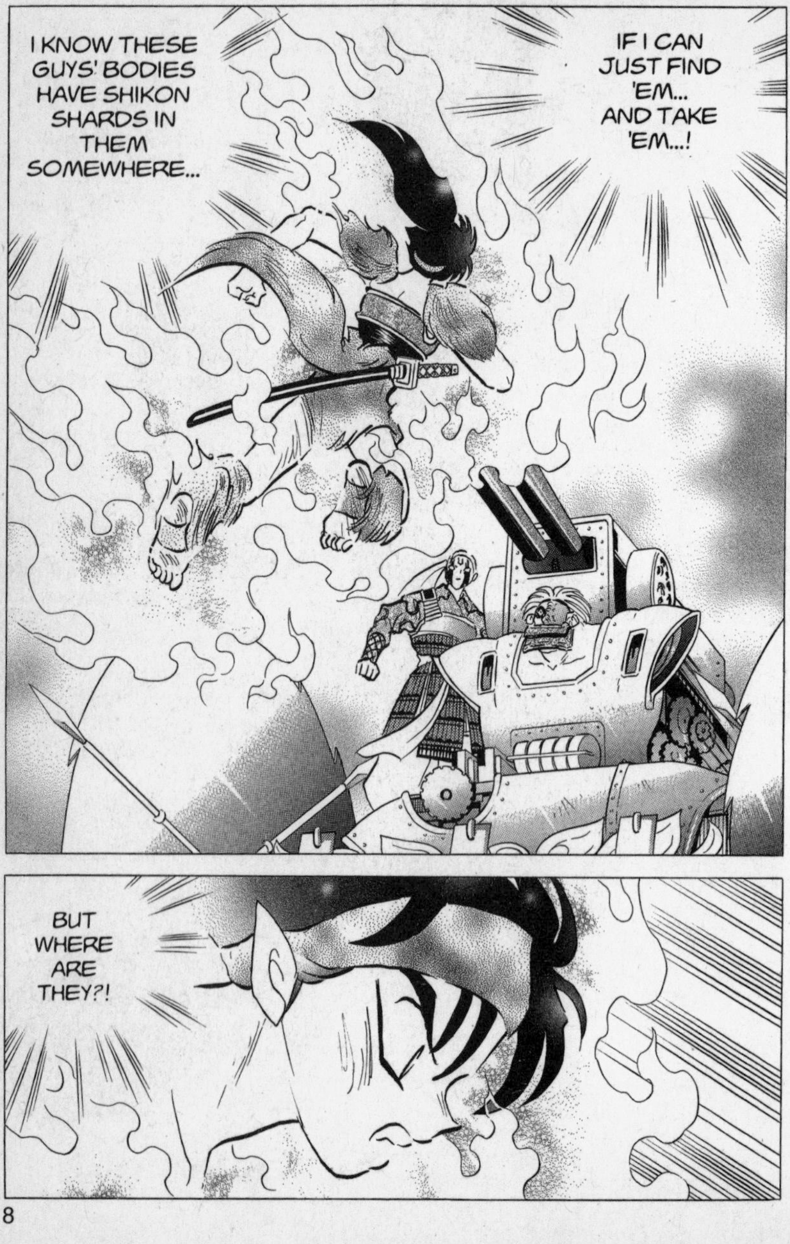
IF I CAN JUST FIND 'EM... AND TAKE 'EM...!
I KNOW THESE GUYS' BODIES HAVE SHIKON SHARDS IN THEM SOMEWHERE...
BUT WHERE ARE THEY?!

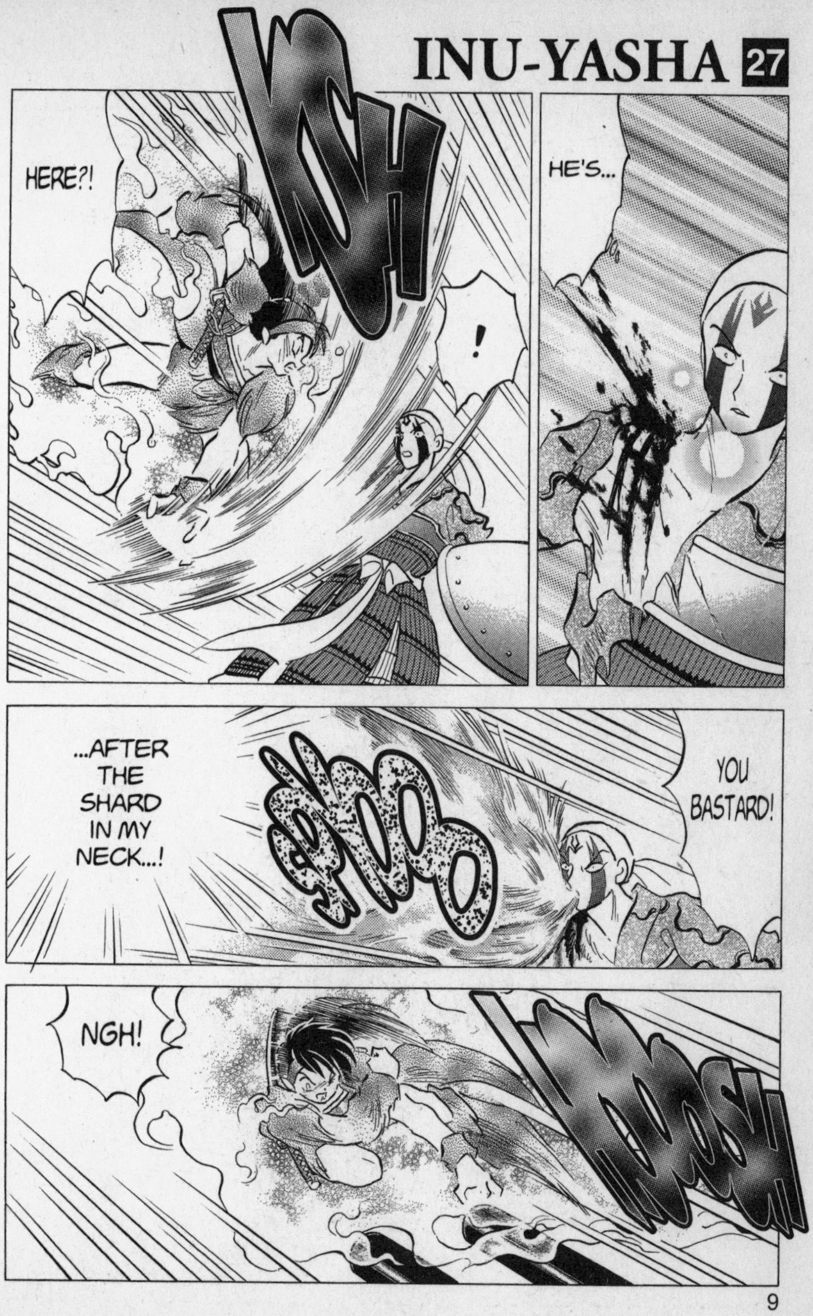
HE'S...
KCH
HERE?!
!
YOU BASTARD!
...AFTER THE SHARD IN MY NECK...!
NGH!

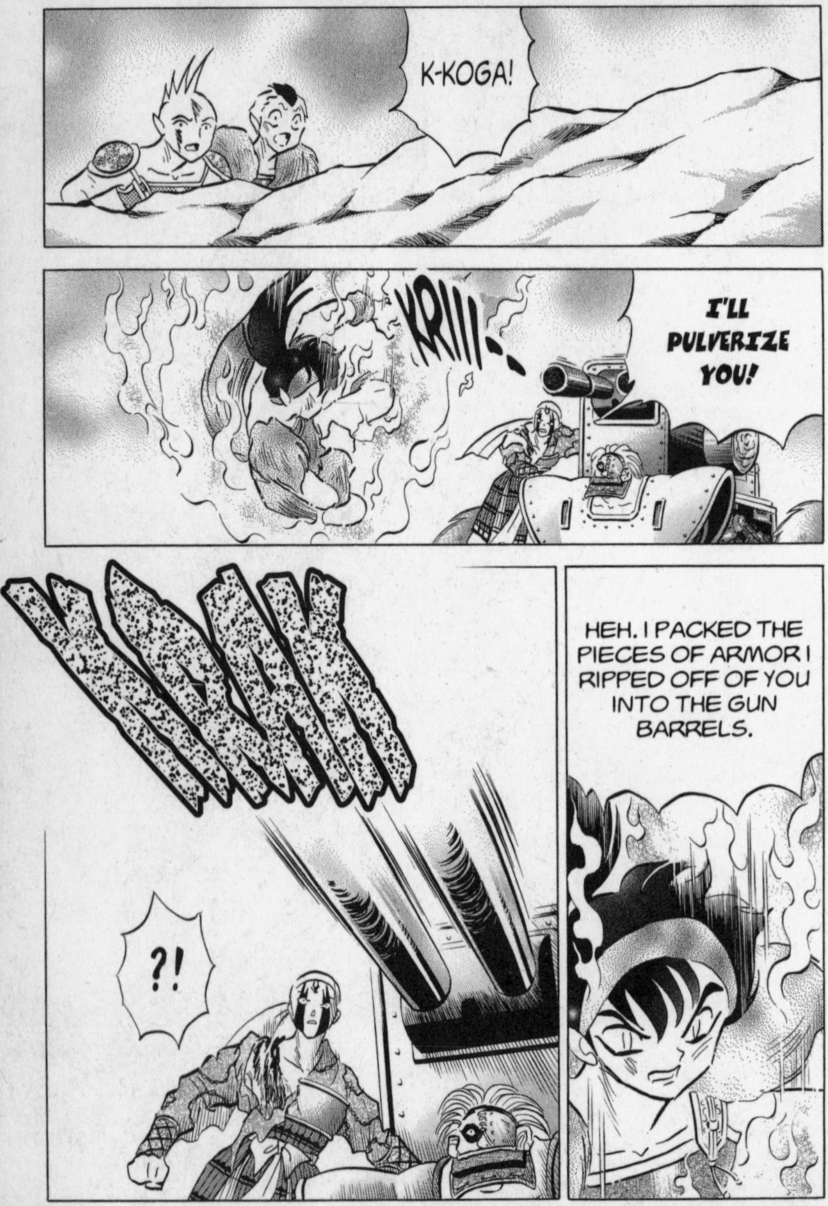
K-KOGA!
KRIIII...
I'LL PULVERIZE YOU!
HEH. I PACKED THE PIECES OF ARMOR I RIPPED OFF OF YOU INTO THE GUN BARRELS.
?!

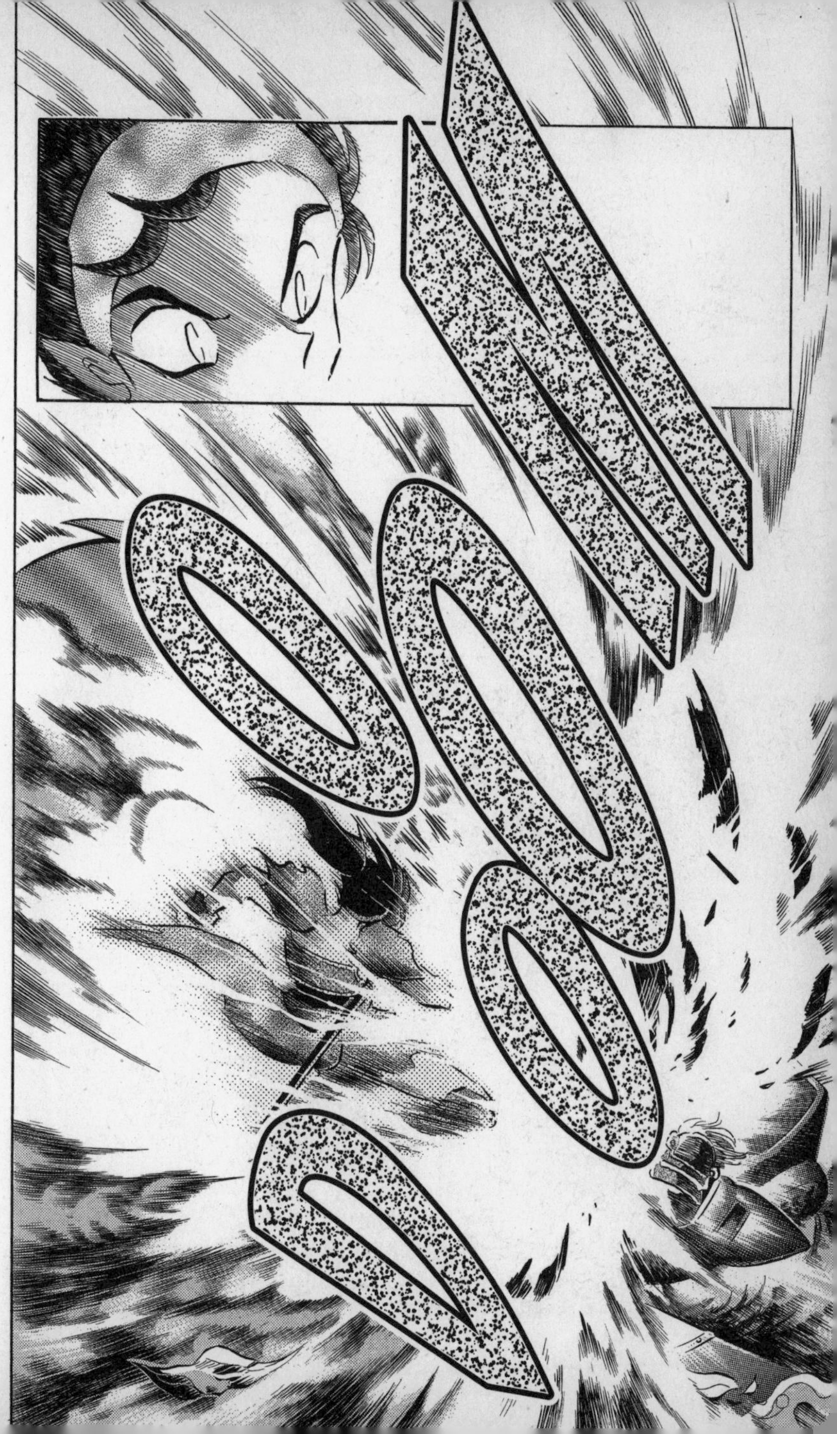
DOOM

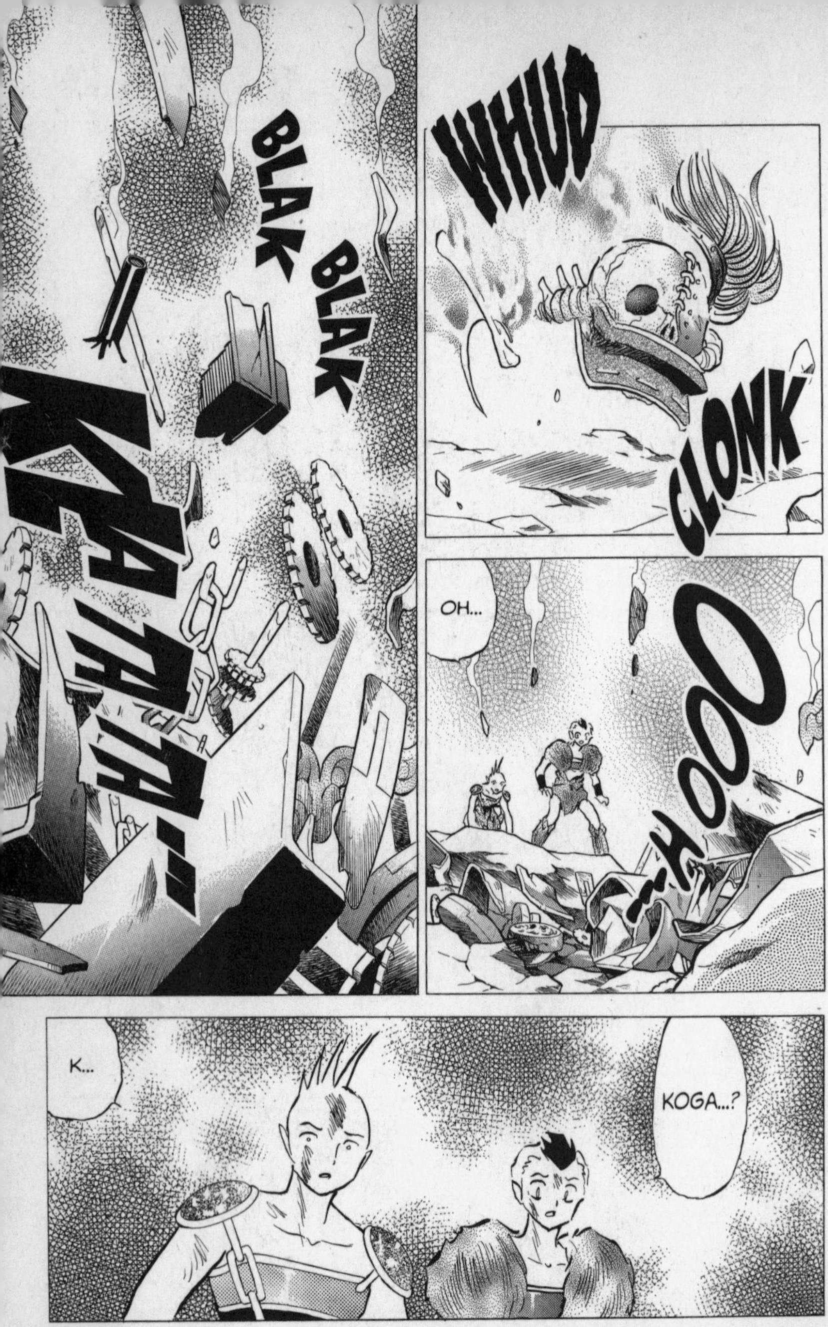
WHUD
CLONK
BLAK BLAK
OH...
--HOOO
KOGA...?
K...

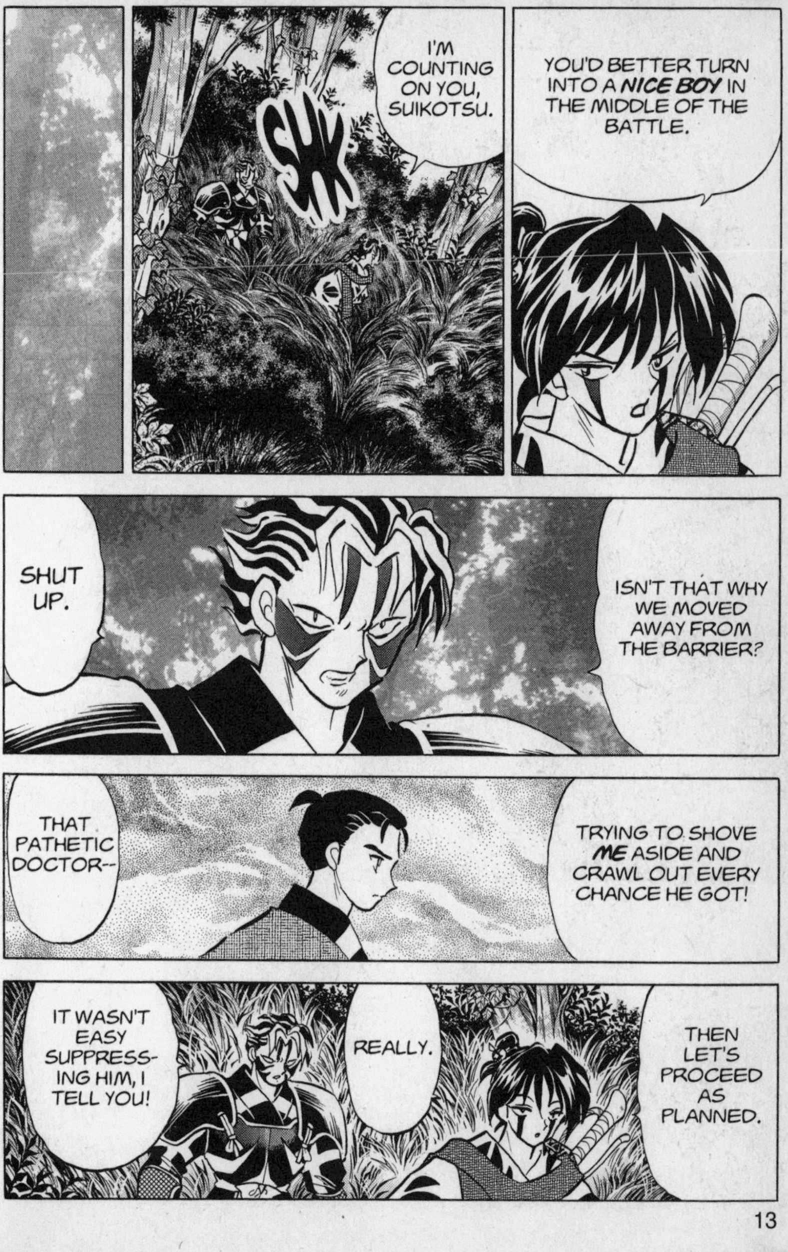
SHK
I'M COUNTING ON YOU, SUIKOTSU.
YOU'D BETTER TURN INTO A ***NICE BOY*** IN THE MIDDLE OF THE BATTLE.
ISN'T THAT WHY WE MOVED AWAY FROM THE BARRIER?
SHUT UP.
THAT PATHETIC DOCTOR--
TRYING TO SHOVE ***ME*** ASIDE AND CRAWL OUT EVERY CHANCE HE GOT!
IT WASN'T EASY SUPPRESS-ING HIM, I TELL YOU!
REALLY.
THEN LET'S PROCEED AS PLANNED.

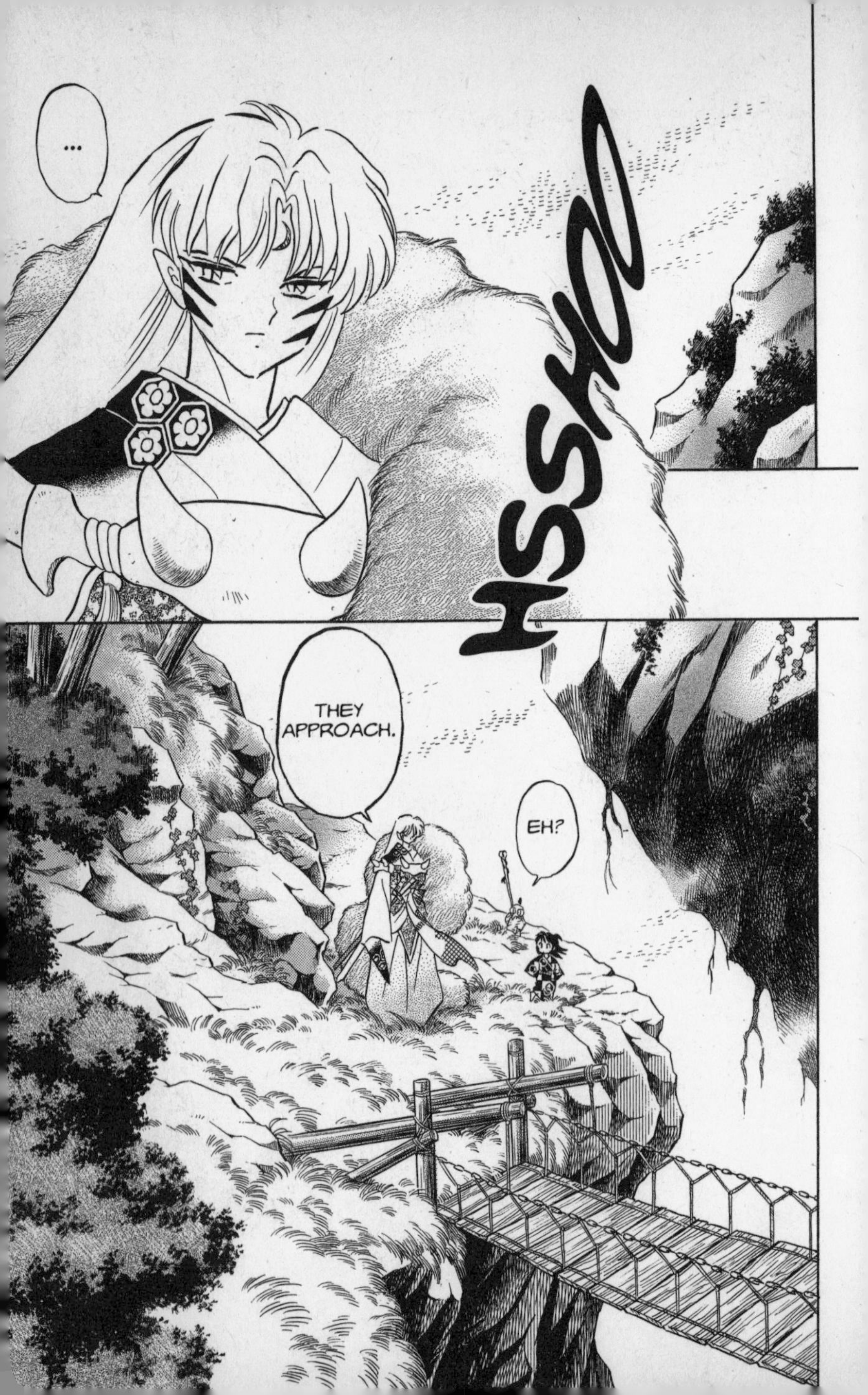
...
HSSHA
THEY APPROACH.
EH?

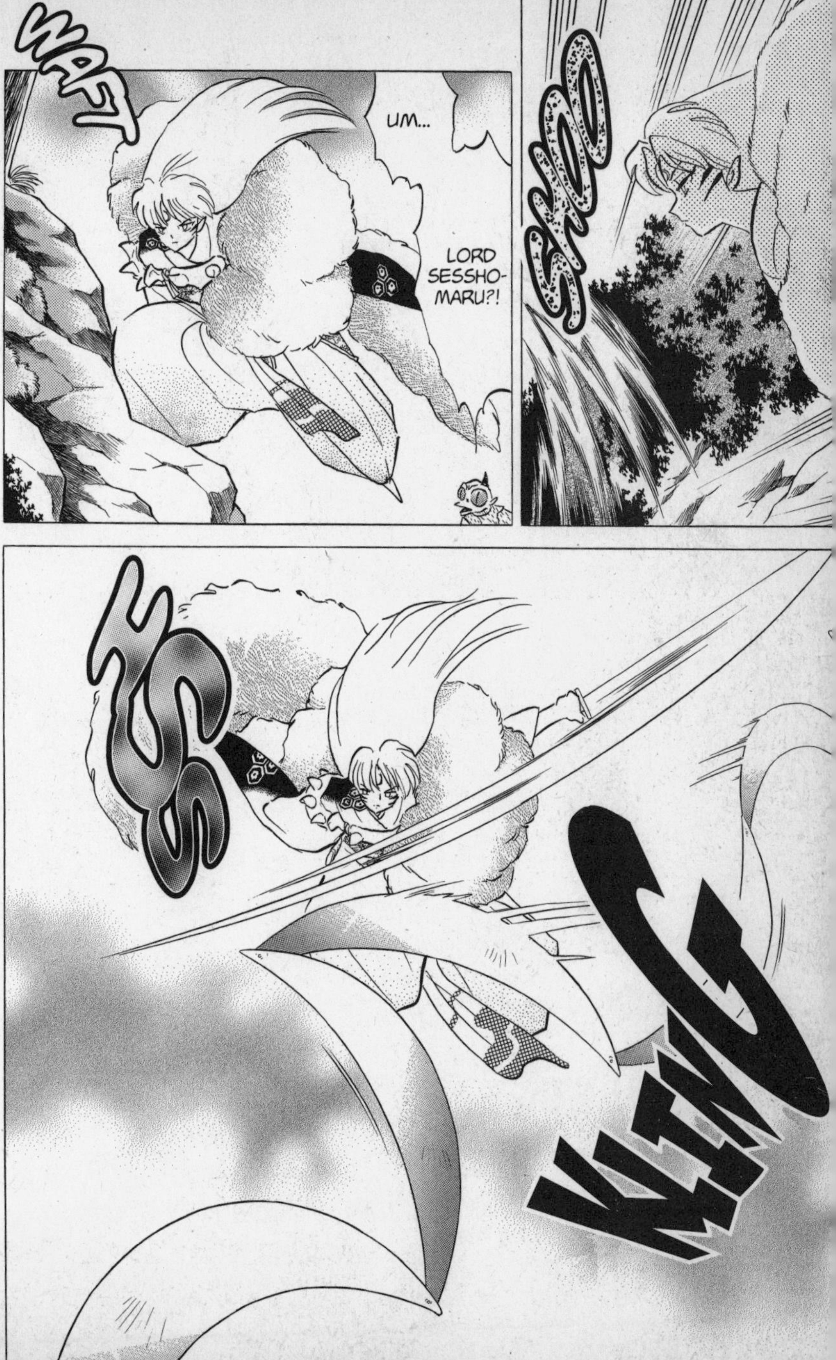
SHOO
LORD SESSHO-MARU?!
UM...
WAFT
KLING
SSH

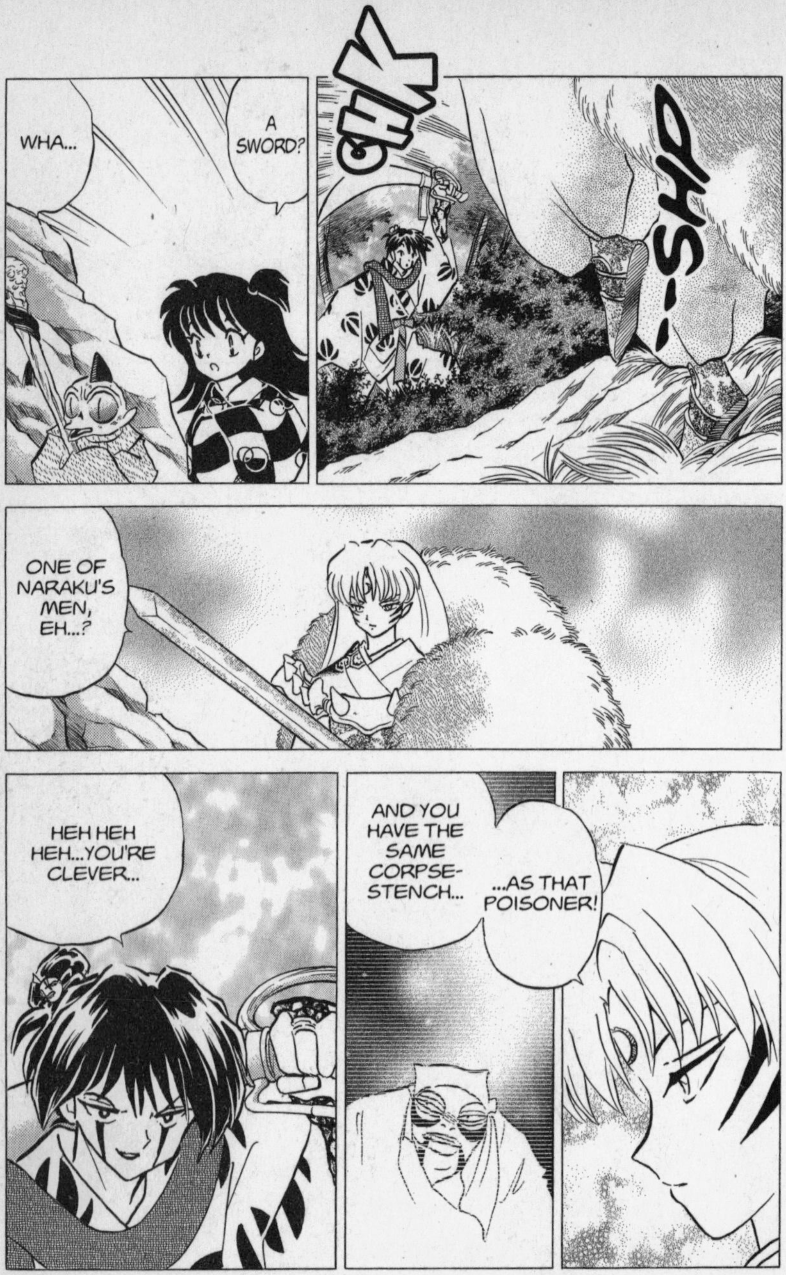
WHA...
A SWORD?
CHK
SHP
ONE OF NARAKU'S MEN, EH...?
HEH HEH HEH...YOU'RE CLEVER...
AND YOU HAVE THE SAME CORPSE-STENCH...
...AS THAT POISONER!

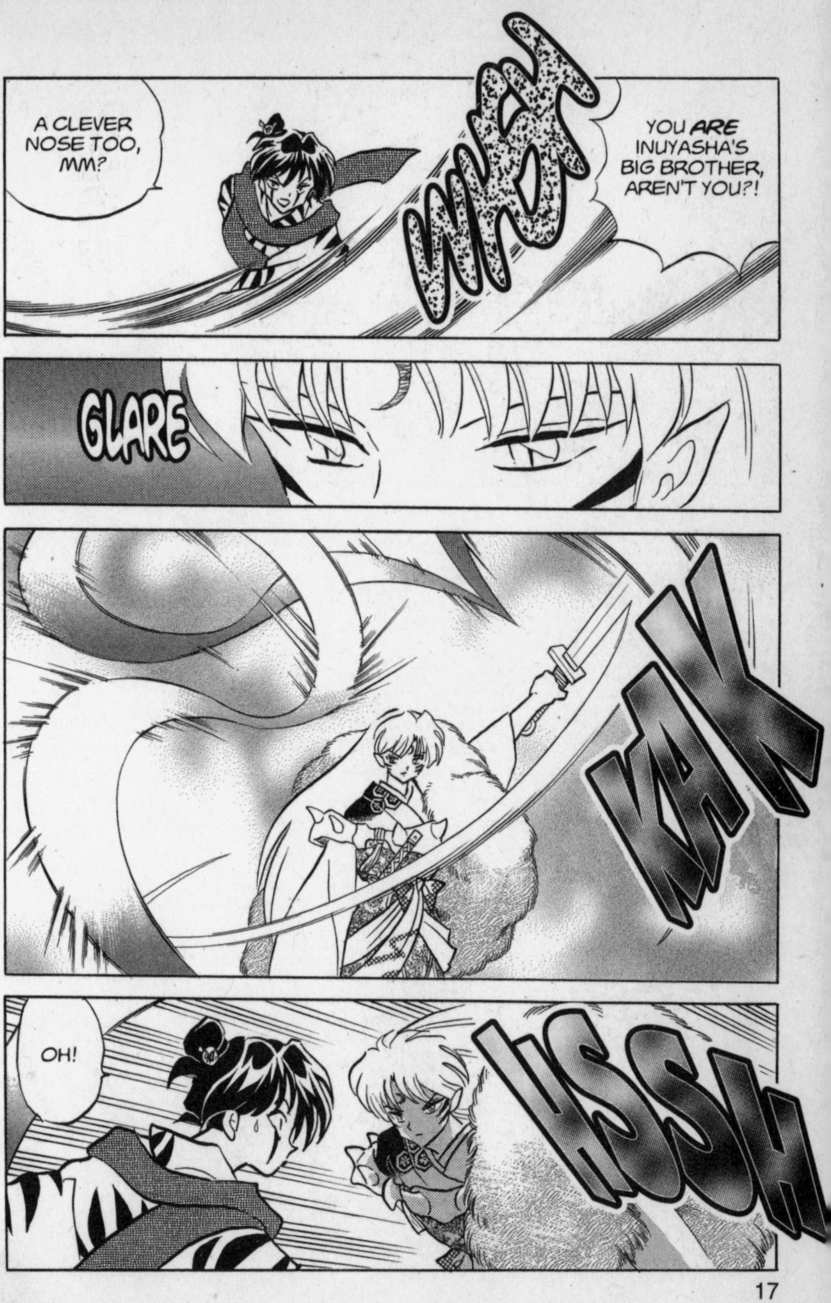
YOU ARE INUYASHA'S BIG BROTHER, AREN'T YOU?!
WHIFF
A CLEVER NOSE TOO, MM?
GLARE
KAK
OH!

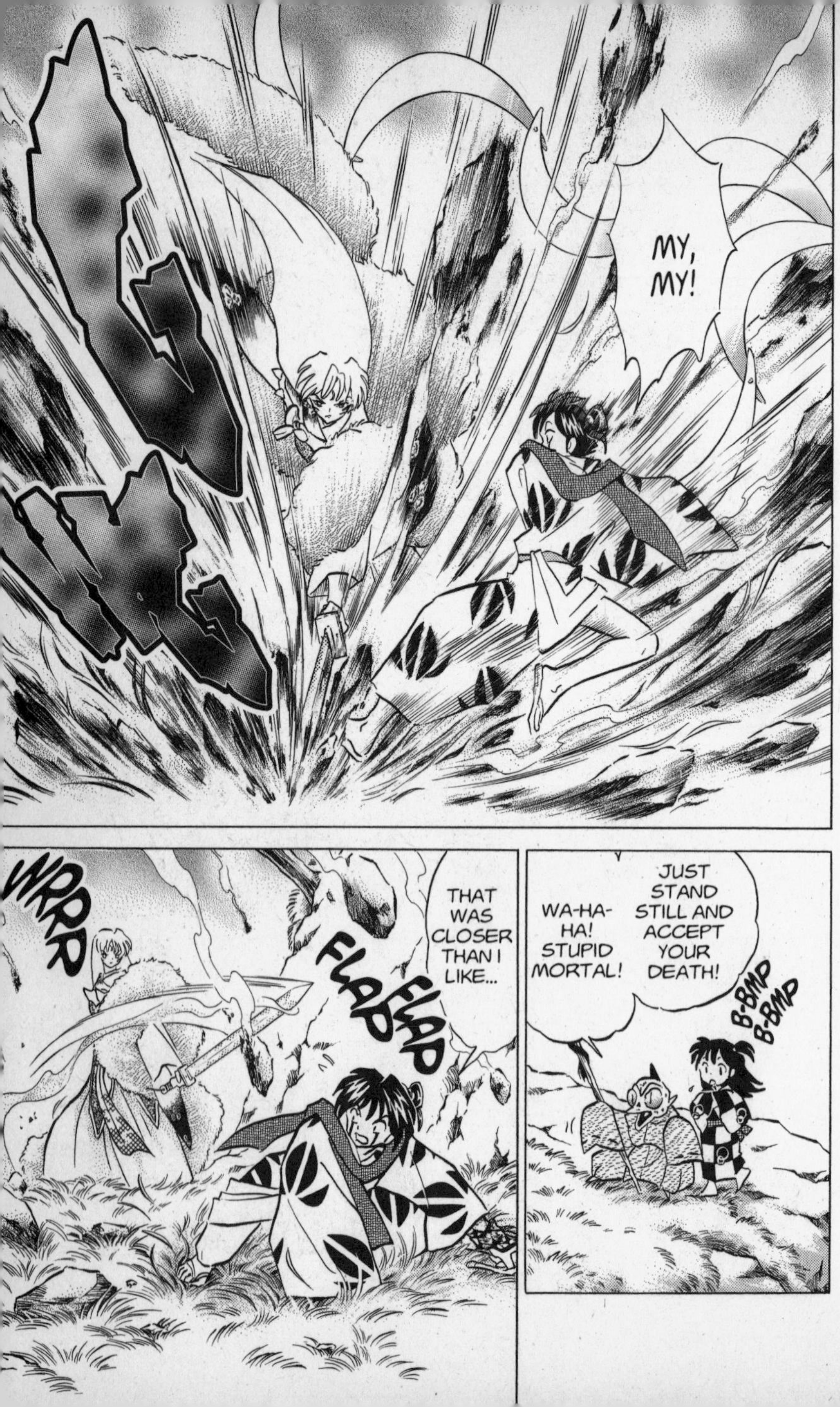
MY, MY!
JUST STAND STILL AND ACCEPT YOUR DEATH!
WA-HA-HA! STUPID MORTAL!
B-BMP B-BMP
THAT WAS CLOSER THAN I LIKE...
FLAP FLAP
WRRR

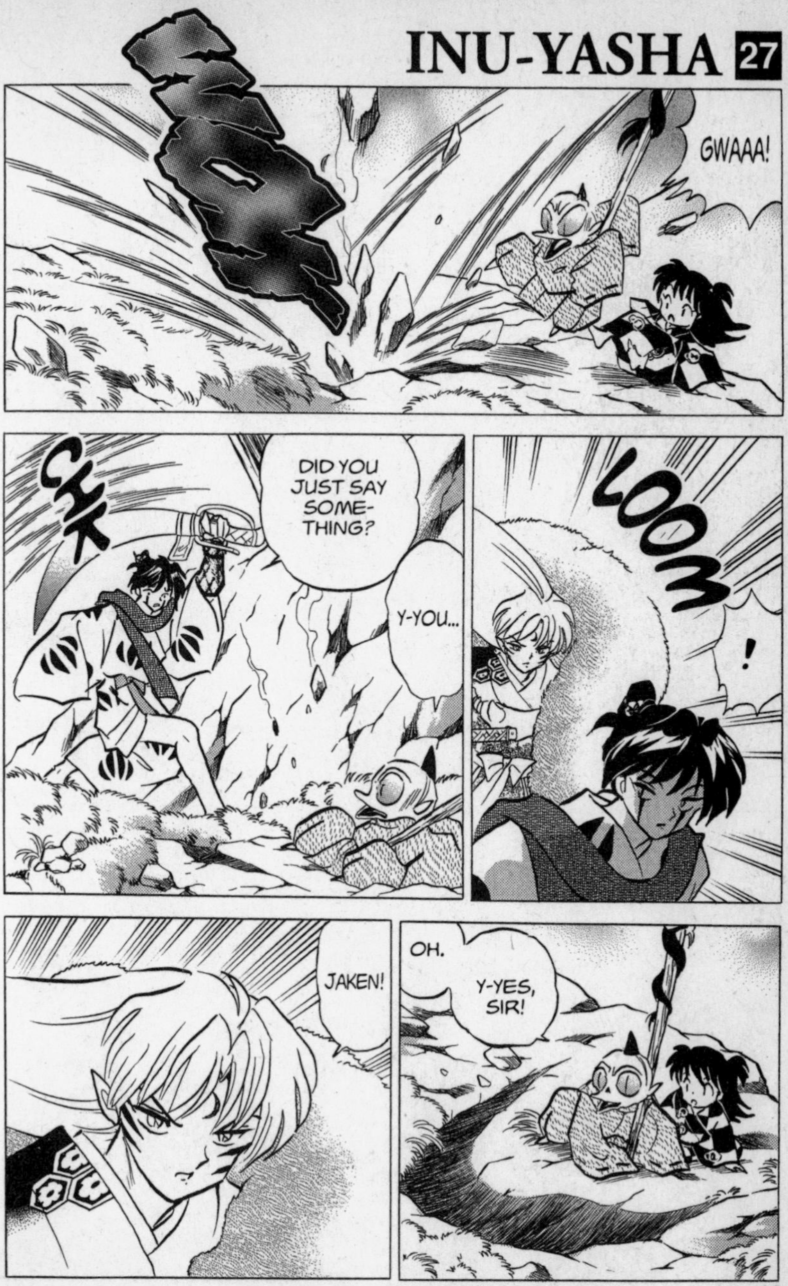
GWAAA!
CHK
DID YOU JUST SAY SOME-THING?
Y-YOU...
LOOM
!
JAKEN!
OH.
Y-YES, SIR!

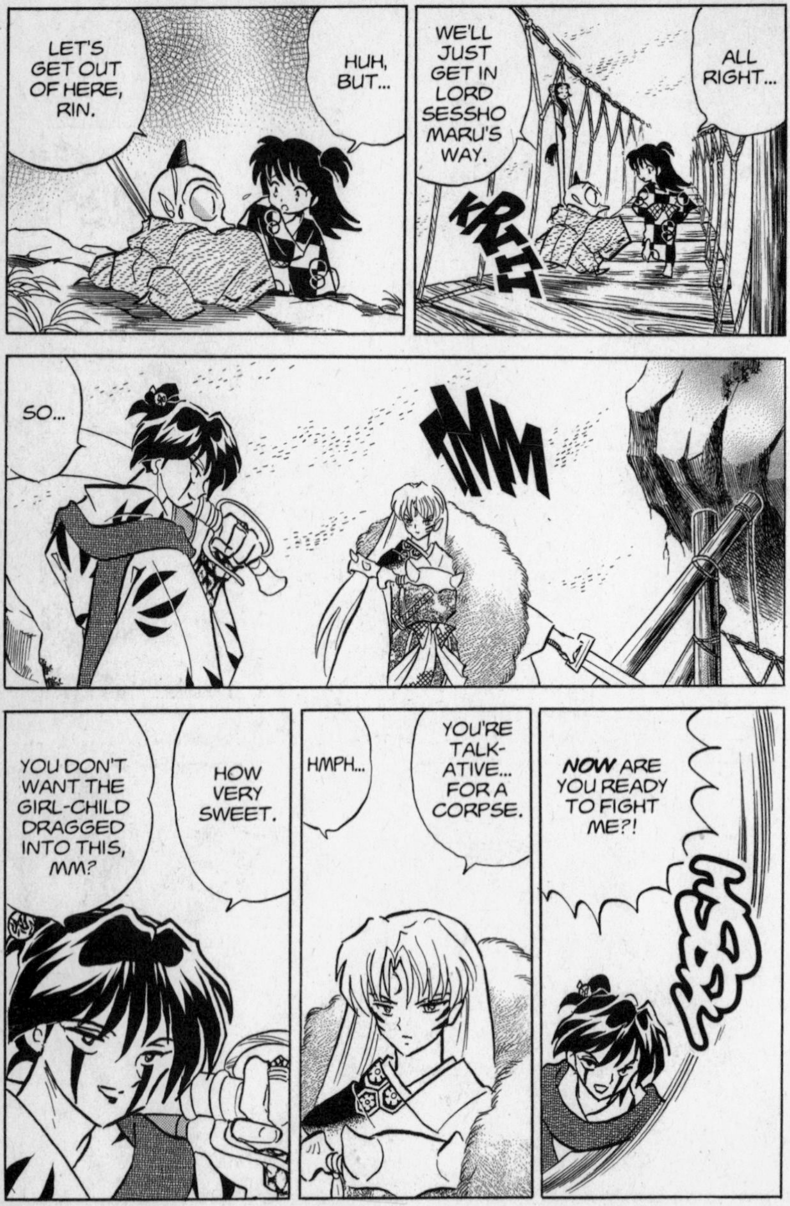
LET'S GET OUT OF HERE, RIN.
HUH, BUT...
WE'LL JUST GET IN LORD SESSHO MARU'S WAY.
KRIII
ALL RIGHT...
SO...
YOU DON'T WANT THE GIRL-CHILD DRAGGED INTO THIS, MM?
HOW VERY SWEET.
HMPH...
YOU'RE TALK-ATIVE... FOR A CORPSE.
NOW ARE YOU READY TO FIGHT ME?!

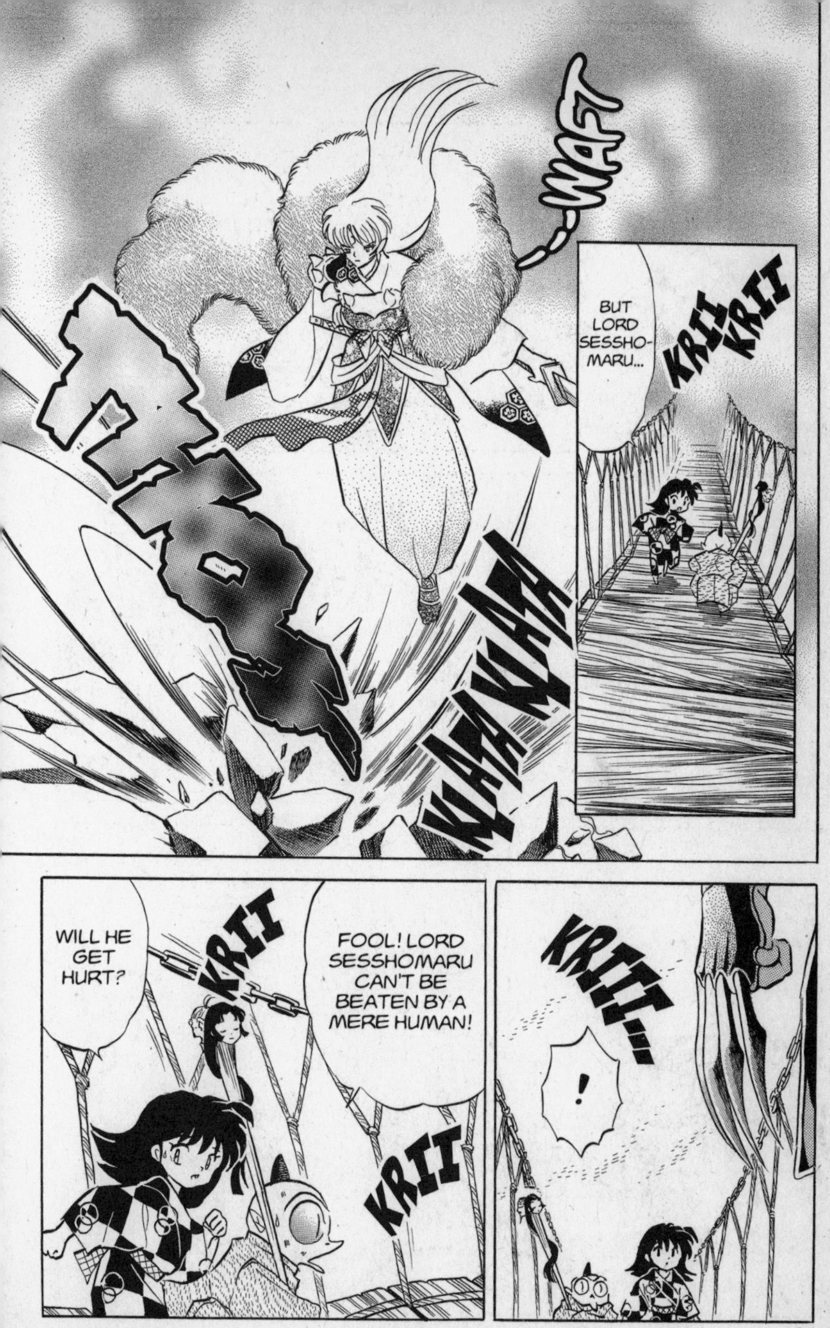
WAFT
BUT LORD SESSHOMARU...
KRII KRII
KRIIT...
!
FOOL! LORD SESSHOMARU CAN'T BE BEATEN BY A MERE HUMAN!
KRIT
WILL HE GET HURT?
KRIT

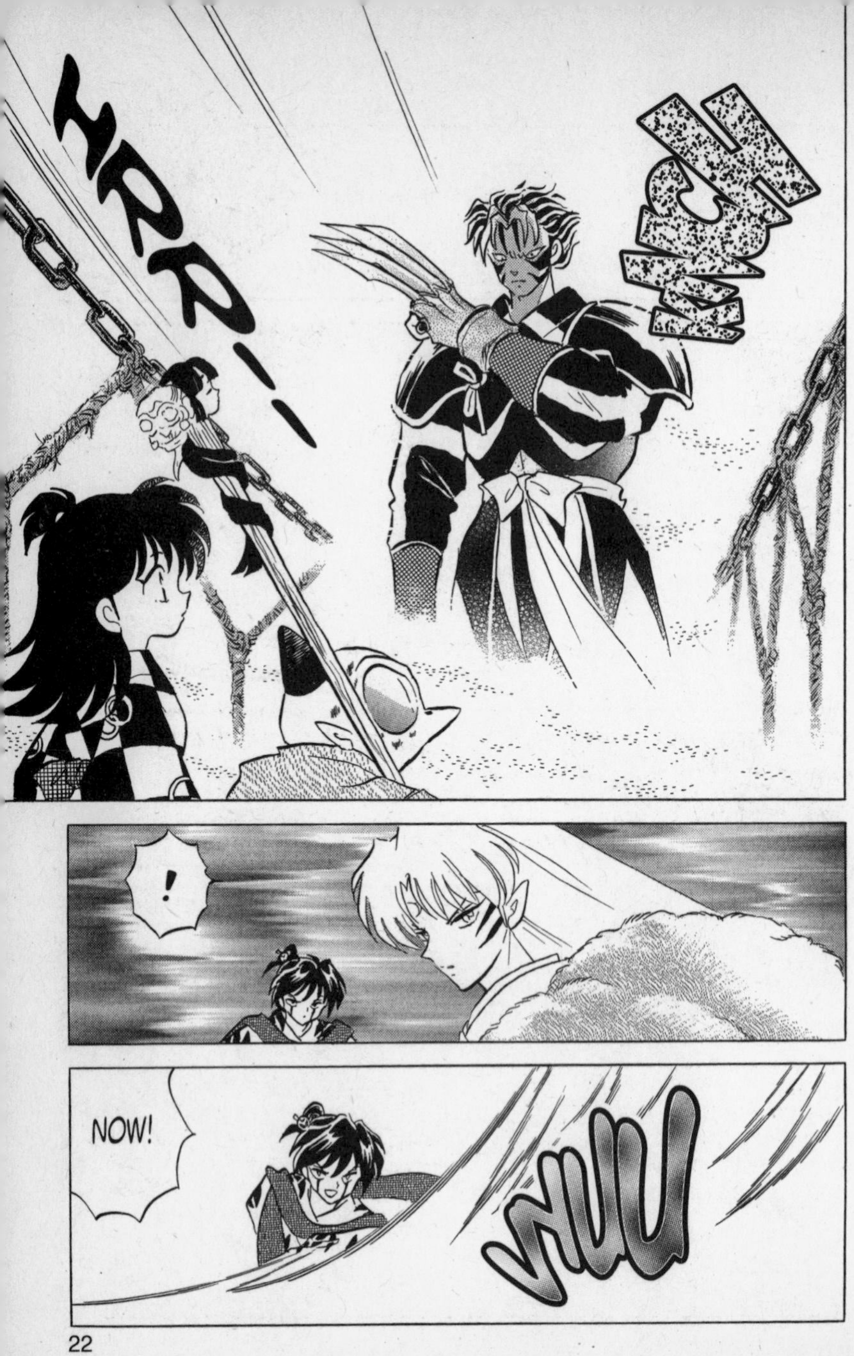

WHACK!
JRR...
!
NOW!
WHU

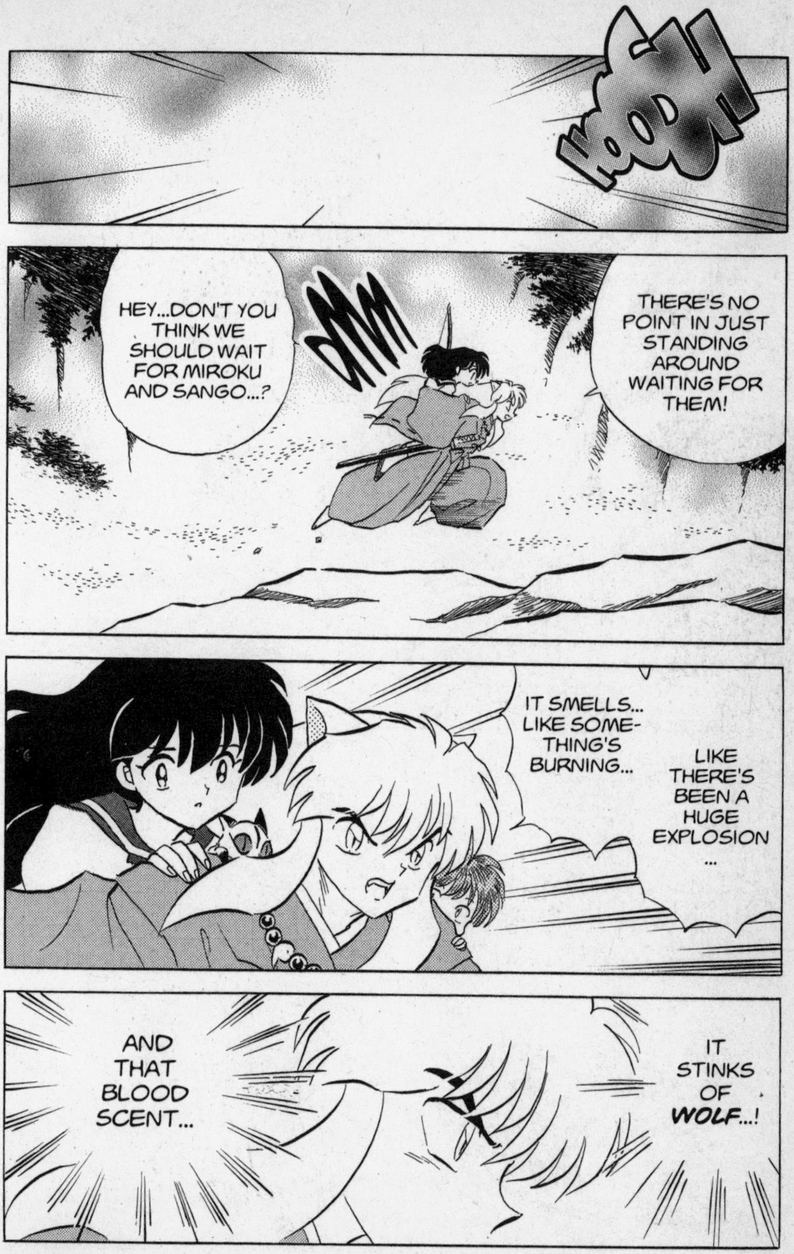
THERE'S NO POINT IN JUST STANDING AROUND WAITING FOR THEM!
HEY...DON'T YOU THINK WE SHOULD WAIT FOR MIROKU AND SANGO...?
LIKE THERE'S BEEN A HUGE EXPLOSION ...
IT SMELLS... LIKE SOME-THING'S BURNING...
IT STINKS OF **WOLF**...!
AND THAT BLOOD SCENT...

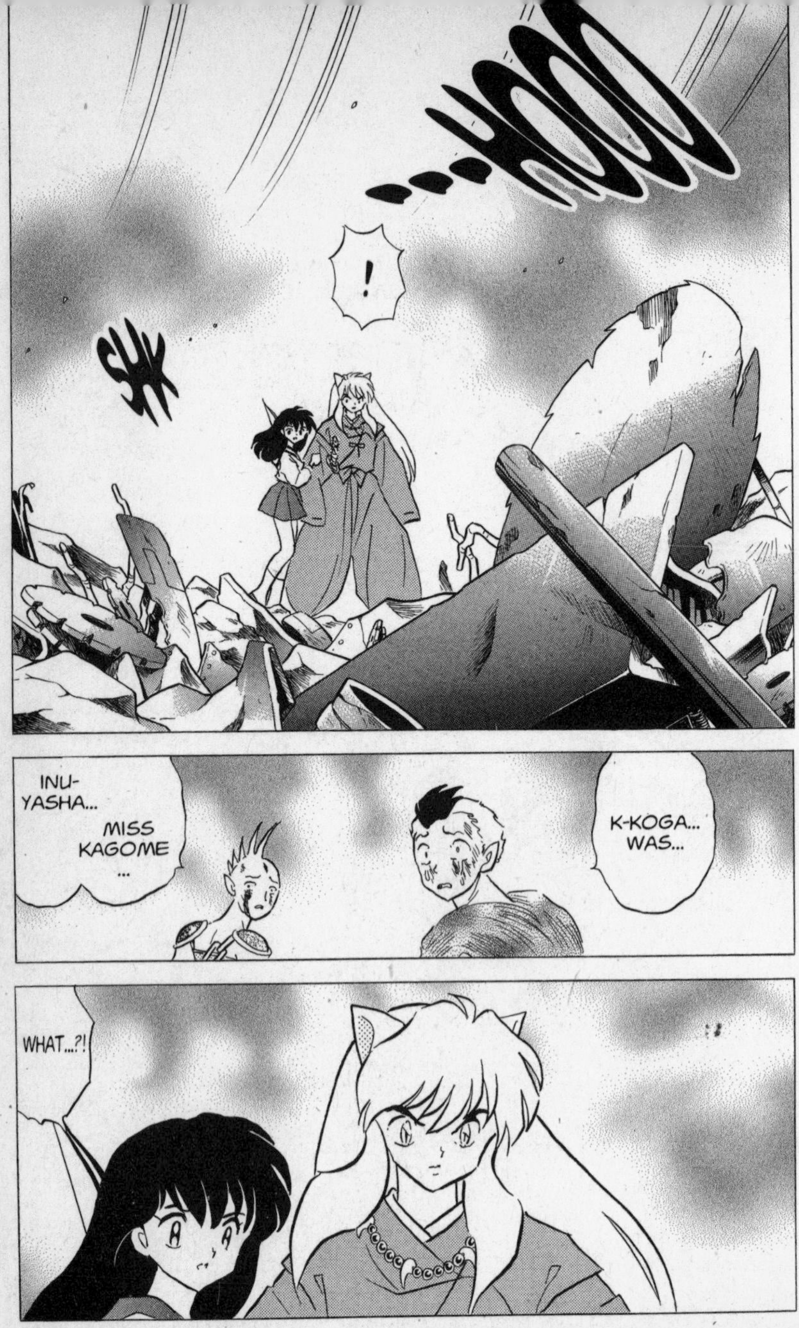

...HOO
!
SHK
K-KOGA... WAS...
INU-YASHA... MISS KAGOME ...
WHAT...?!

SCROLL TWO
FACES

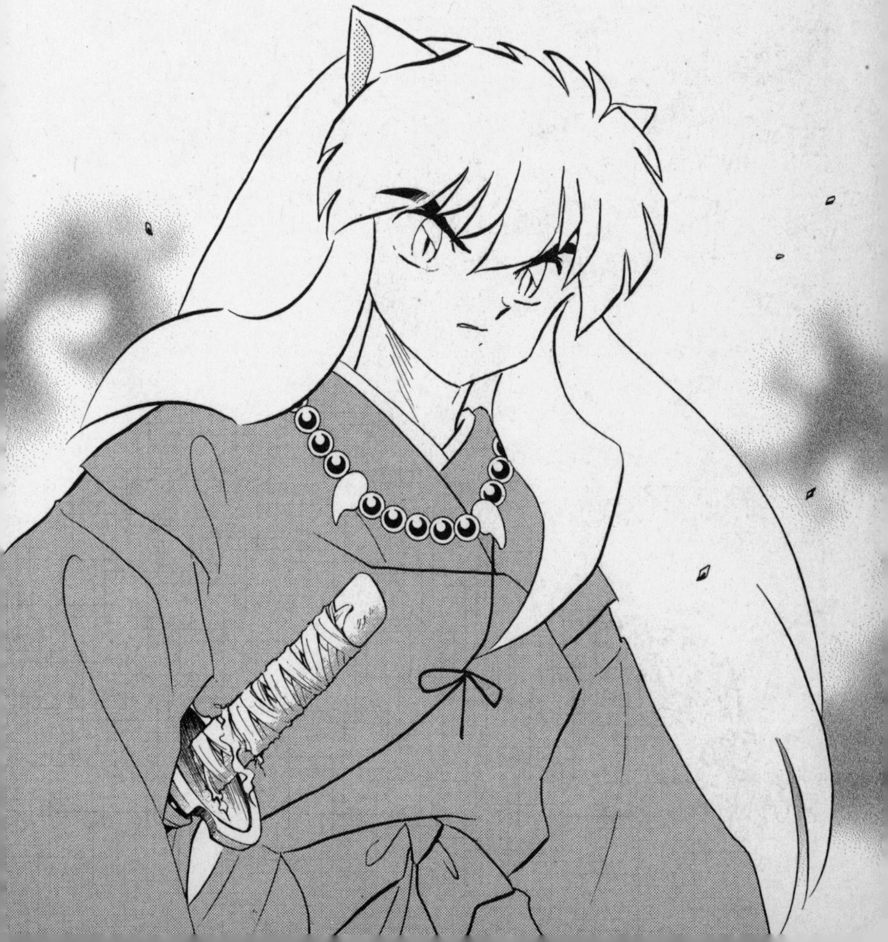

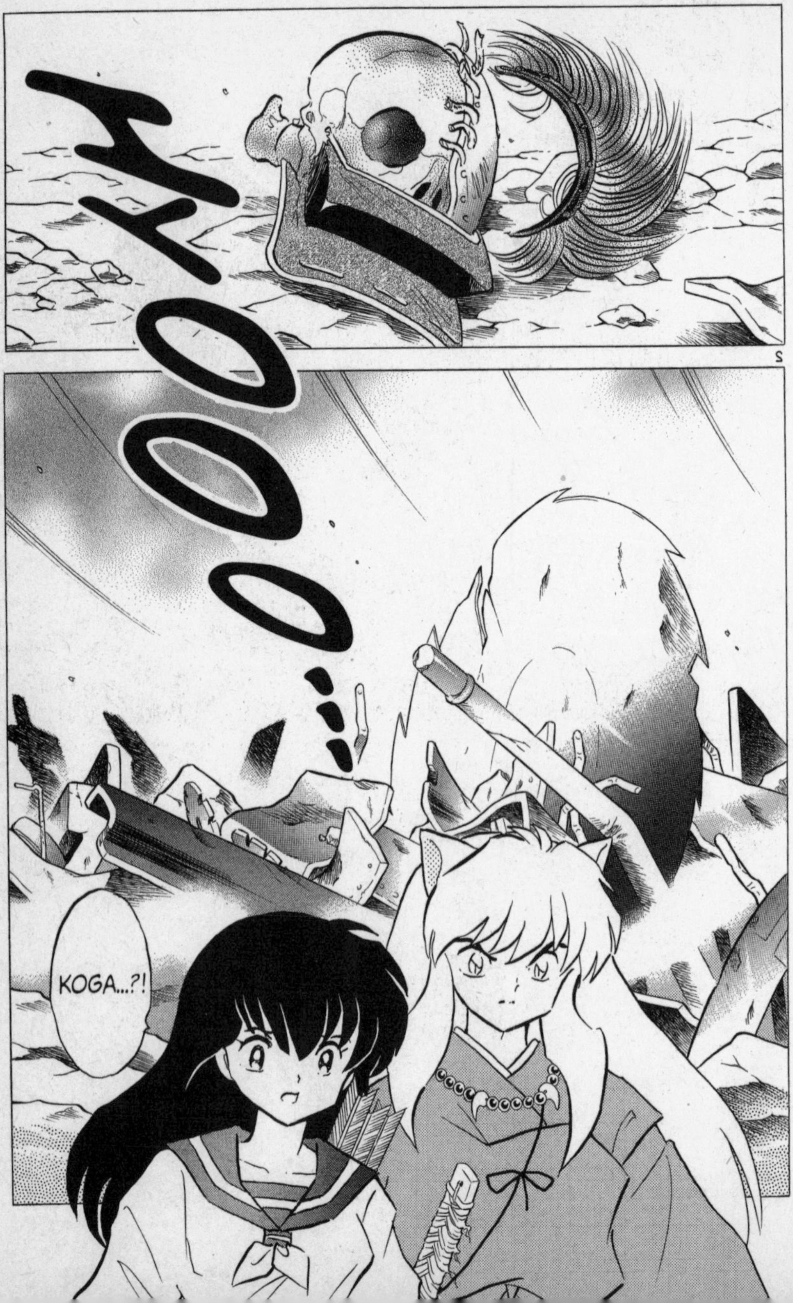
KOGA...?!

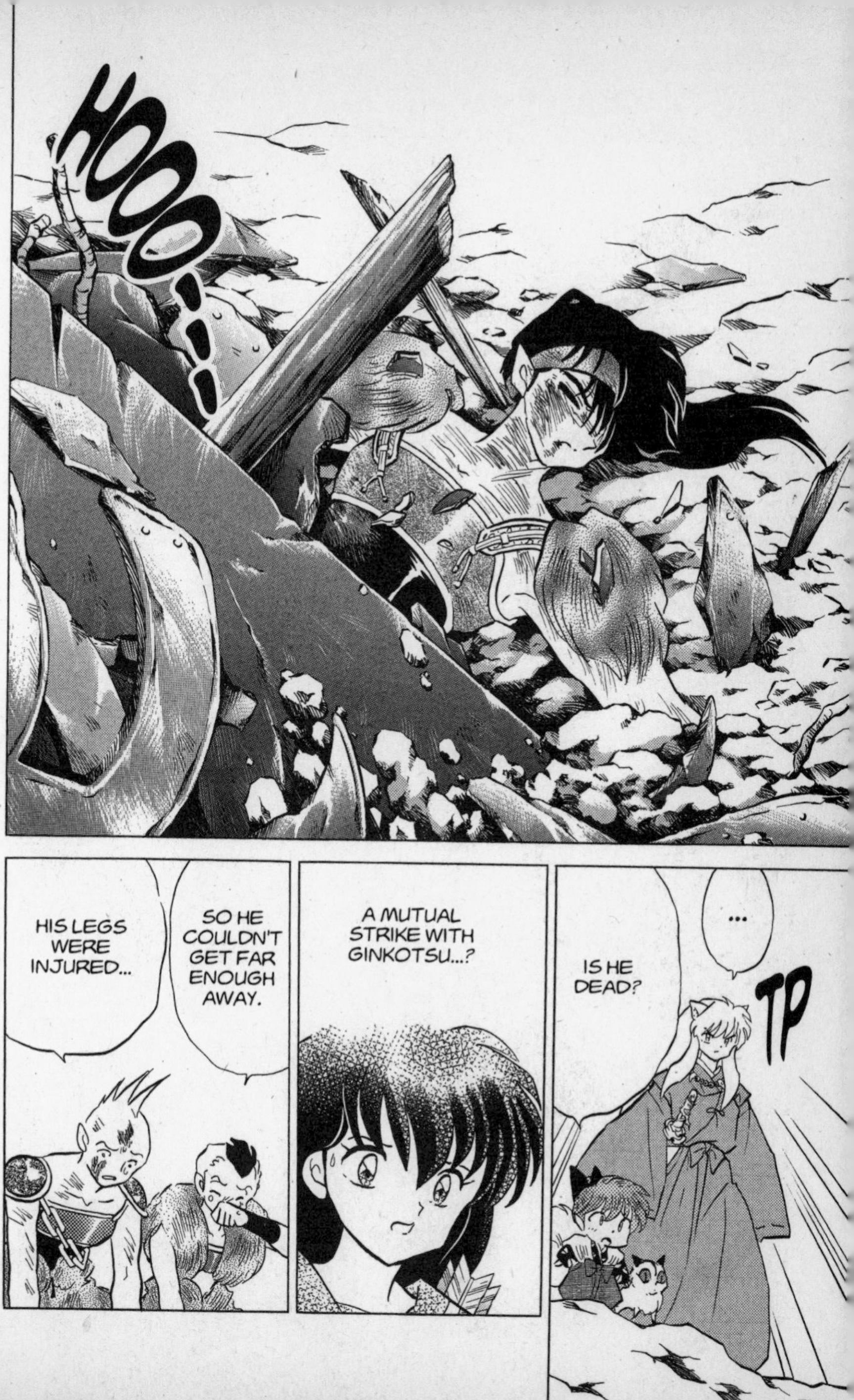
HOOO...
...
IS HE DEAD?
TP
A MUTUAL STRIKE WITH GINKOTSU...?
HIS LEGS WERE INJURED...
SO HE COULDN'T GET FAR ENOUGH AWAY.

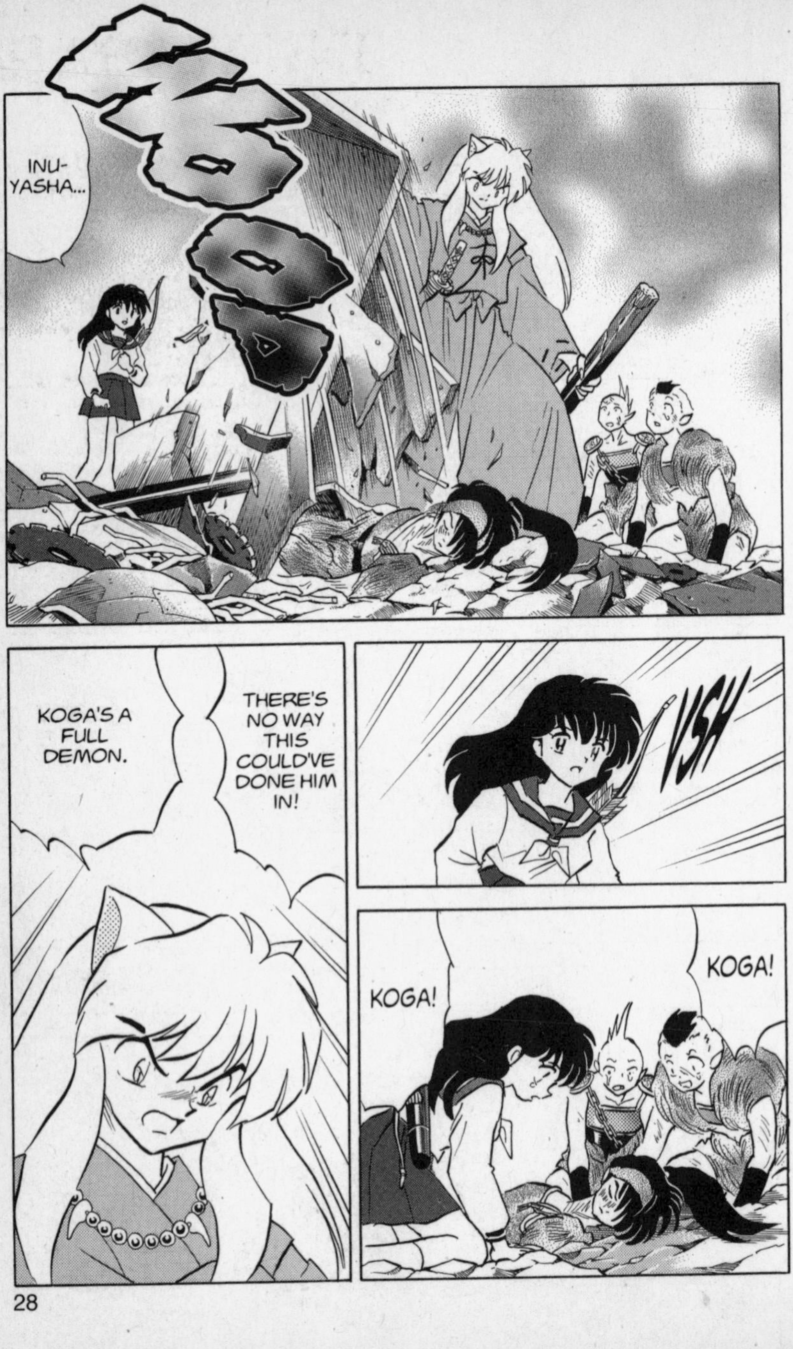
INU-YASHA...
VSH
THERE'S NO WAY THIS COULD'VE DONE HIM IN!
KOGA'S A FULL DEMON.
KOGA!
KOGA!

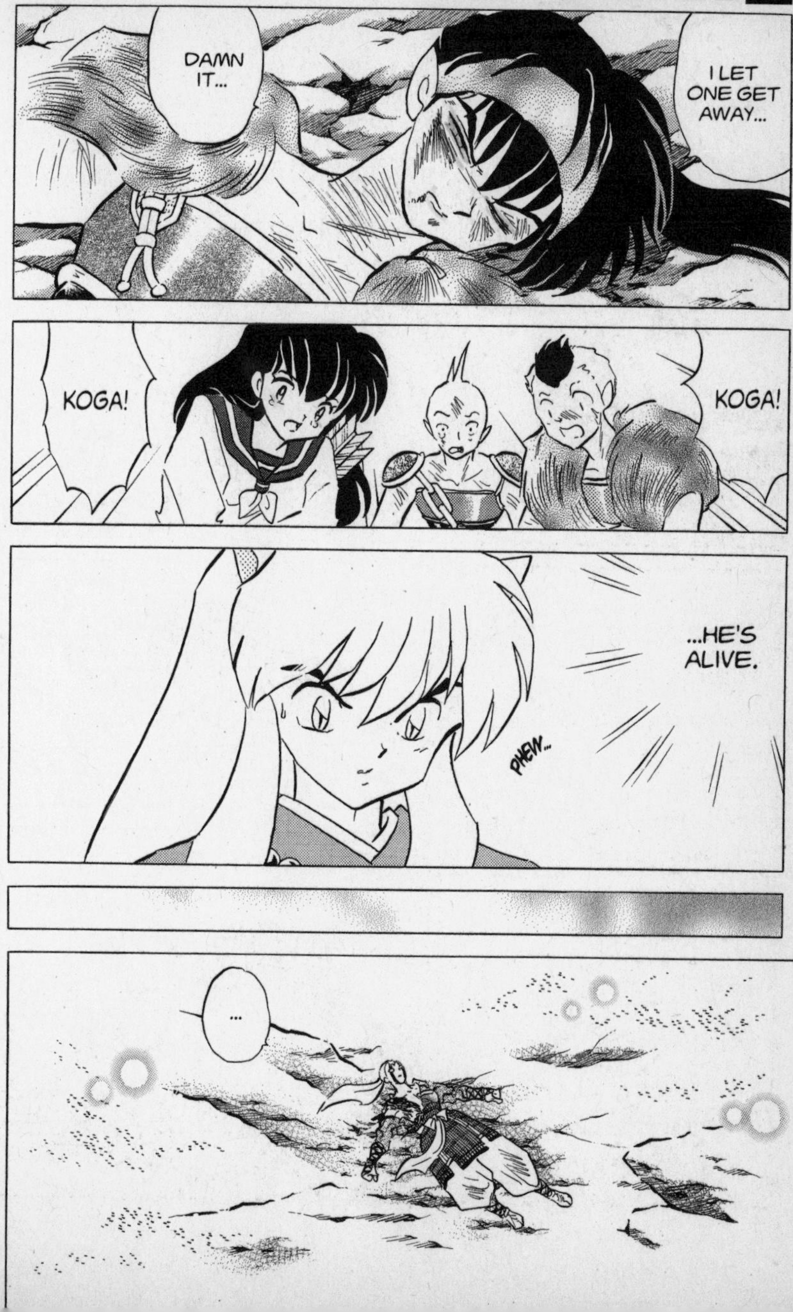
DAMN IT...
I LET ONE GET AWAY...
KOGA!
KOGA!
...HE'S ALIVE.
PHEW...
...

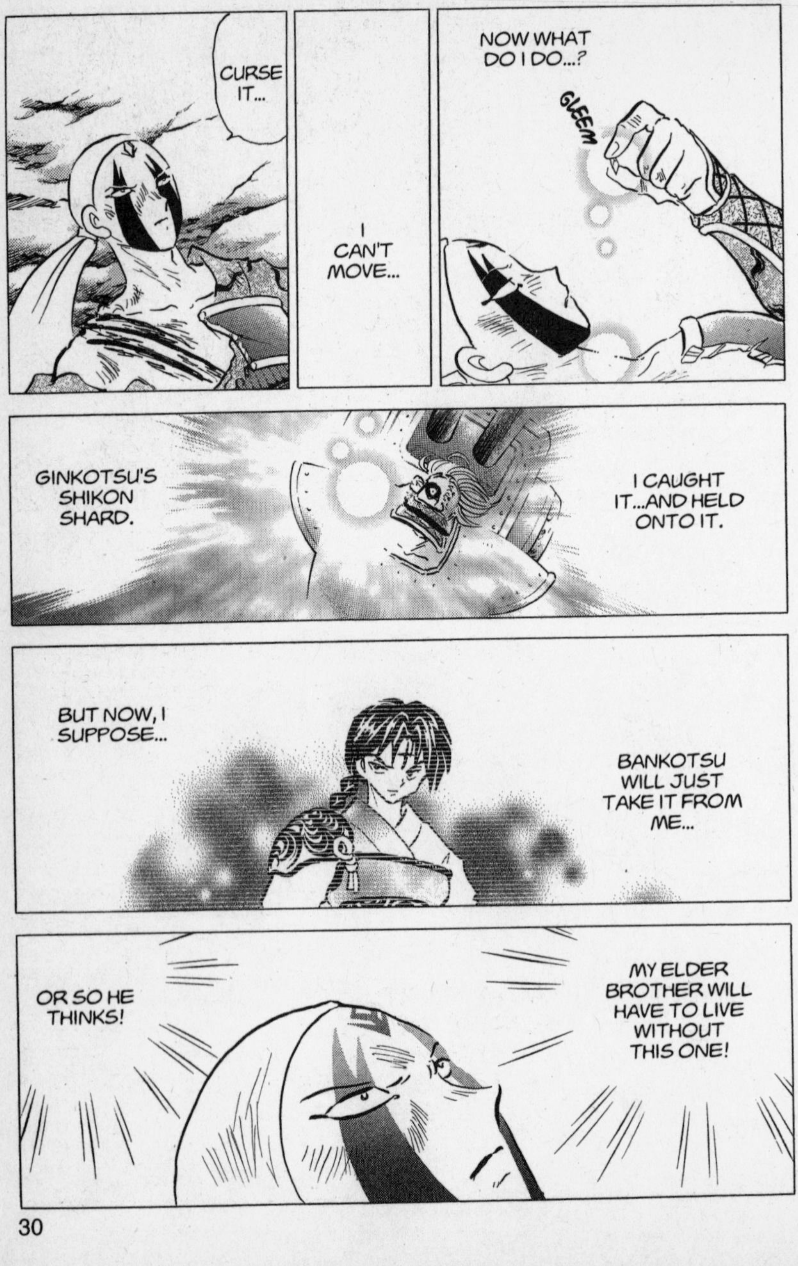

CURSE IT...
I CAN'T MOVE...
NOW WHAT DO I DO...?
GLEEM
GINKOTSU'S SHIKON SHARD.
I CAUGHT IT...AND HELD ONTO IT.
BUT NOW, I SUPPOSE...
BANKOTSU WILL JUST TAKE IT FROM ME...
OR SO HE THINKS!
MY ELDER BROTHER WILL HAVE TO LIVE WITHOUT THIS ONE!

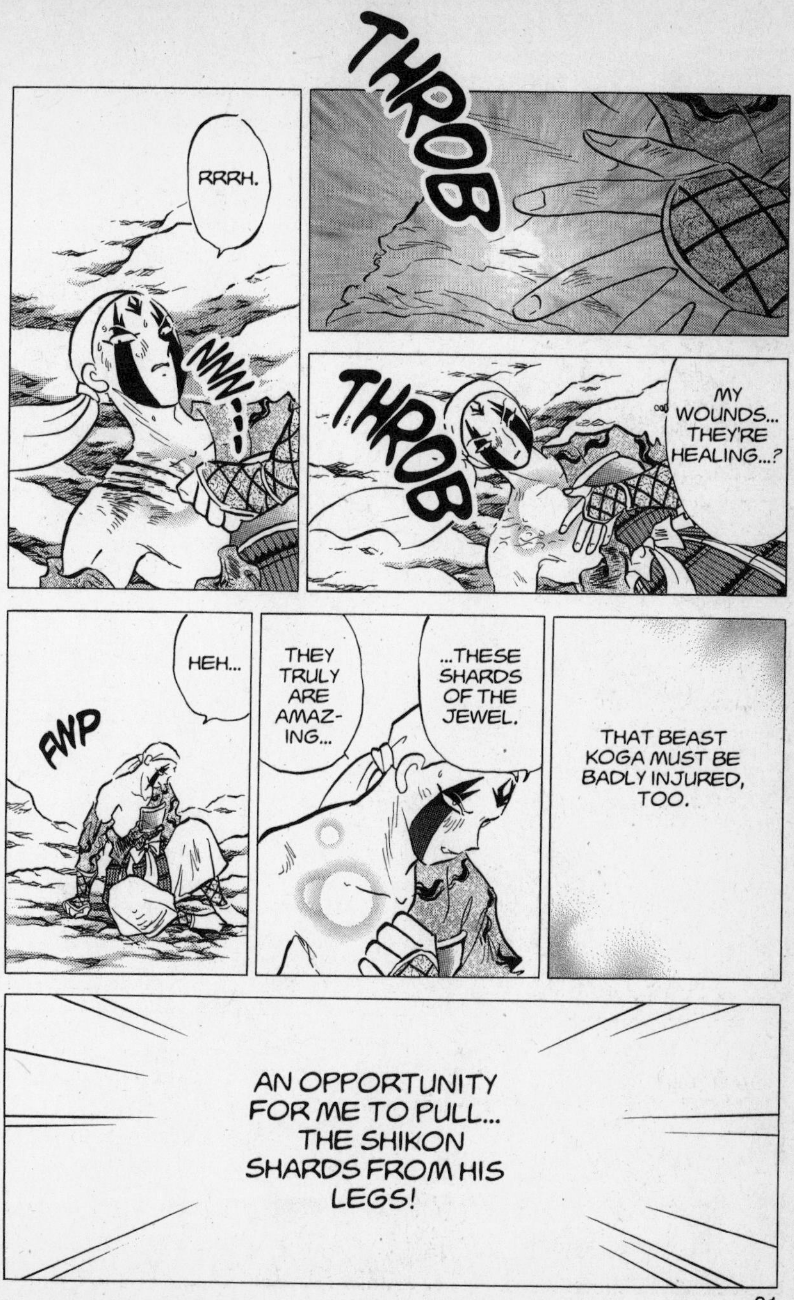
RRRH.
NNN...
THROB
THROB
MY WOUNDS... THEY'RE HEALING...?
FWP
HEH...
THEY TRULY ARE AMAZ-ING...
...THESE SHARDS OF THE JEWEL.
THAT BEAST KOGA MUST BE BADLY INJURED, TOO.
AN OPPORTUNITY FOR ME TO PULL... THE SHIKON SHARDS FROM HIS LEGS!

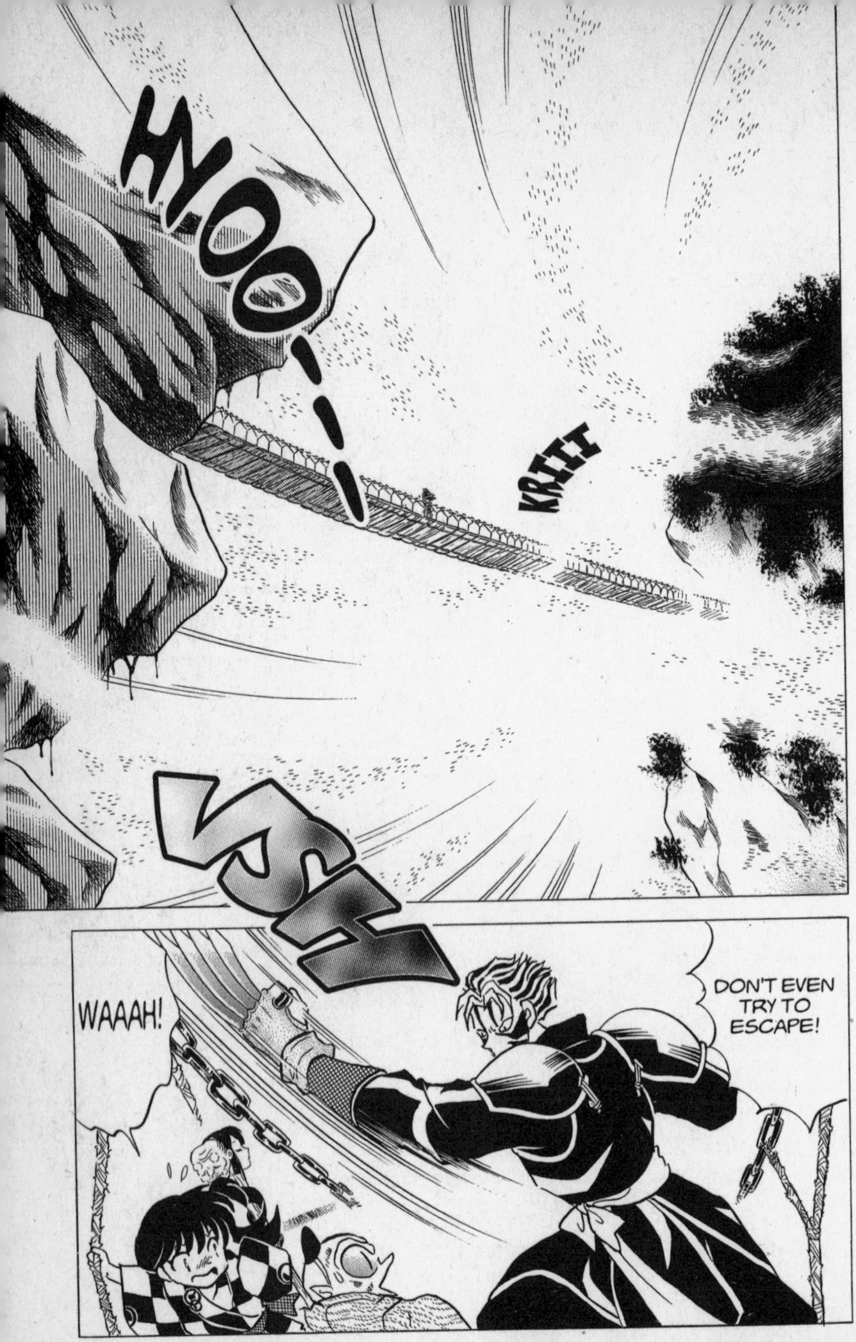
HYOO---
KRIII
VSSH
DON'T EVEN TRY TO ESCAPE!
WAAAH!

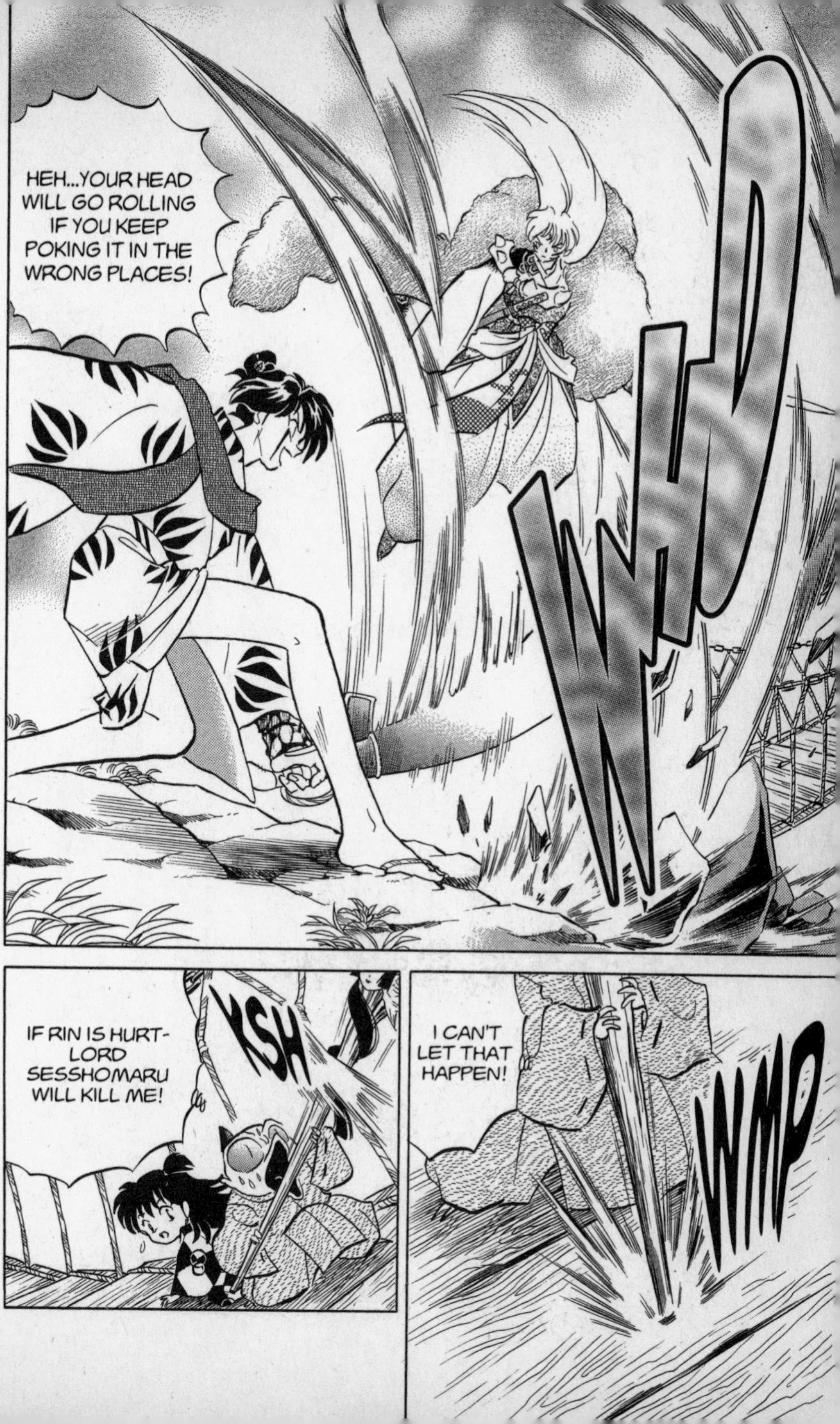
HEH...YOUR HEAD WILL GO ROLLING IF YOU KEEP POKING IT IN THE WRONG PLACES!
WHD
IF RIN IS HURT- LORD SESSHOMARU WILL KILL ME!
YSH
I CAN'T LET THAT HAPPEN!
WMP

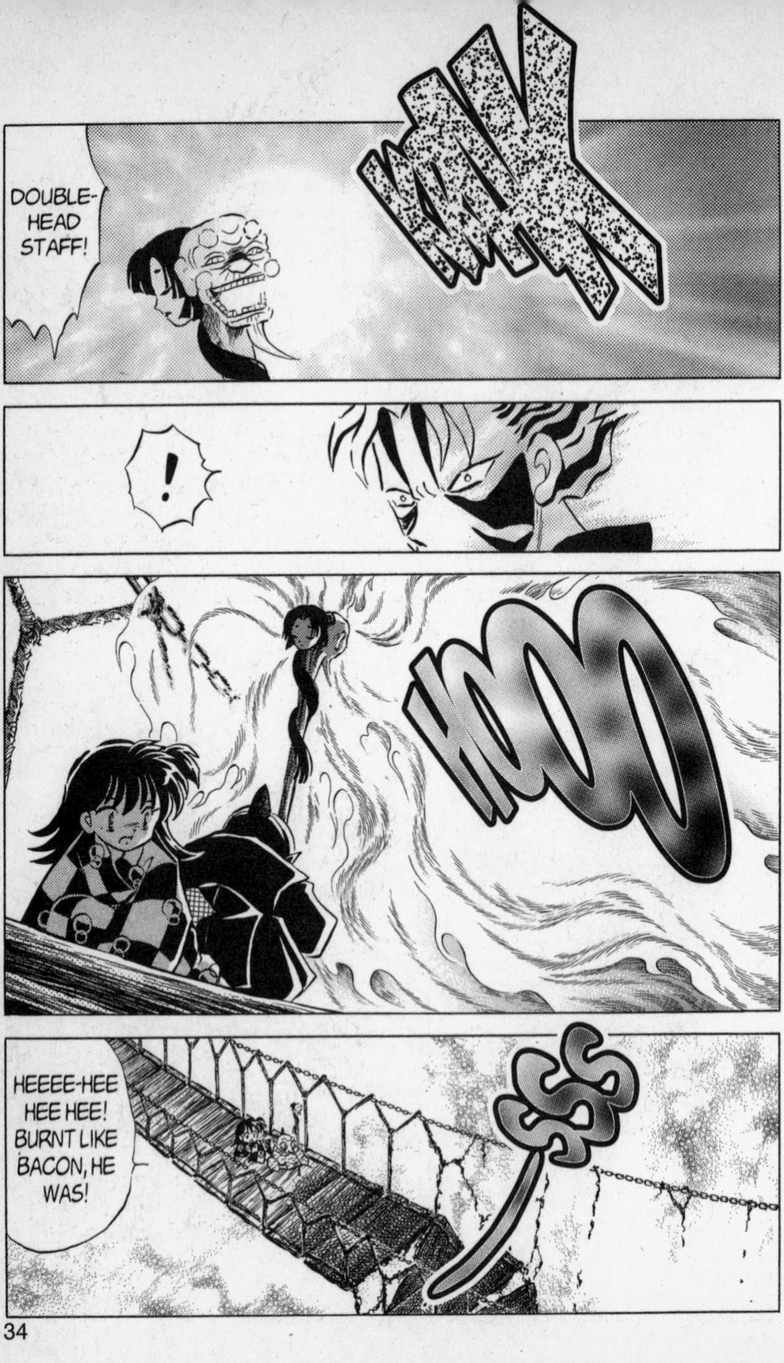
DOUBLE-HEAD STAFF!
!
HEEEE-HEE HEE HEE! BURNT LIKE BACON, HE WAS!

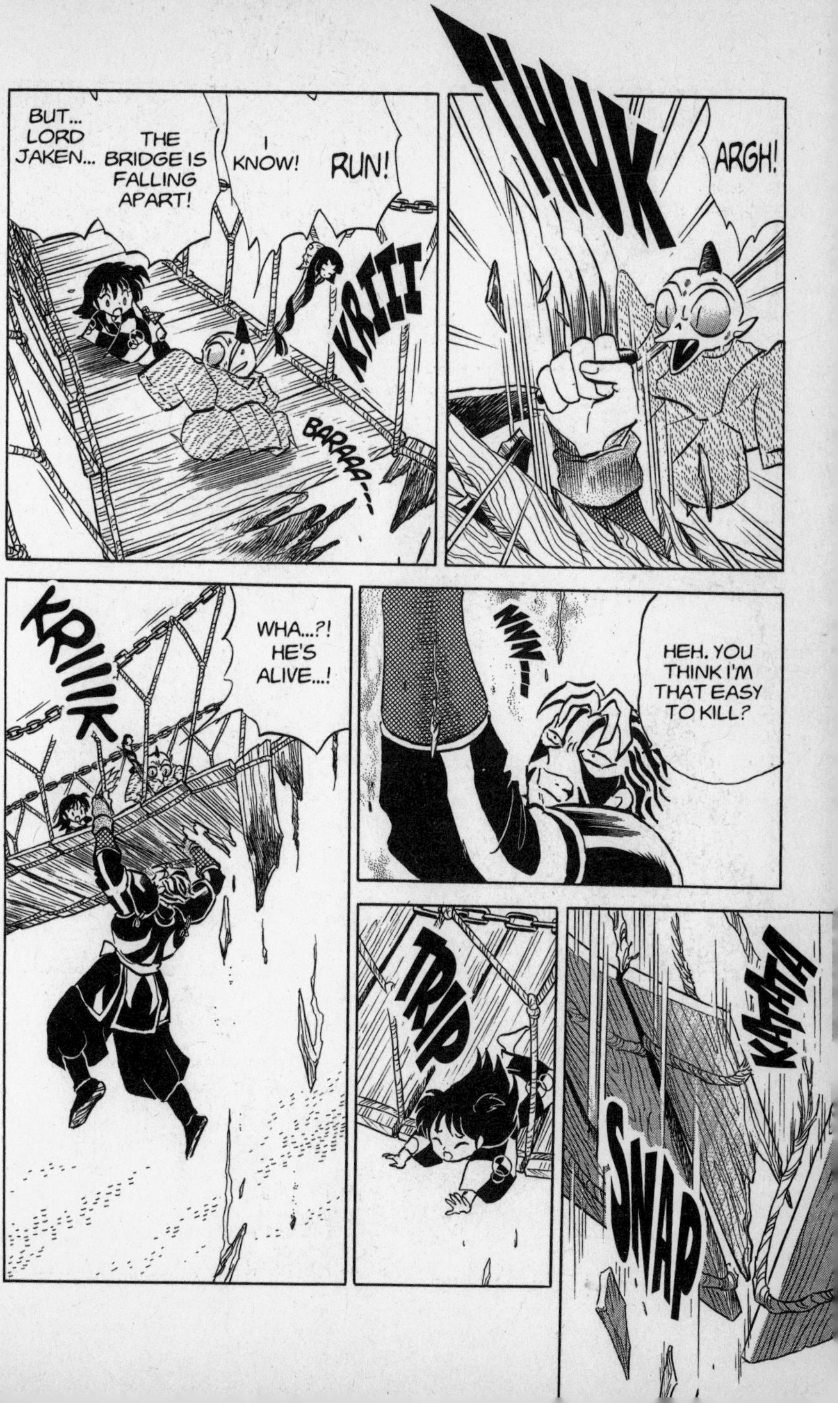
THUNK
ARGH!
RUN!
BUT... LORD JAKEN...
THE BRIDGE IS FALLING APART!
I KNOW!
KRIII
BARAAA...
NNN...
HEH. YOU THINK I'M THAT EASY TO KILL?
WHA...?! HE'S ALIVE...!
KRIIIIK
KATATA
SNAP
TRIP

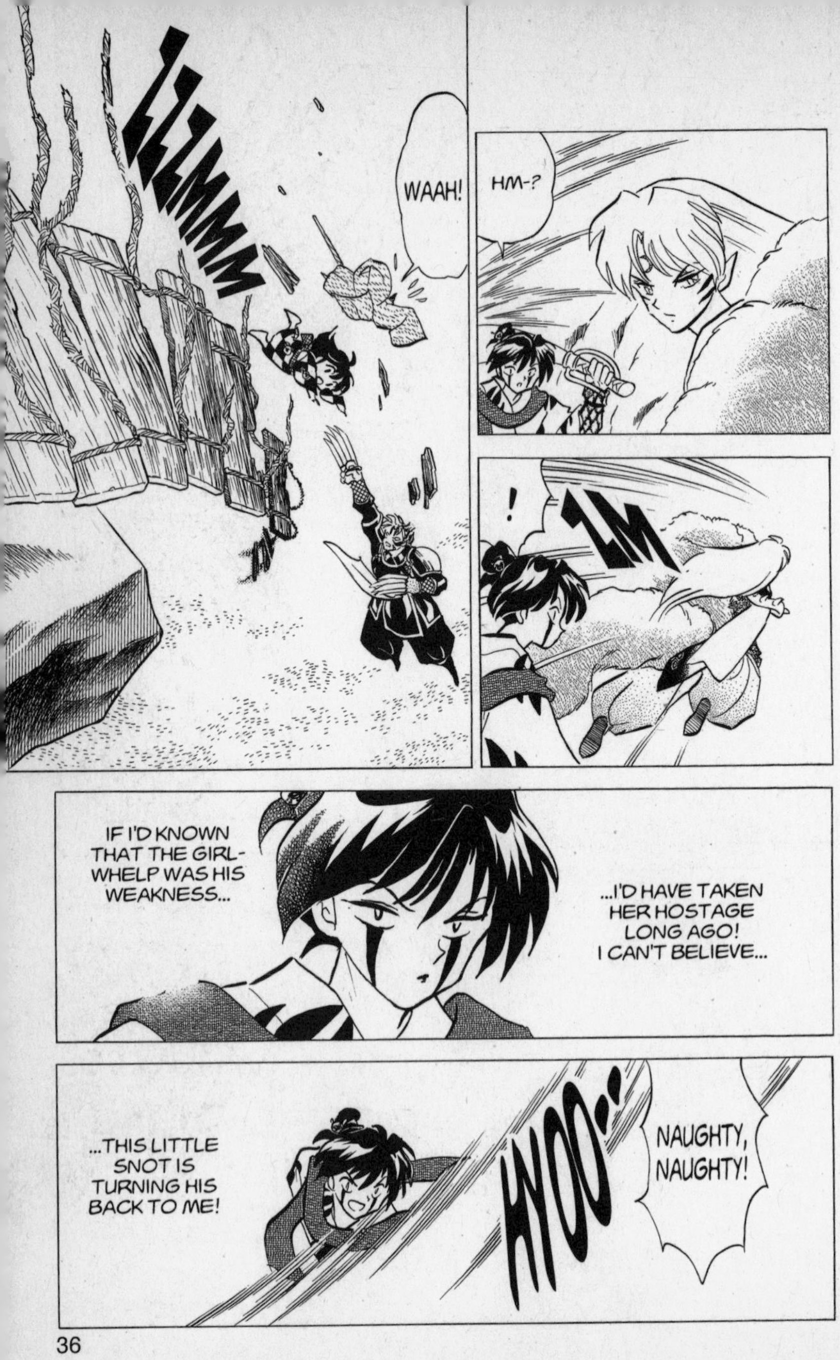
HM-?
!
ZM
WAAH!
ZZZMMMM
IF I'D KNOWN THAT THE GIRL-WHELP WAS HIS WEAKNESS...
...I'D HAVE TAKEN HER HOSTAGE LONG AGO! I CAN'T BELIEVE...
NAUGHTY, NAUGHTY!
HYOO...
...THIS LITTLE SNOT IS TURNING HIS BACK TO ME!

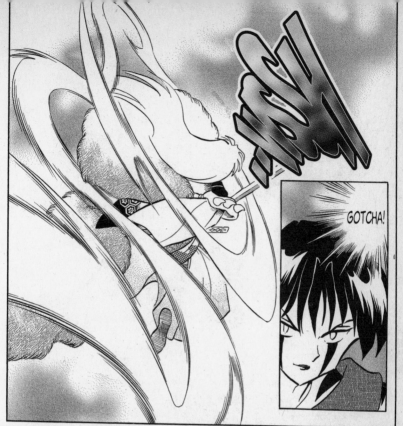

GOTCHA!

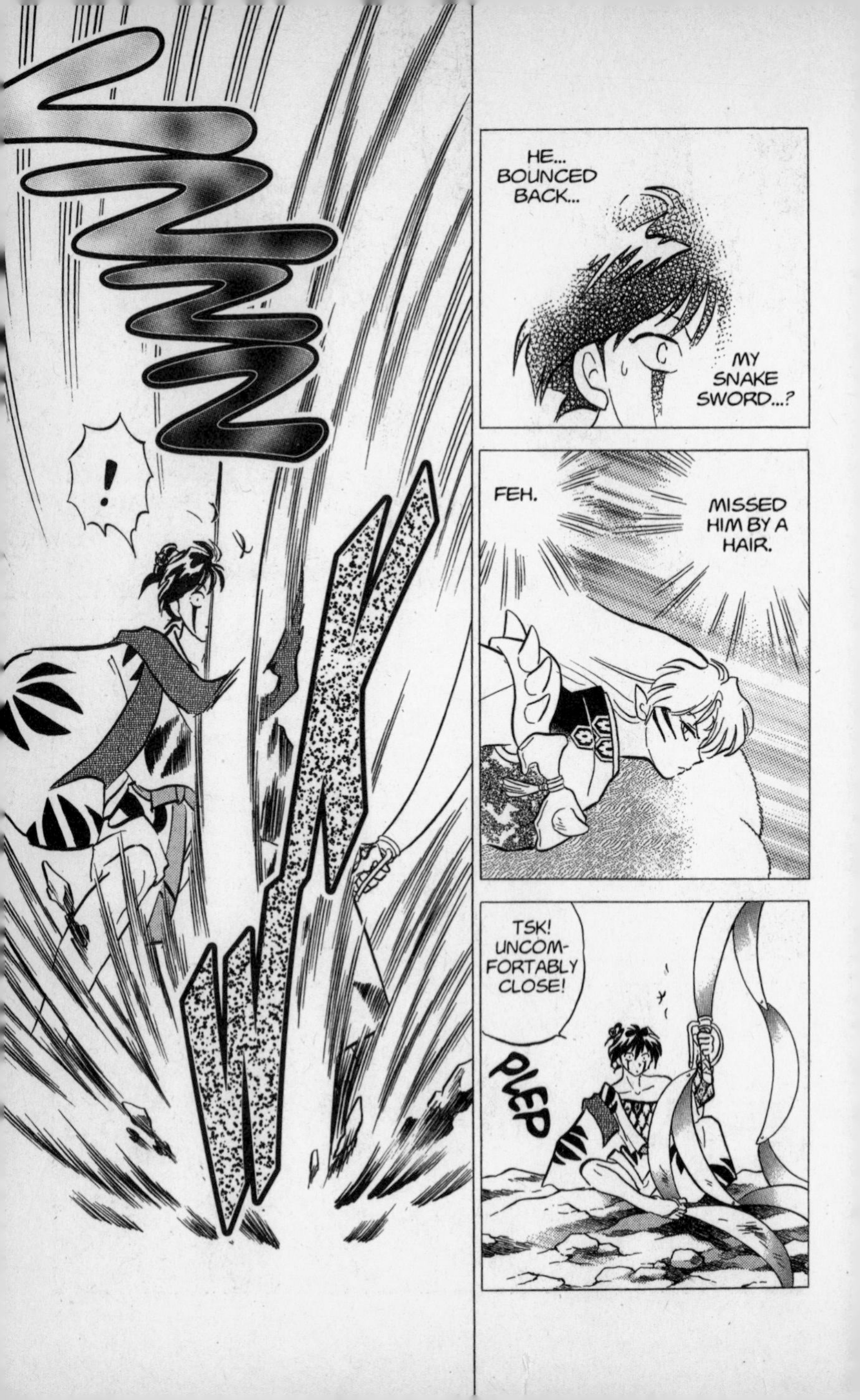
HE... BOUNCED BACK...
MY SNAKE SWORD...?
FEH.
MISSED HIM BY A HAIR.
TSK! UNCOM-FORTABLY CLOSE!
PLEP
!

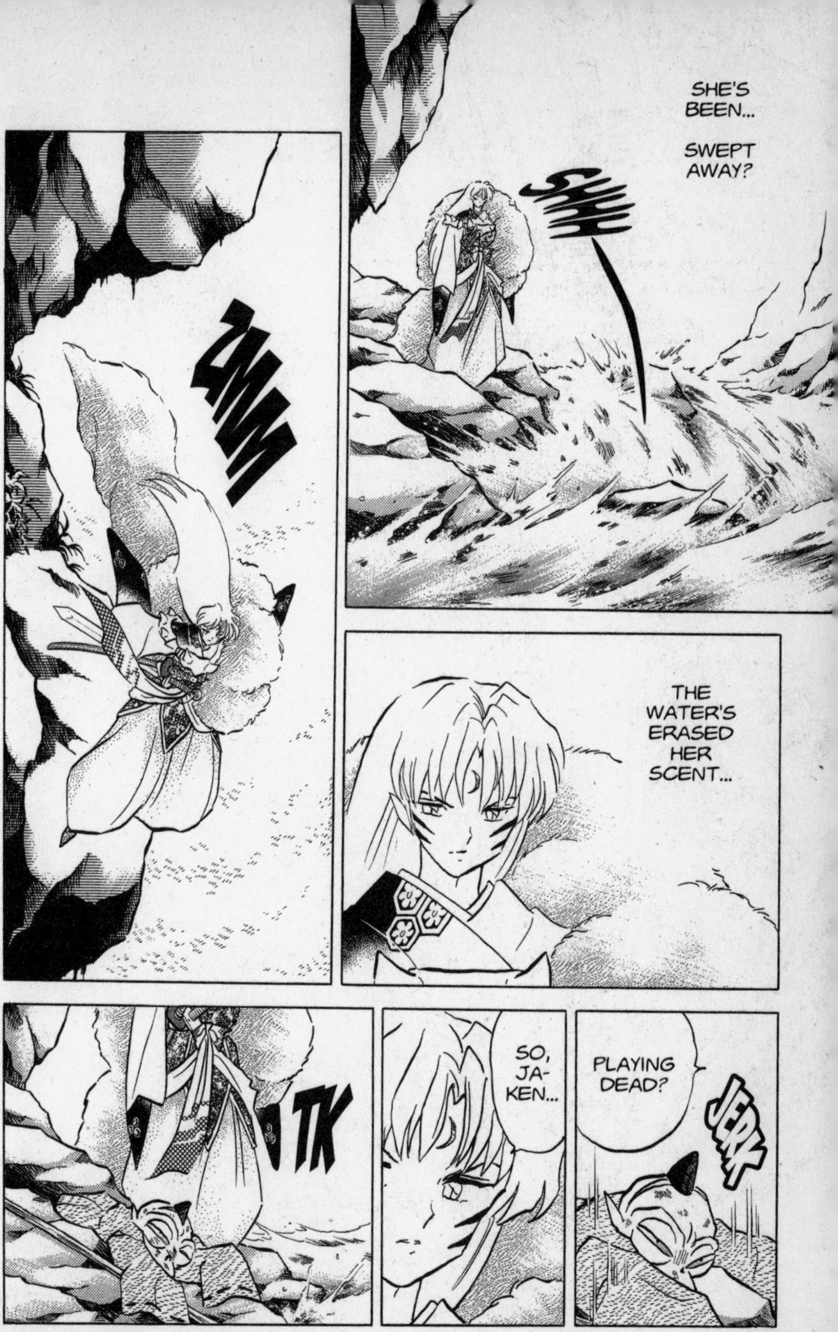
SHE'S BEEN...
SWEPT AWAY?
SHHH
THE WATER'S ERASED HER SCENT...
PLAYING DEAD?
JERK
SO, JA-KEN...
TK

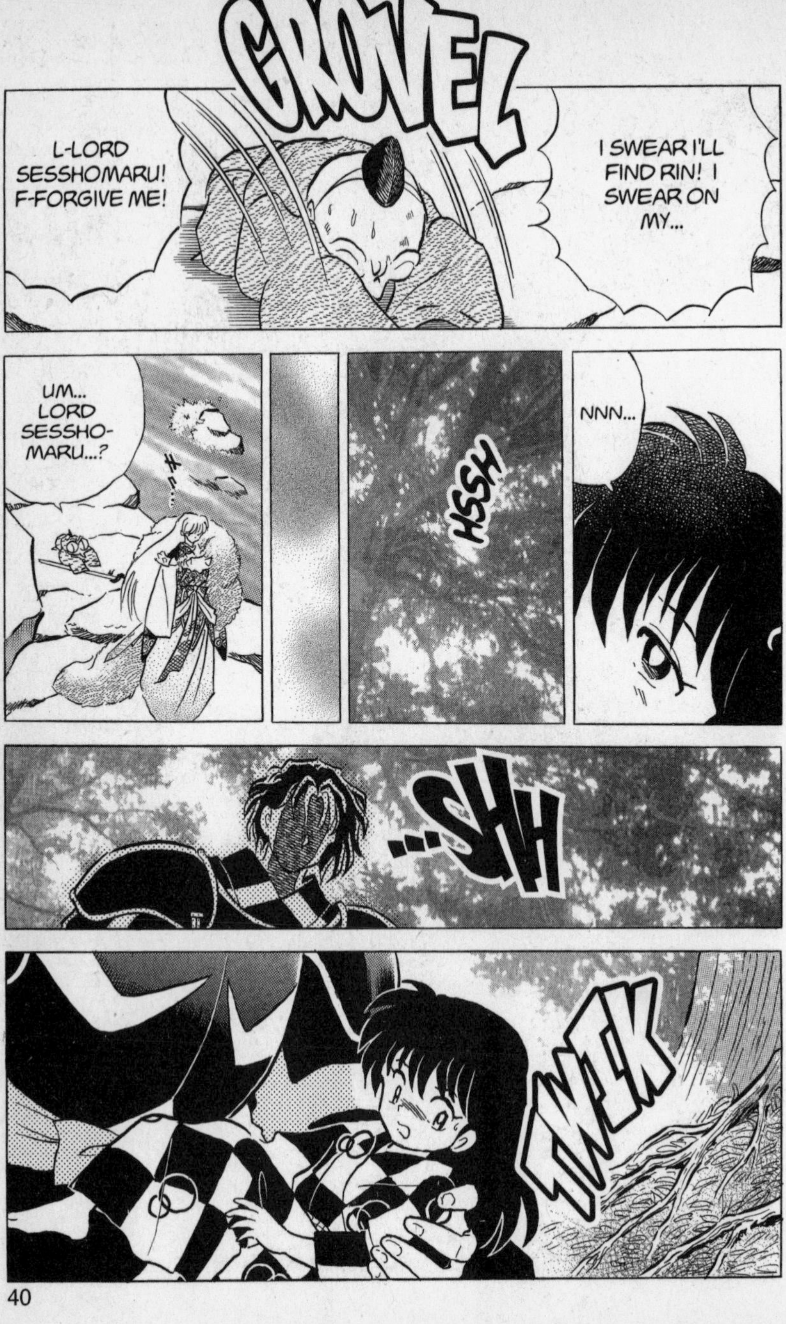
GROVEL
L-LORD SESSHOMARU! F-FORGIVE ME!
I SWEAR I'LL FIND RIN! I SWEAR ON MY...
UM... LORD SESSHOMARU...?
HSSH
NNN...
...SHH

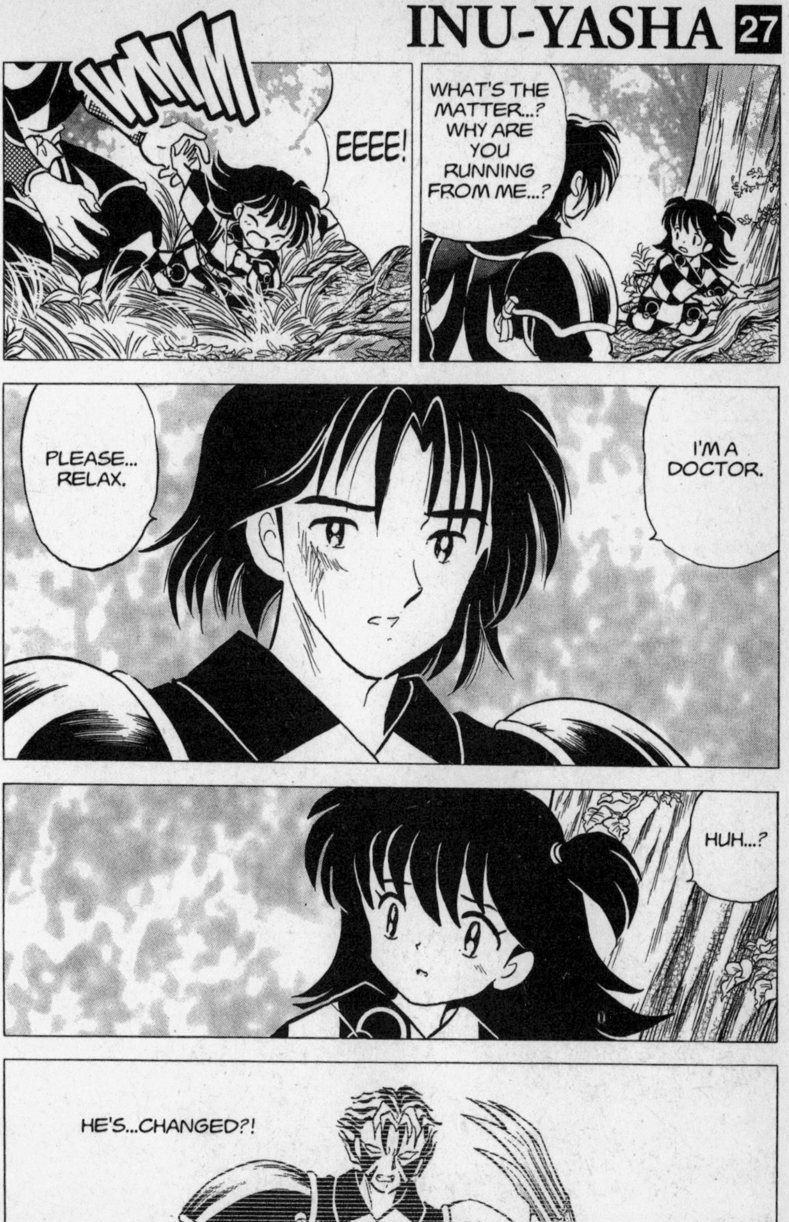
WMM
EEEE!
WHAT'S THE MATTER...? WHY ARE YOU RUNNING FROM ME...?
PLEASE... RELAX.
I'M A DOCTOR.
HUH...?
HE'S...CHANGED?!

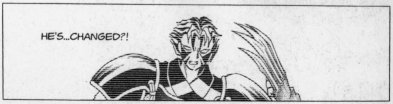

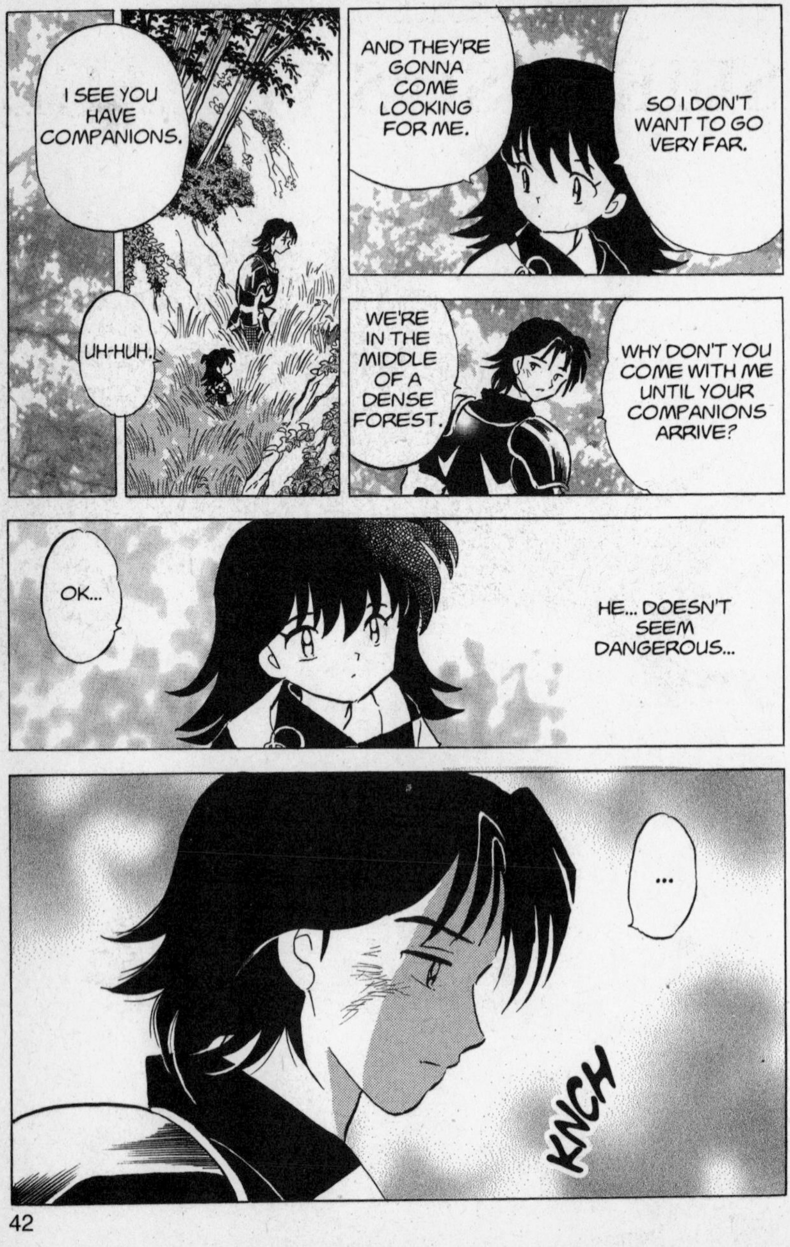
I SEE YOU HAVE COMPANIONS.
UH-HUH.
AND THEY'RE GONNA COME LOOKING FOR ME.
SO I DON'T WANT TO GO VERY FAR.
WE'RE IN THE MIDDLE OF A DENSE FOREST.
WHY DON'T YOU COME WITH ME UNTIL YOUR COMPANIONS ARRIVE?
OK...
HE... DOESN'T SEEM DANGEROUS...
...
KNCH

SCROLL THREE
SUIKOTSU'S VILLAGE

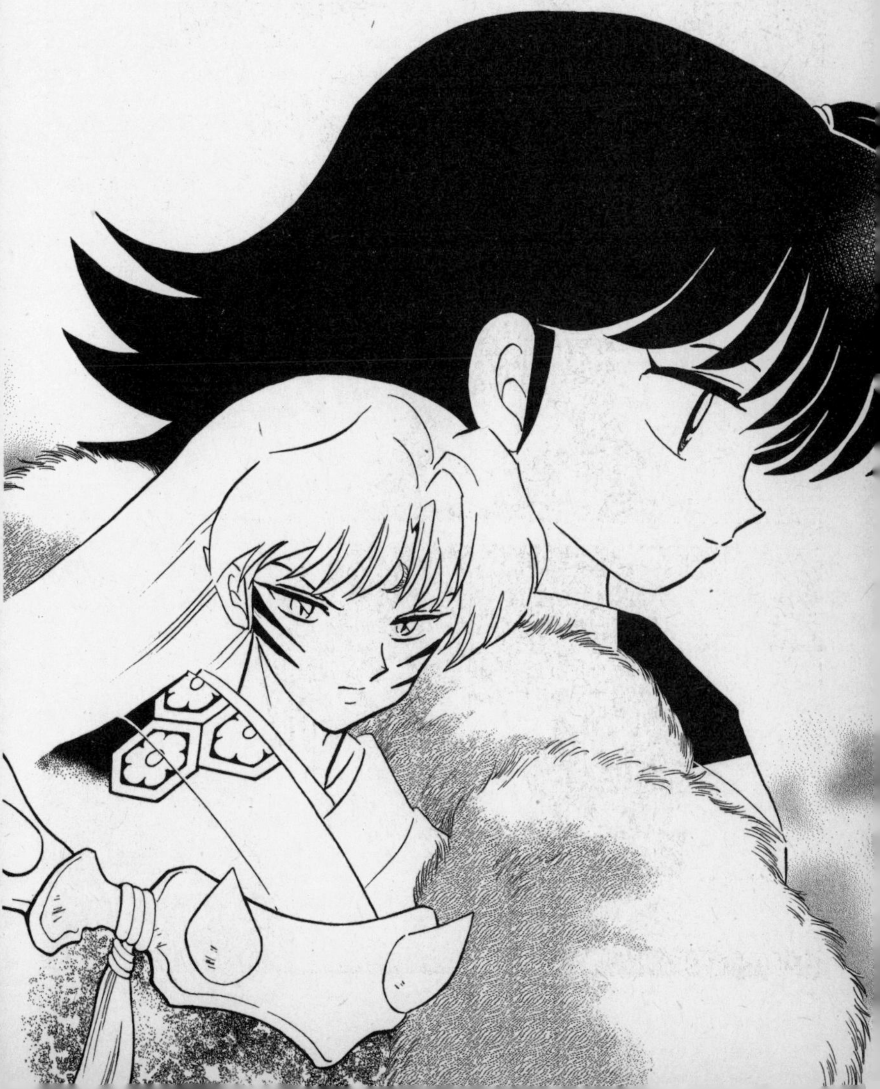

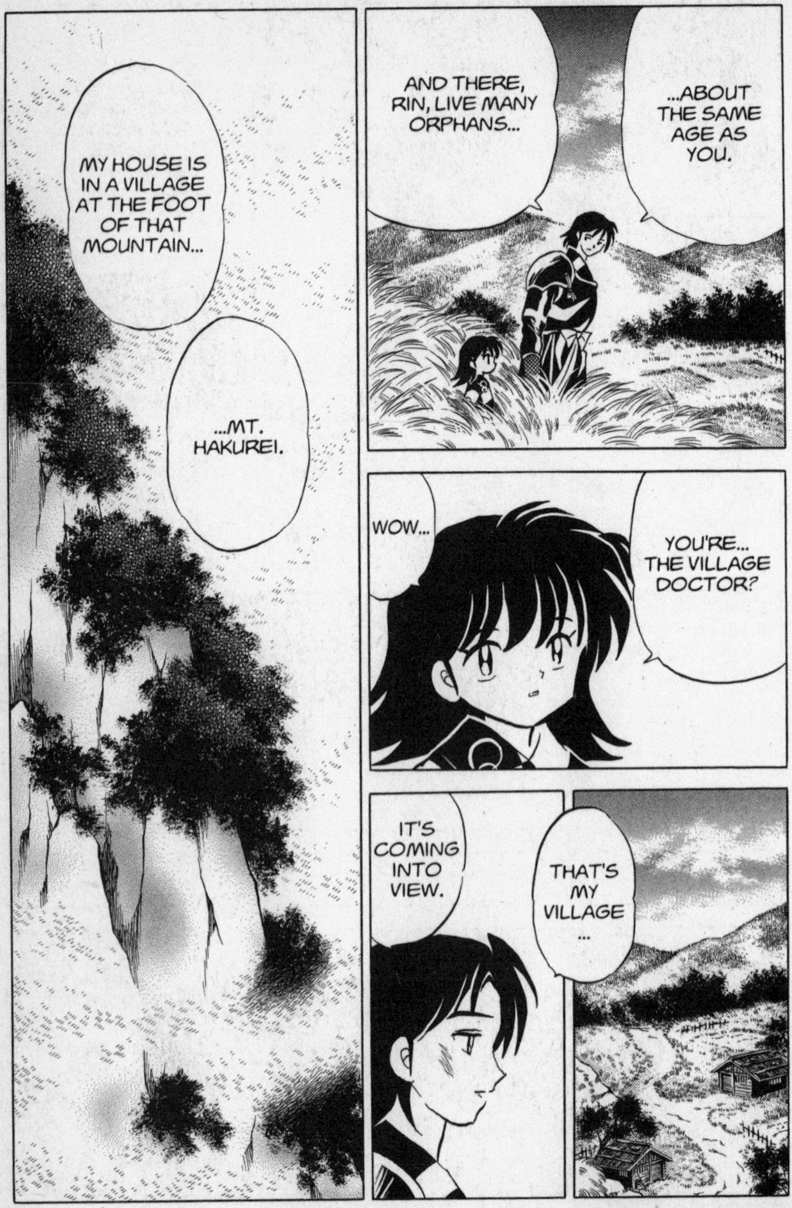
MY HOUSE IS IN A VILLAGE AT THE FOOT OF THAT MOUNTAIN...
...MT. HAKUREI.
AND THERE, RIN, LIVE MANY ORPHANS...
...ABOUT THE SAME AGE AS YOU.
WOW...
YOU'RE... THE VILLAGE DOCTOR?
IT'S COMING INTO VIEW.
THAT'S MY VILLAGE ...

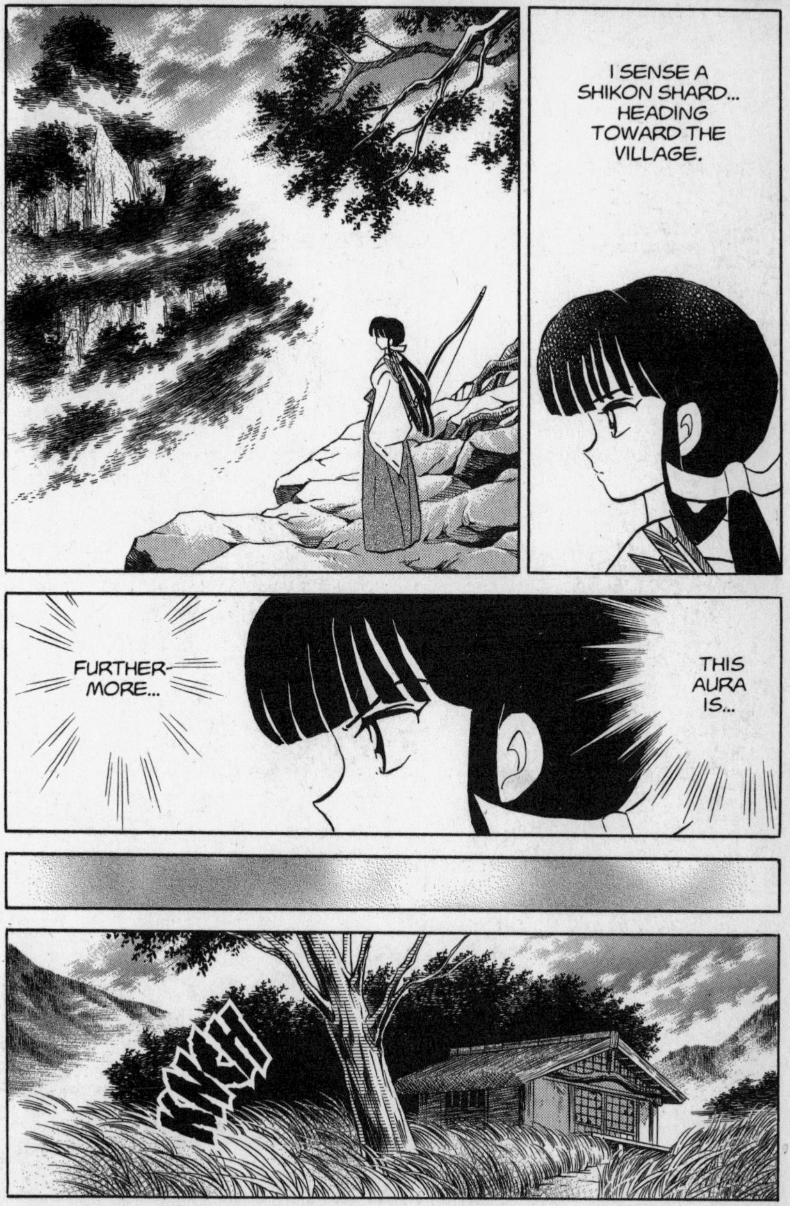
I SENSE A SHIKON SHARD... HEADING TOWARD THE VILLAGE.
FURTHER-MORE...
THIS AURA IS...

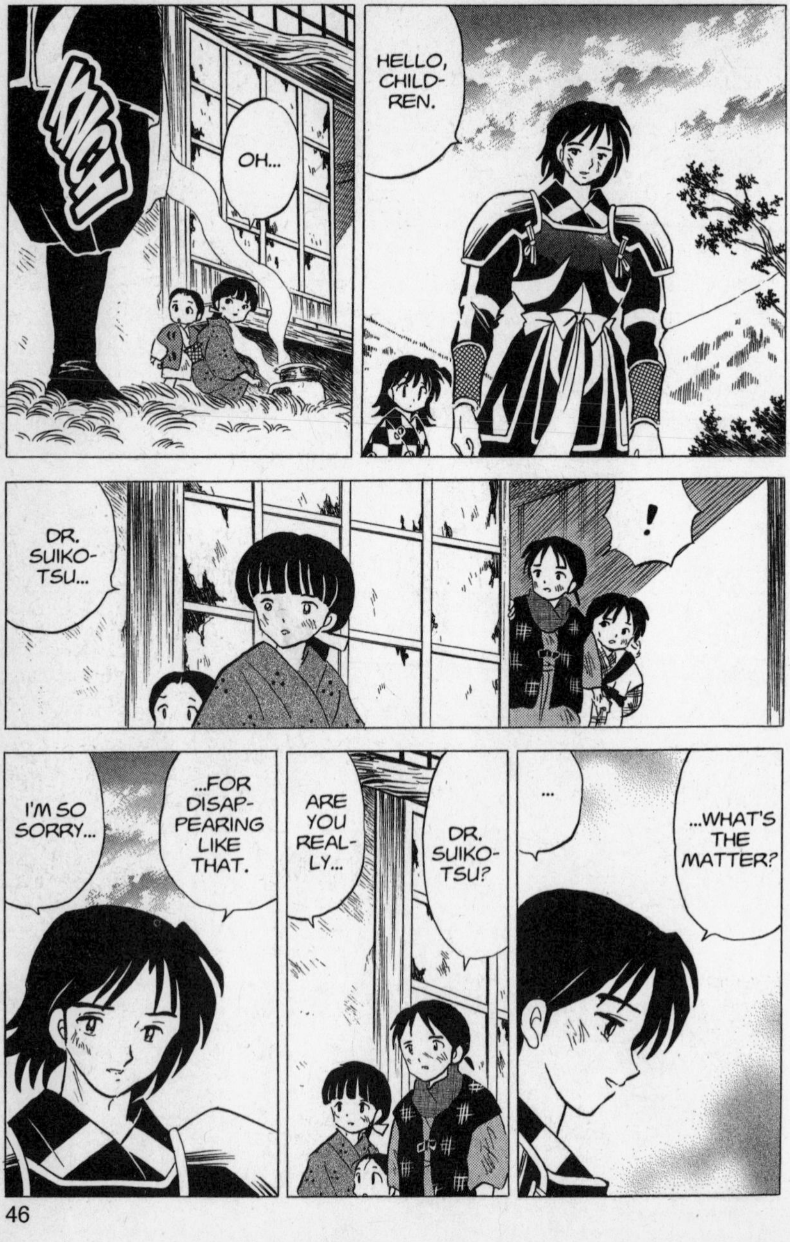

KNCH!
OH...
HELLO, CHILD-REN.
DR. SUIKO-TSU...
!
I'M SO SORRY...
...FOR DISAP-PEARING LIKE THAT.
ARE YOU REAL-LY...
DR. SUIKO-TSU?
...
...WHAT'S THE MATTER?

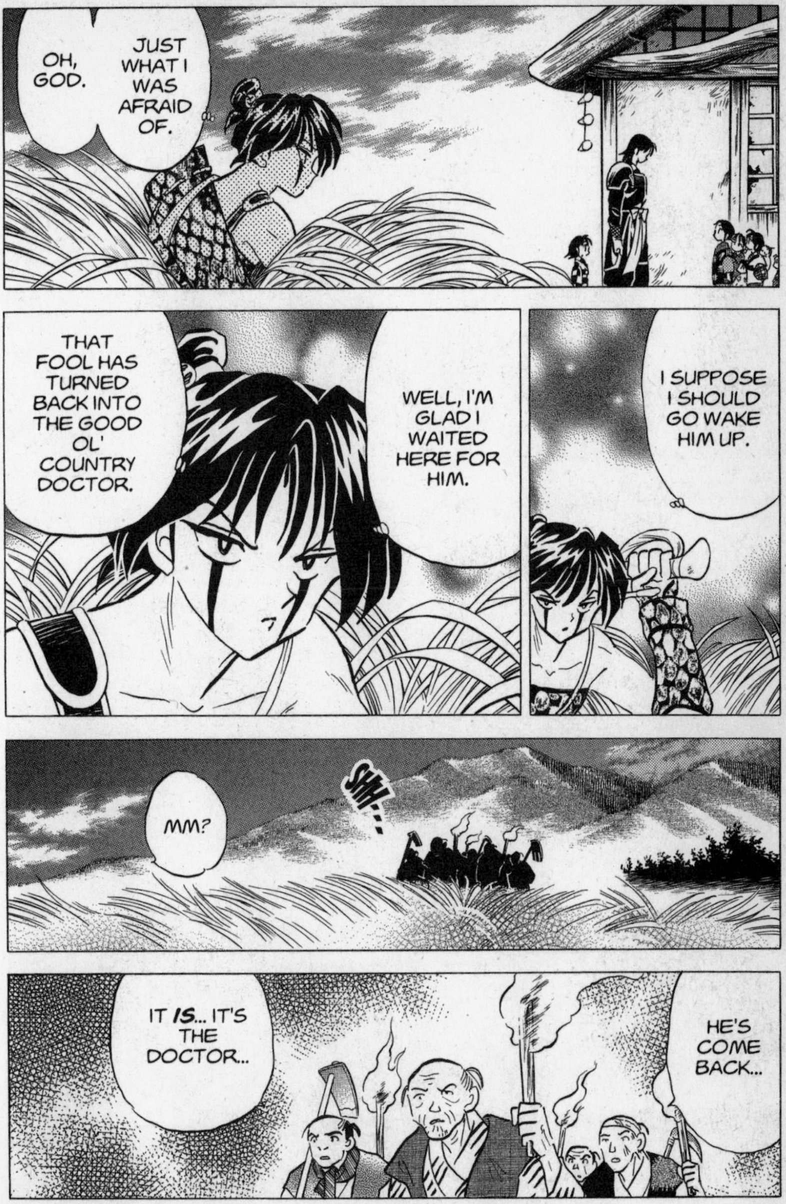
OH, GOD.
JUST WHAT I WAS AFRAID OF.
THAT FOOL HAS TURNED BACK INTO THE GOOD OL' COUNTRY DOCTOR.
WELL, I'M GLAD I WAITED HERE FOR HIM.
I SUPPOSE I SHOULD GO WAKE HIM UP.
MM?
SHH...
IT IS... IT'S THE DOCTOR...
HE'S COME BACK...

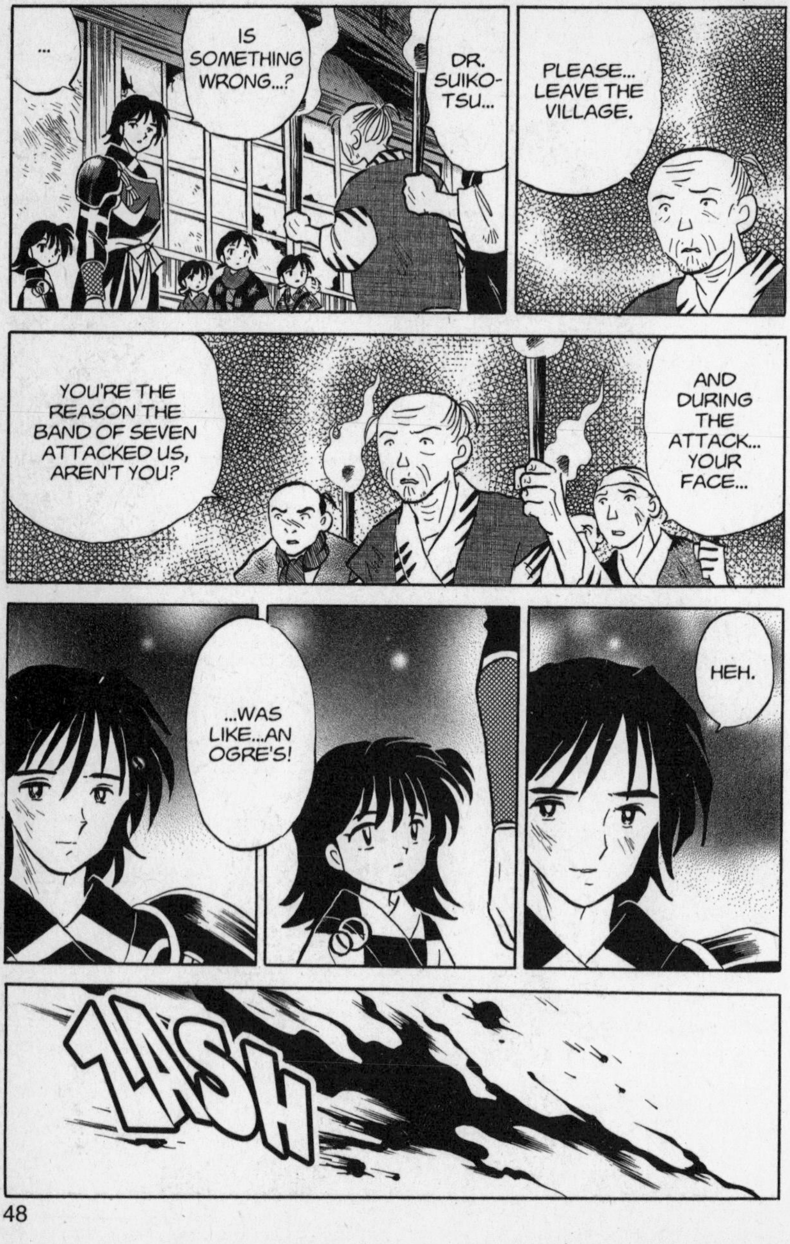
DR. SUIKO-TSU...
IS SOMETHING WRONG...?
...
PLEASE... LEAVE THE VILLAGE.
YOU'RE THE REASON THE BAND OF SEVEN ATTACKED US, AREN'T YOU?
AND DURING THE ATTACK... YOUR FACE...
...WAS LIKE...AN OGRE'S!
HEH.
ZASH

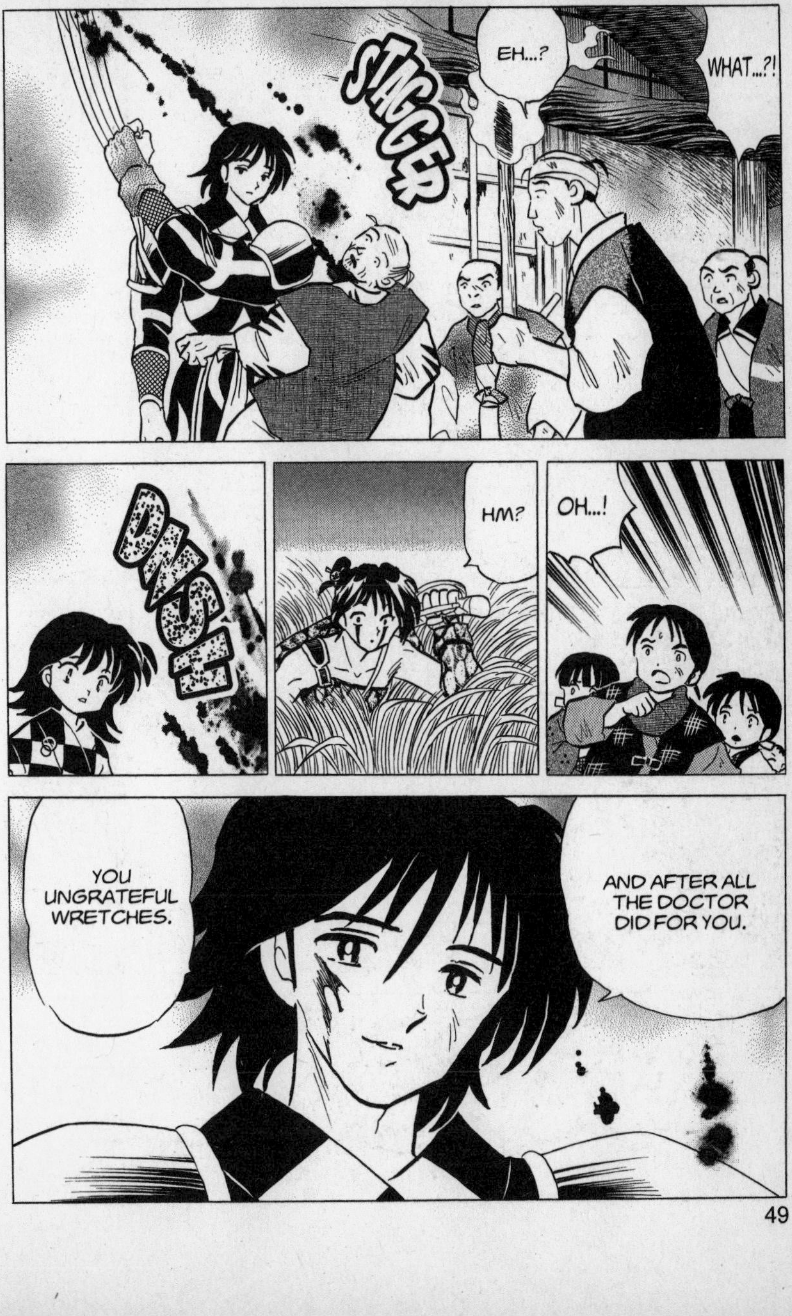
STAGGER
EH...?
WHAT...?!
DWSH
HM?
OH...!
YOU UNGRATEFUL WRETCHES.
AND AFTER ALL THE DOCTOR DID FOR YOU.

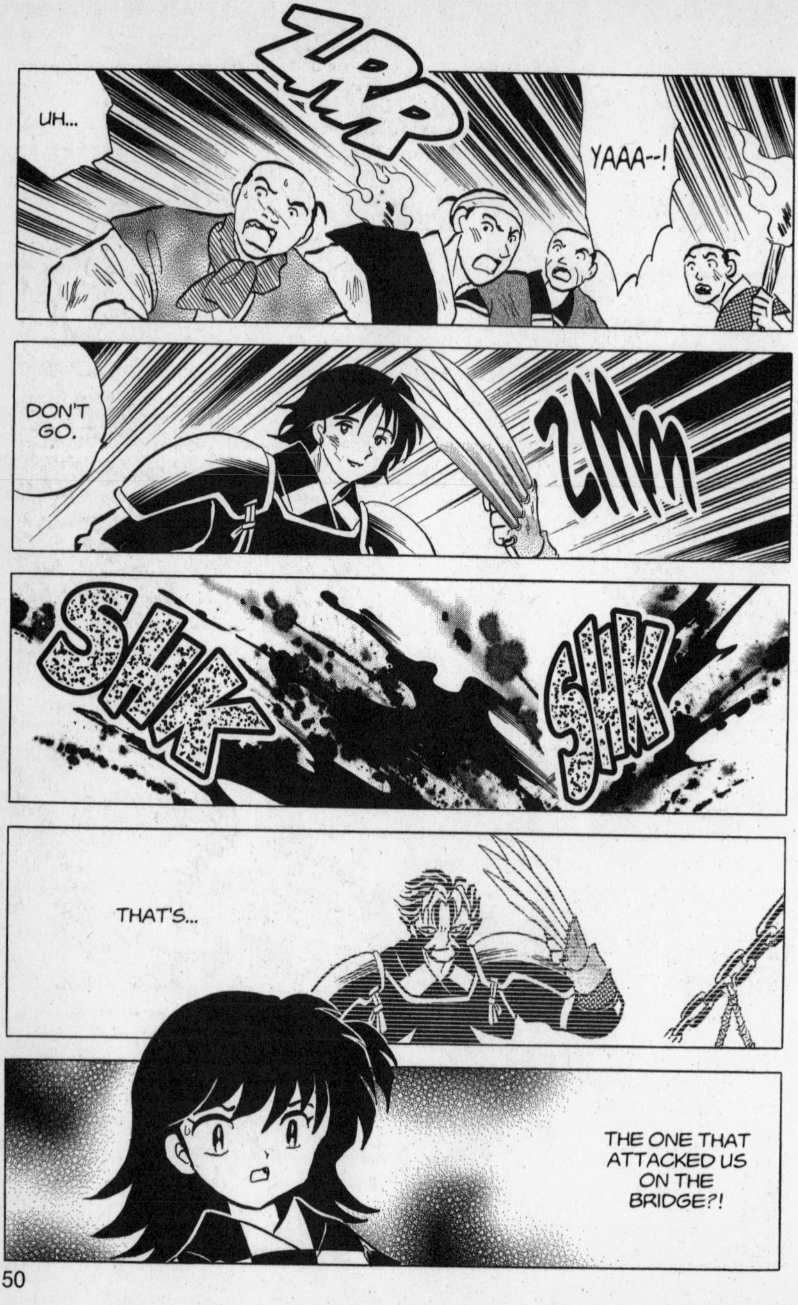
ZRP
YAAA--!
UH...
ZMM
DON'T GO.
SHK
SHK
THAT'S...
THE ONE THAT ATTACKED US ON THE BRIDGE?!

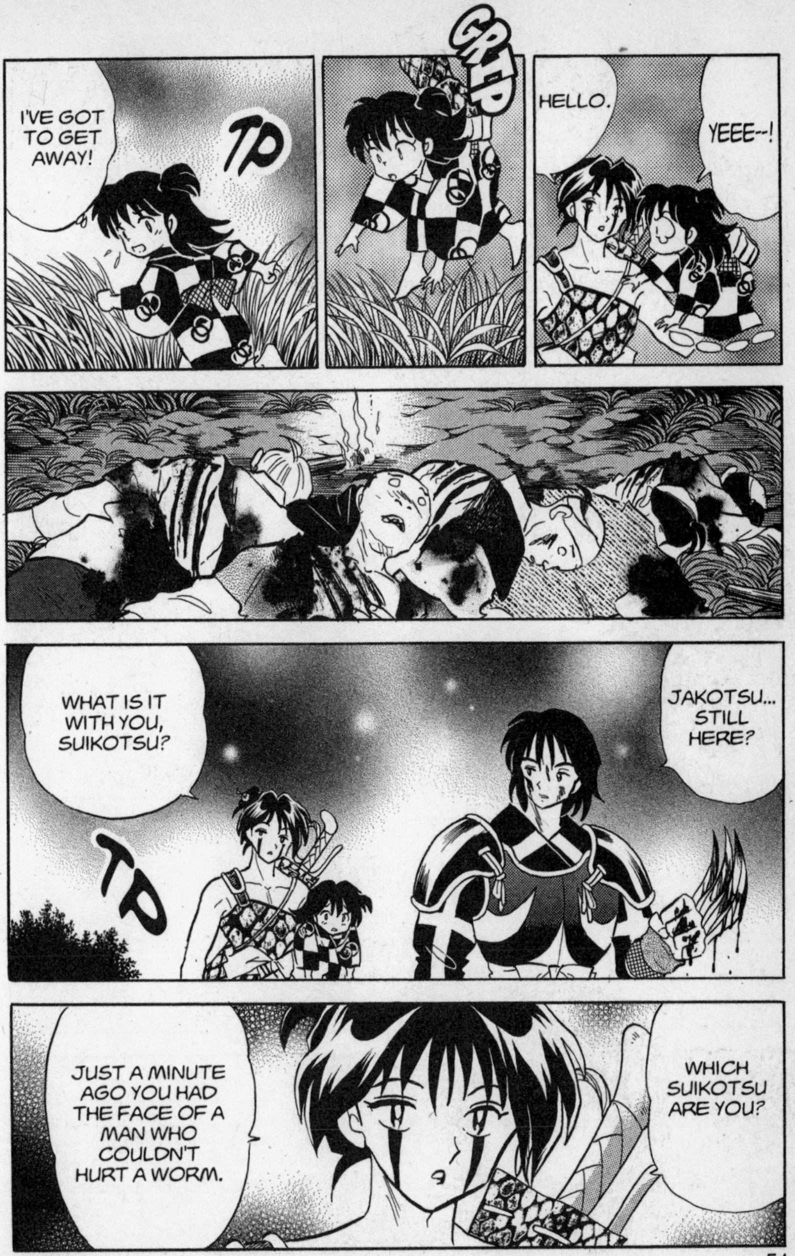

I'VE GOT TO GET AWAY!
TP
GRIP
HELLO.
YEEE--!
WHAT IS IT WITH YOU, SUIKOTSU?
TP
JAKOTSU... STILL HERE?
JUST A MINUTE AGO YOU HAD THE FACE OF A MAN WHO COULDN'T HURT A WORM.
WHICH SUIKOTSU ARE YOU?

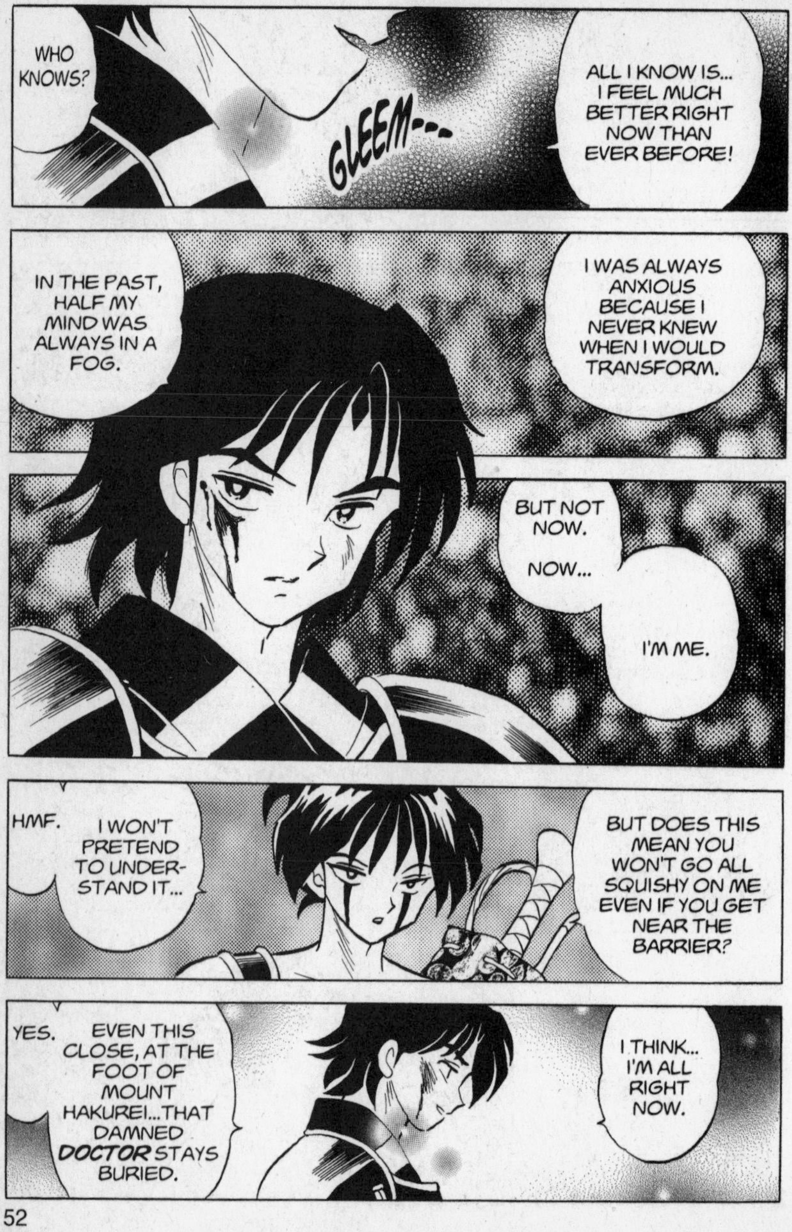
WHO KNOWS?
GLEEM...
ALL I KNOW IS... I FEEL MUCH BETTER RIGHT NOW THAN EVER BEFORE!
IN THE PAST, HALF MY MIND WAS ALWAYS IN A FOG.
I WAS ALWAYS ANXIOUS BECAUSE I NEVER KNEW WHEN I WOULD TRANSFORM.
BUT NOT NOW.
NOW...
I'M ME.
HMF.
I WON'T PRETEND TO UNDER-STAND IT...
BUT DOES THIS MEAN YOU WON'T GO ALL SQUISHY ON ME EVEN IF YOU GET NEAR THE BARRIER?
YES.
EVEN THIS CLOSE, AT THE FOOT OF MOUNT HAKUREI...THAT DAMNED DOCTOR STAYS BURIED.
I THINK... I'M ALL RIGHT NOW.

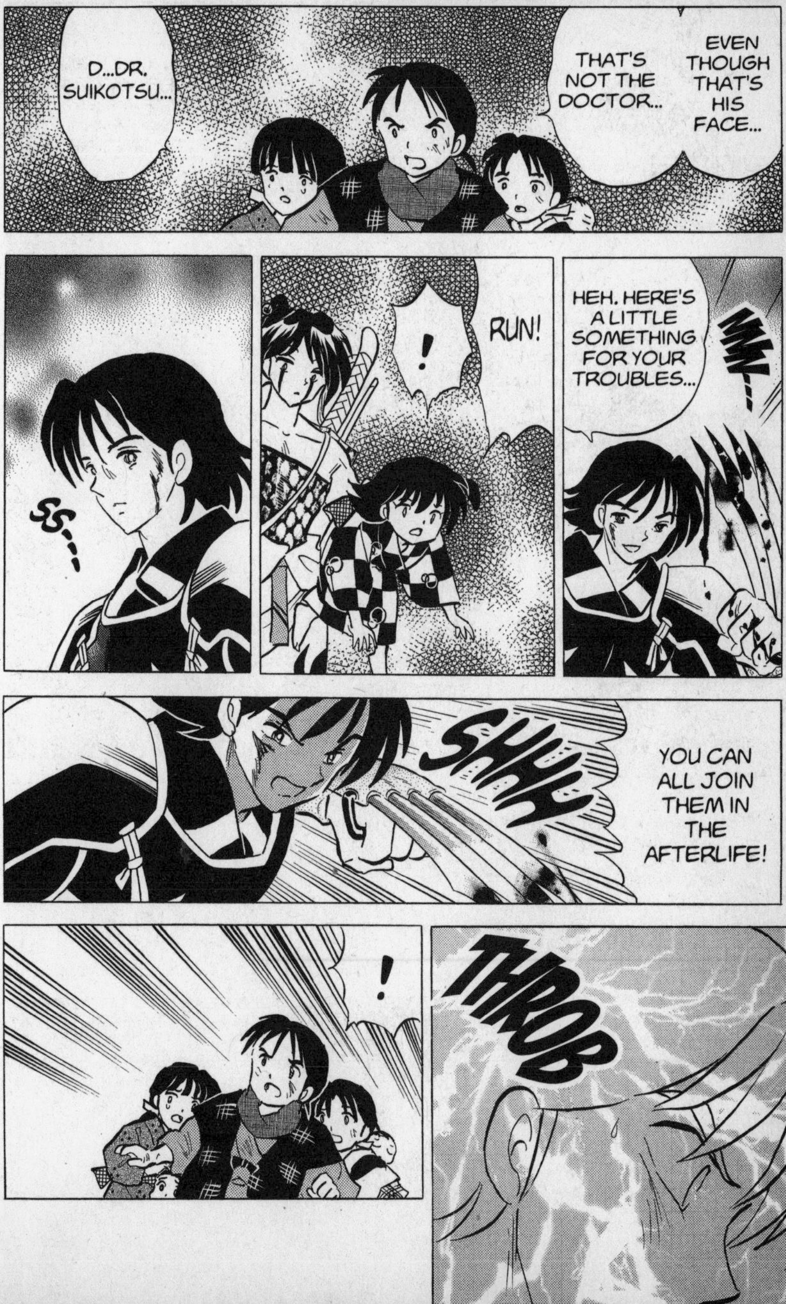
D...DR. SUIKOTSU...
THAT'S NOT THE DOCTOR...
EVEN THOUGH THAT'S HIS FACE...
SS...
!
RUN!
HEH. HERE'S A LITTLE SOMETHING FOR YOUR TROUBLES...
MMM...
SHHH
YOU CAN ALL JOIN THEM IN THE AFTERLIFE!
!
THROB

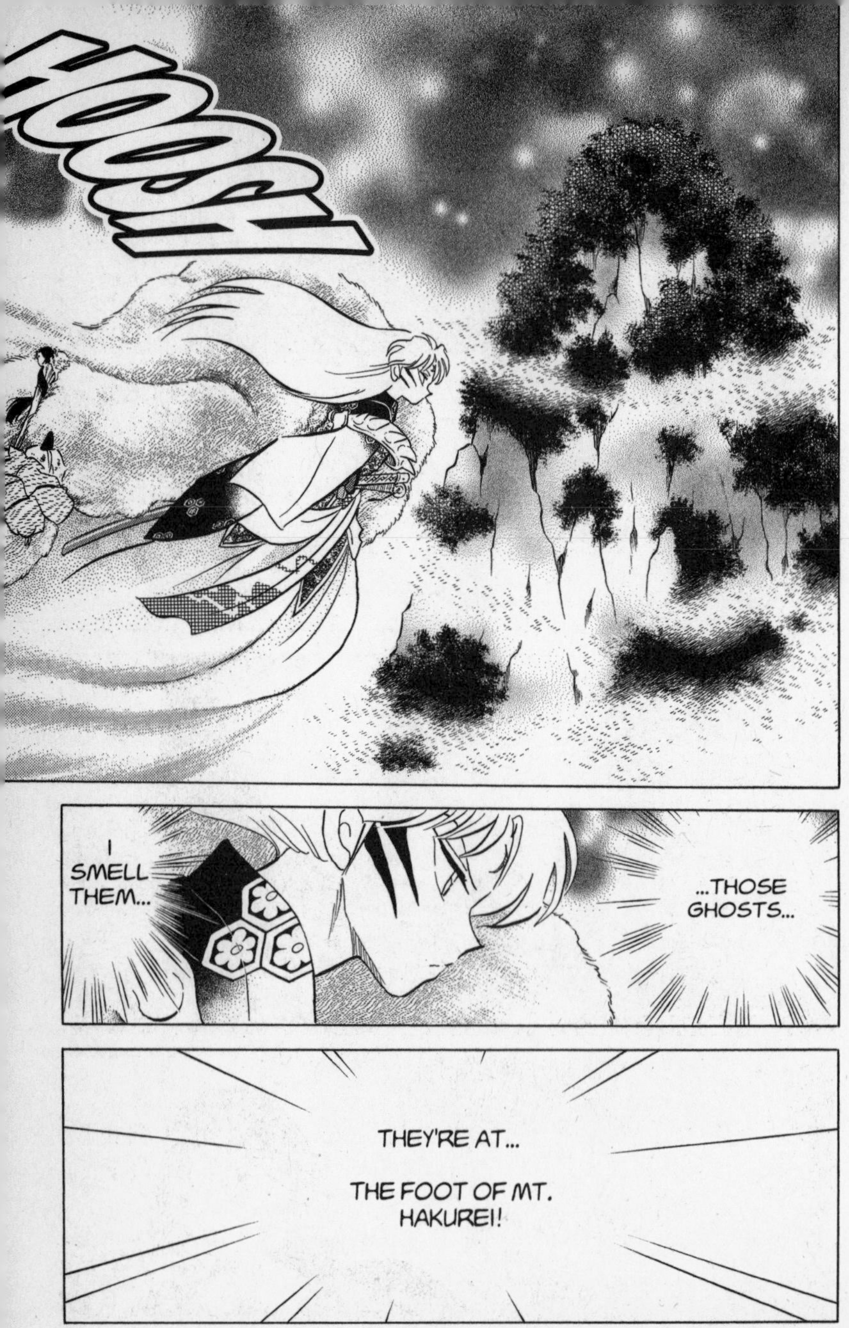
WHOOSH
I SMELL THEM...
...THOSE GHOSTS...
THEY'RE AT...
THE FOOT OF MT. HAKUREI!

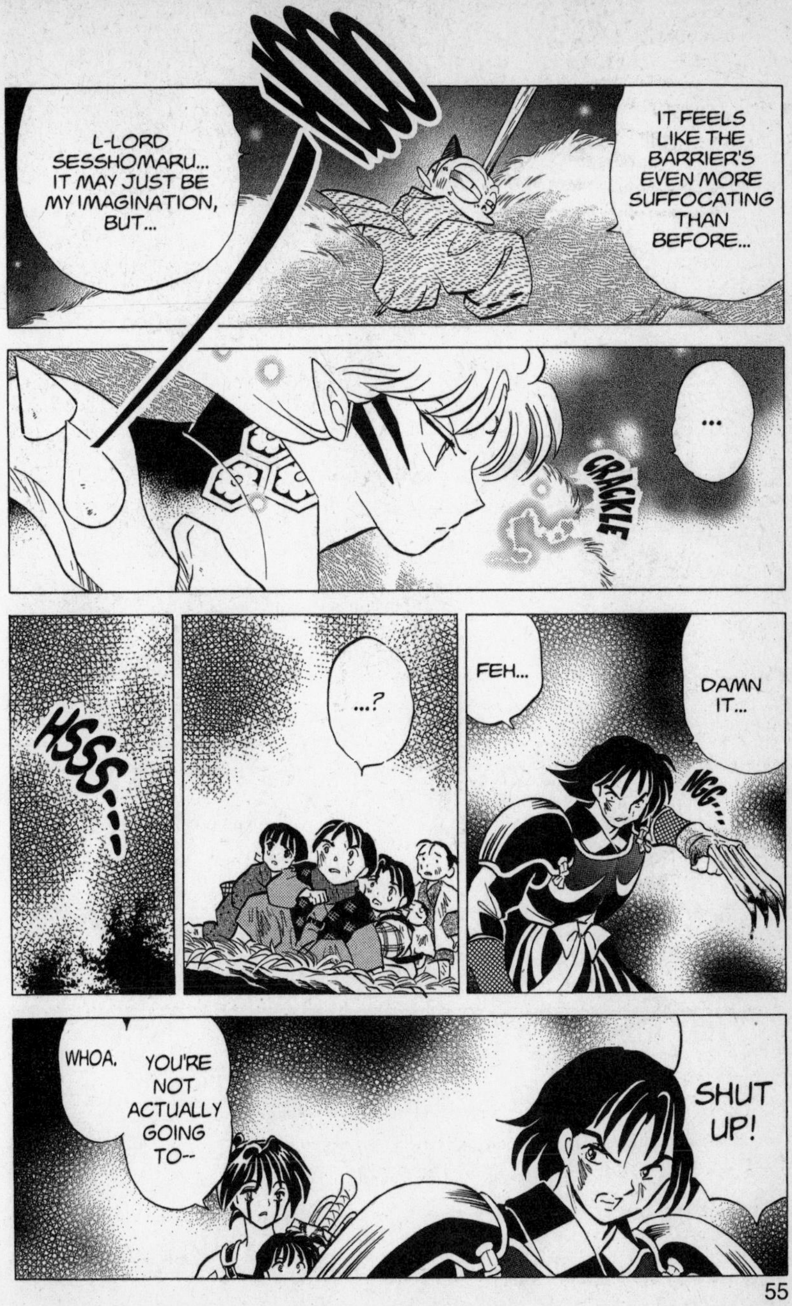
L-LORD SESSHOMARU... IT MAY JUST BE MY IMAGINATION, BUT...
IT FEELS LIKE THE BARRIER'S EVEN MORE SUFFOCATING THAN BEFORE...
...
CRACKLE
DAMN IT...
NGG...
FEH...
...?
HSSS...
SHUT UP!
WHOA.
YOU'RE NOT ACTUALLY GOING TO--

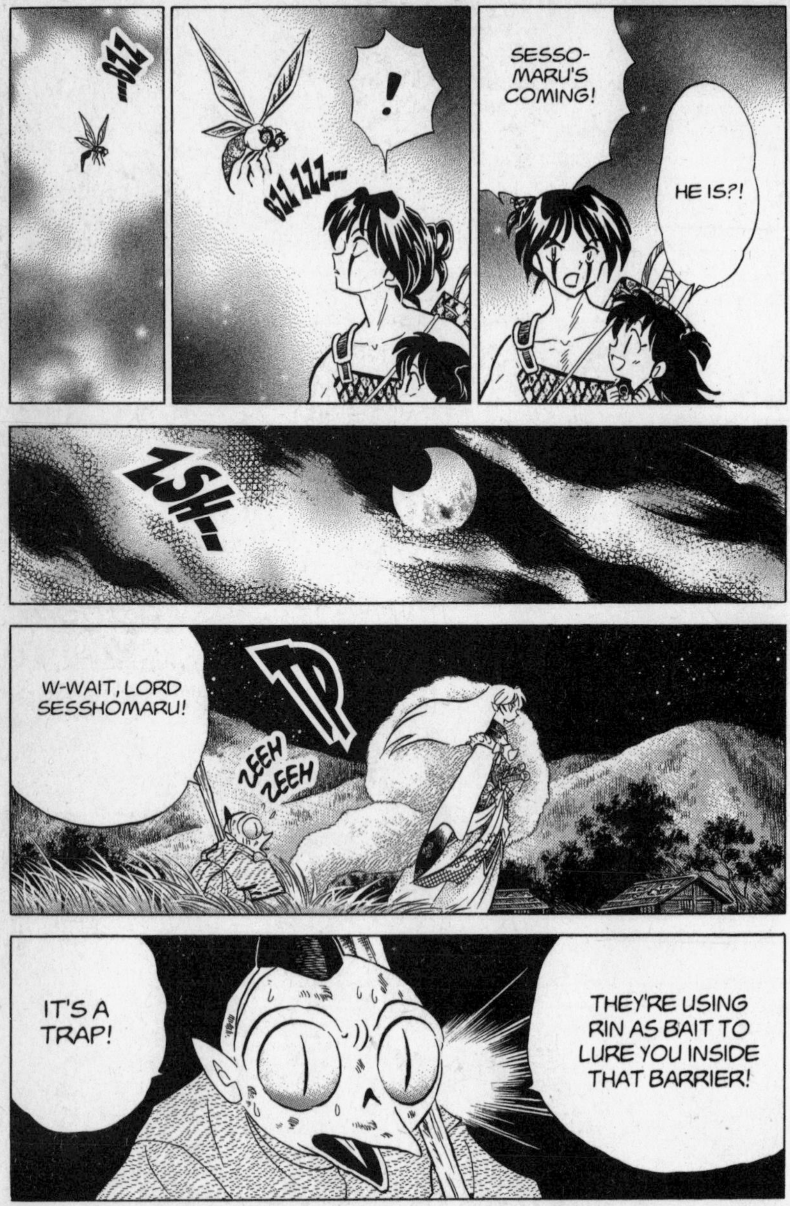
BZZ...
BZZ ZZZ...
!
SESSO-MARU'S COMING!
HE IS?!
ZSH--
W-WAIT, LORD SESSHOMARU!
TP
ZEEH ZEEH
IT'S A TRAP!
THEY'RE USING RIN AS BAIT TO LURE YOU INSIDE THAT BARRIER!

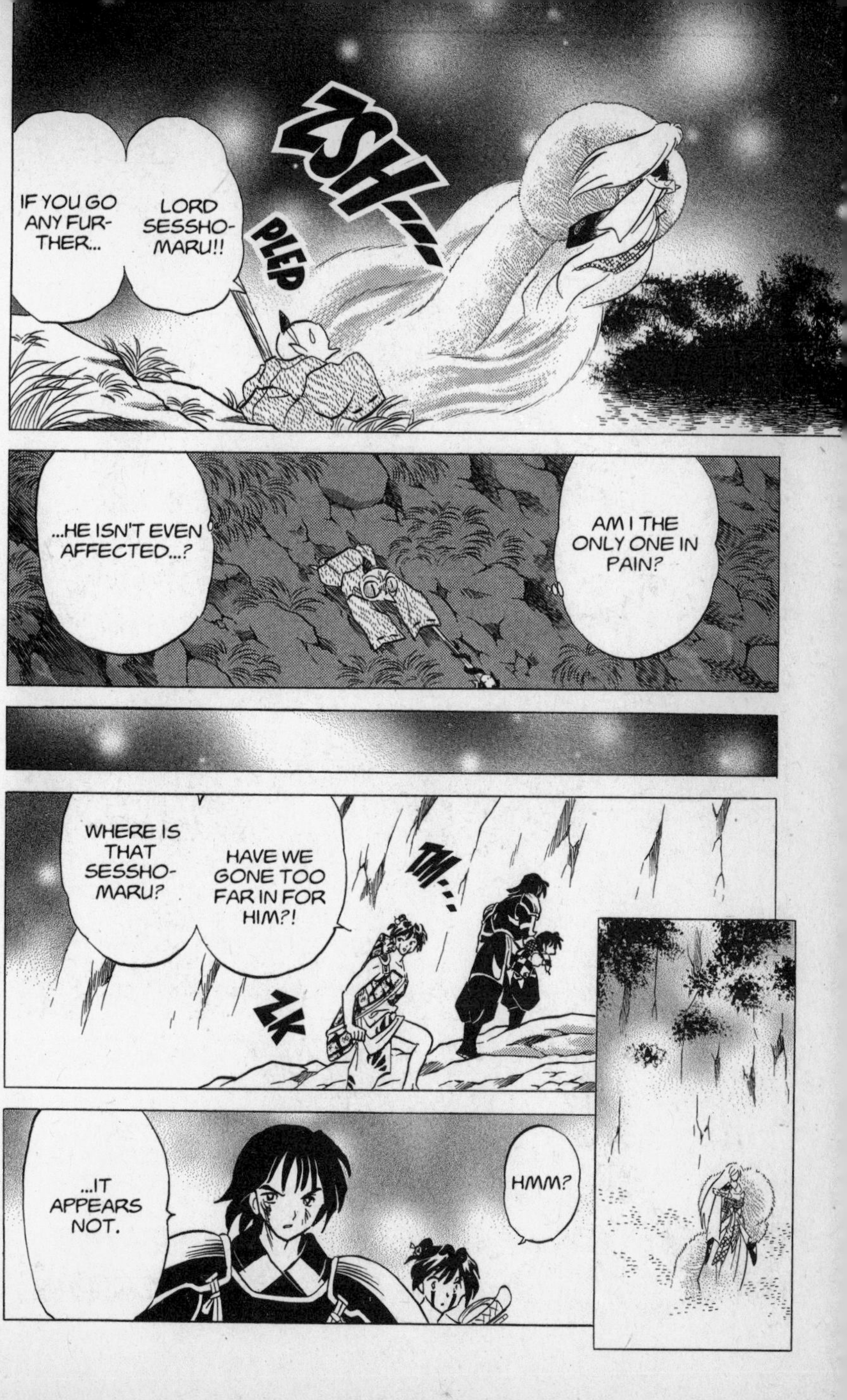
TSH—
LORD SESSHO-MARU!!
IF YOU GO ANY FUR-THER...
PLEP
AM I THE ONLY ONE IN PAIN?
...HE ISN'T EVEN AFFECTED...?
TM...
HAVE WE GONE TOO FAR IN FOR HIM?!
WHERE IS THAT SESSHO-MARU?
ZK
HMM?
...IT APPEARS NOT.

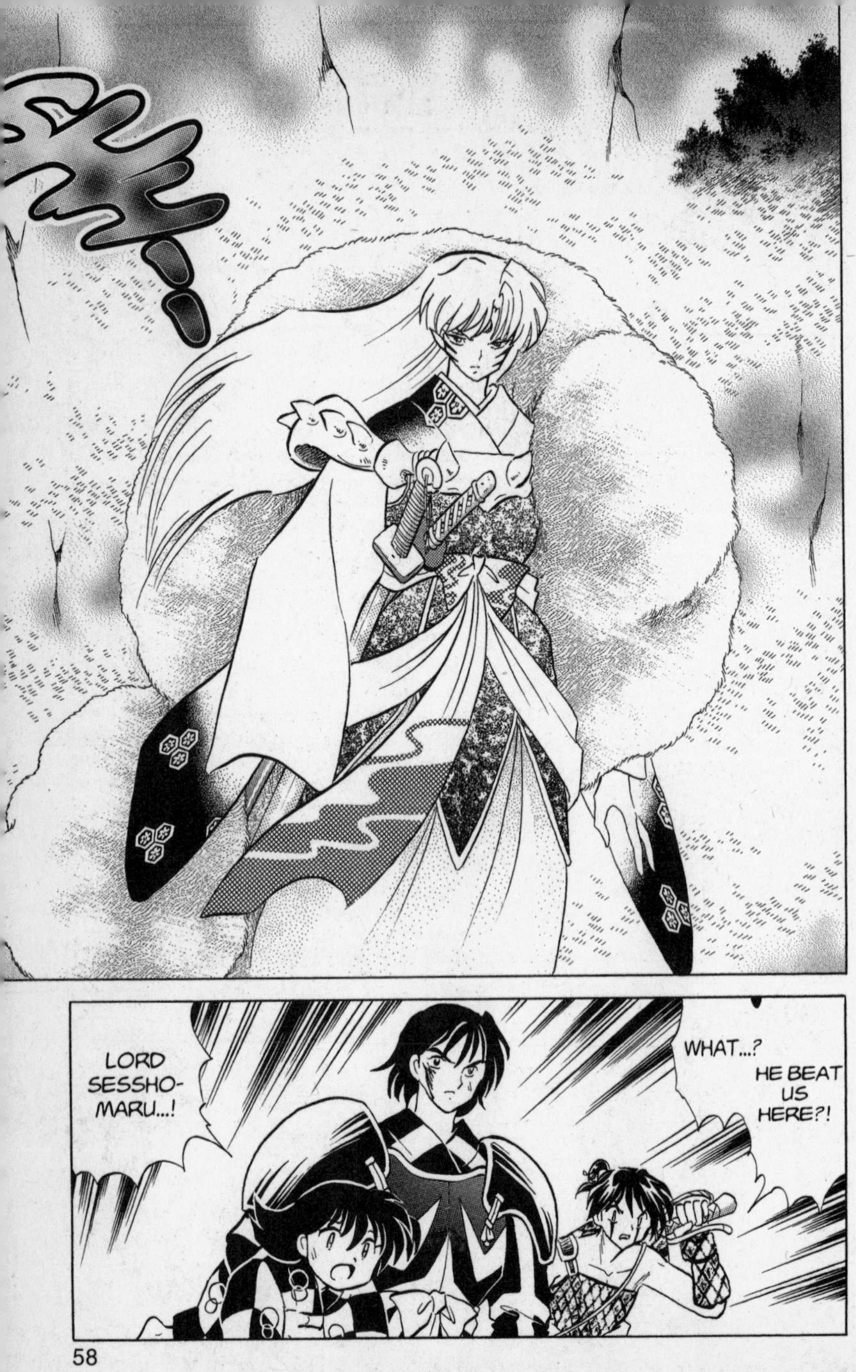
WHAT...?
HE BEAT US HERE?!
LORD SESSHO-MARU...!

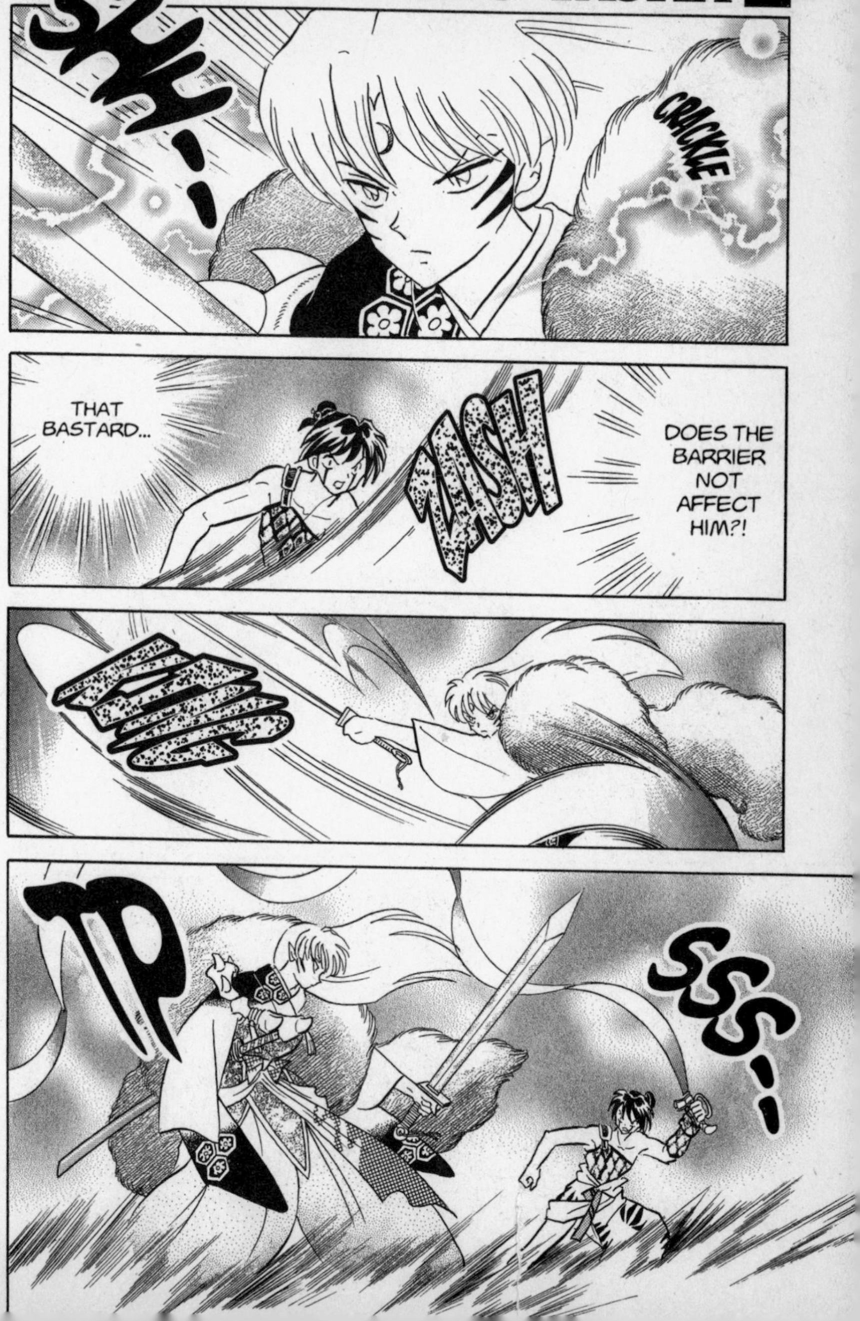
SHH
CRACKLE
THAT BASTARD...
ZASH
DOES THE BARRIER NOT AFFECT HIM?!
TP
SSS

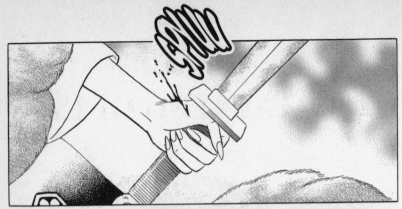

LORD SESSHO-MARU...!

HEH... SLOW, ISN'T HE?

HSSH!

SCROLL FOUR

THE TAINTED GLEAM

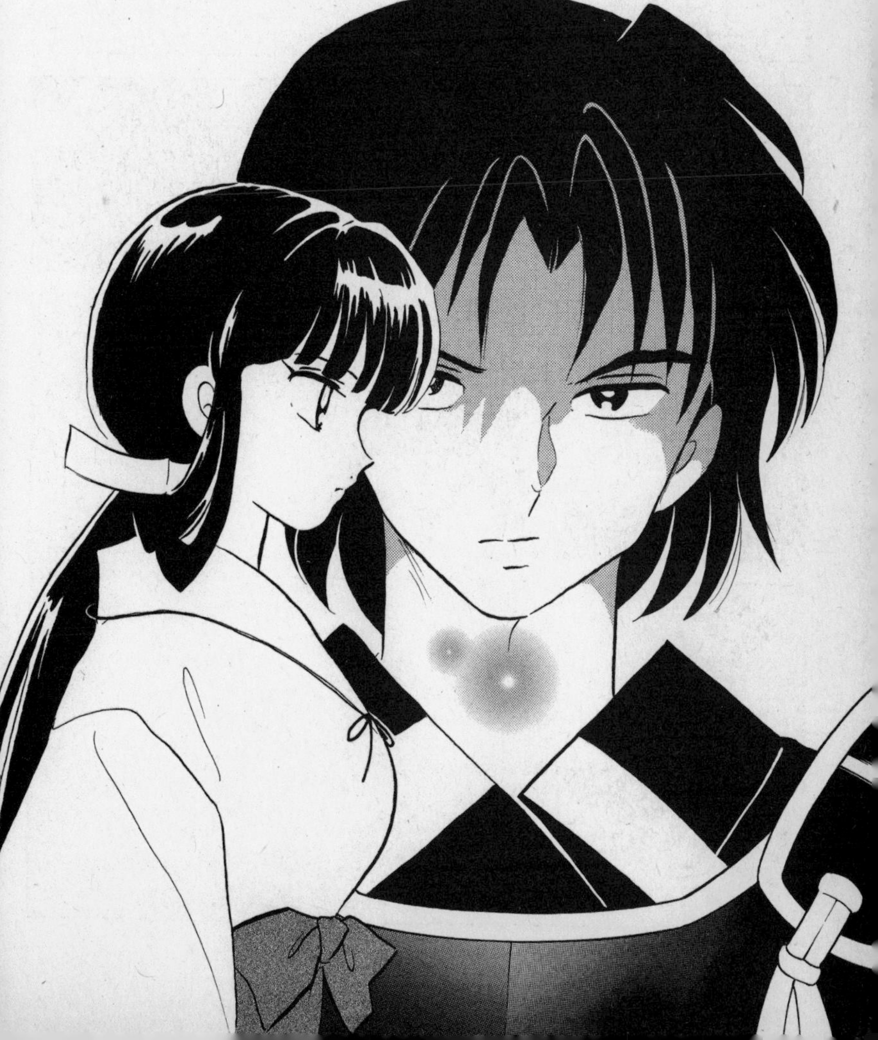

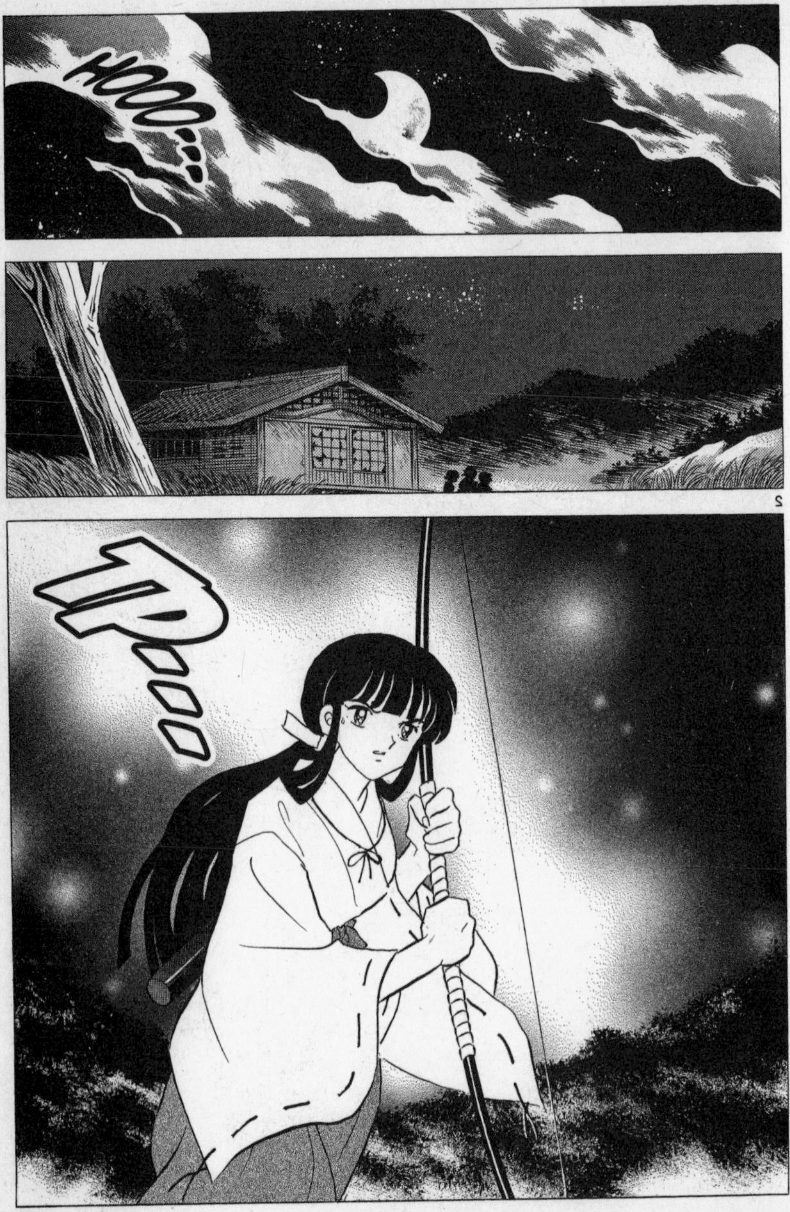
HOOO...

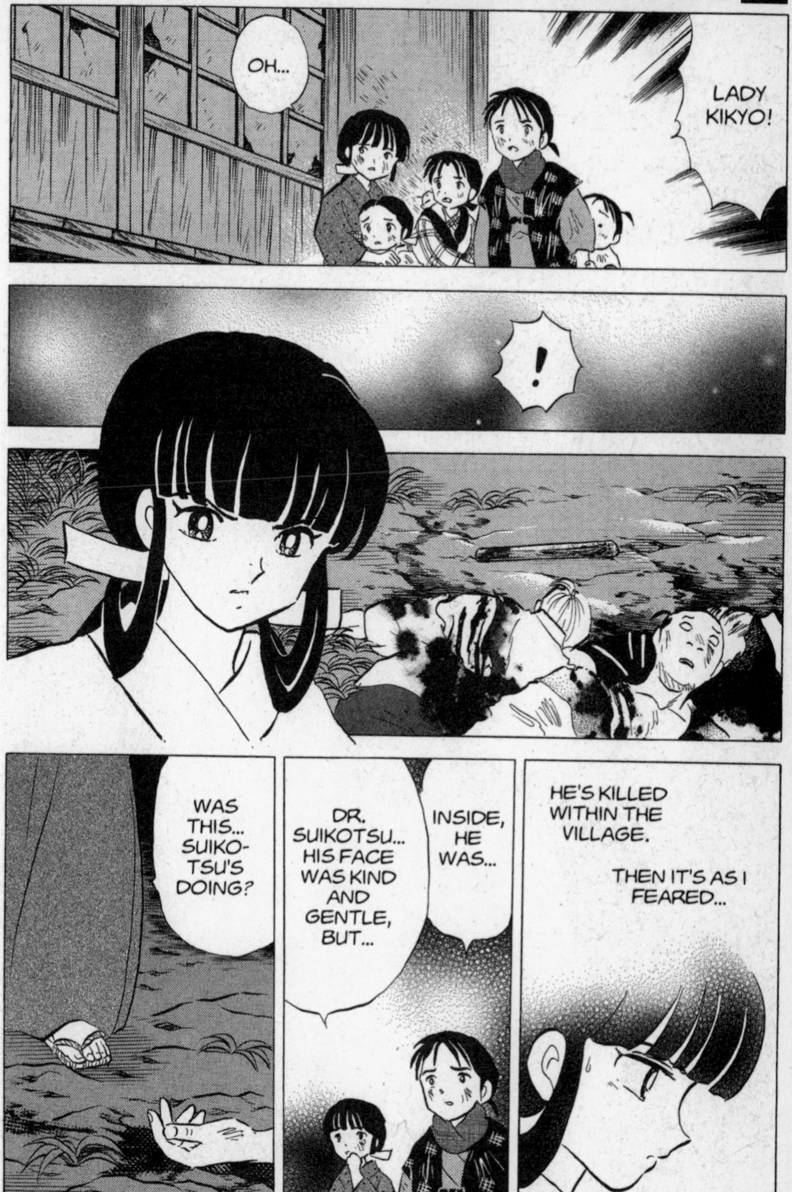
LADY KIKYO!
OH...
!
HE'S KILLED WITHIN THE VILLAGE.
THEN IT'S AS I FEARED...
INSIDE, HE WAS...
DR. SUIKOTSU... HIS FACE WAS KIND AND GENTLE, BUT...
WAS THIS... SUIKO-TSU'S DOING?

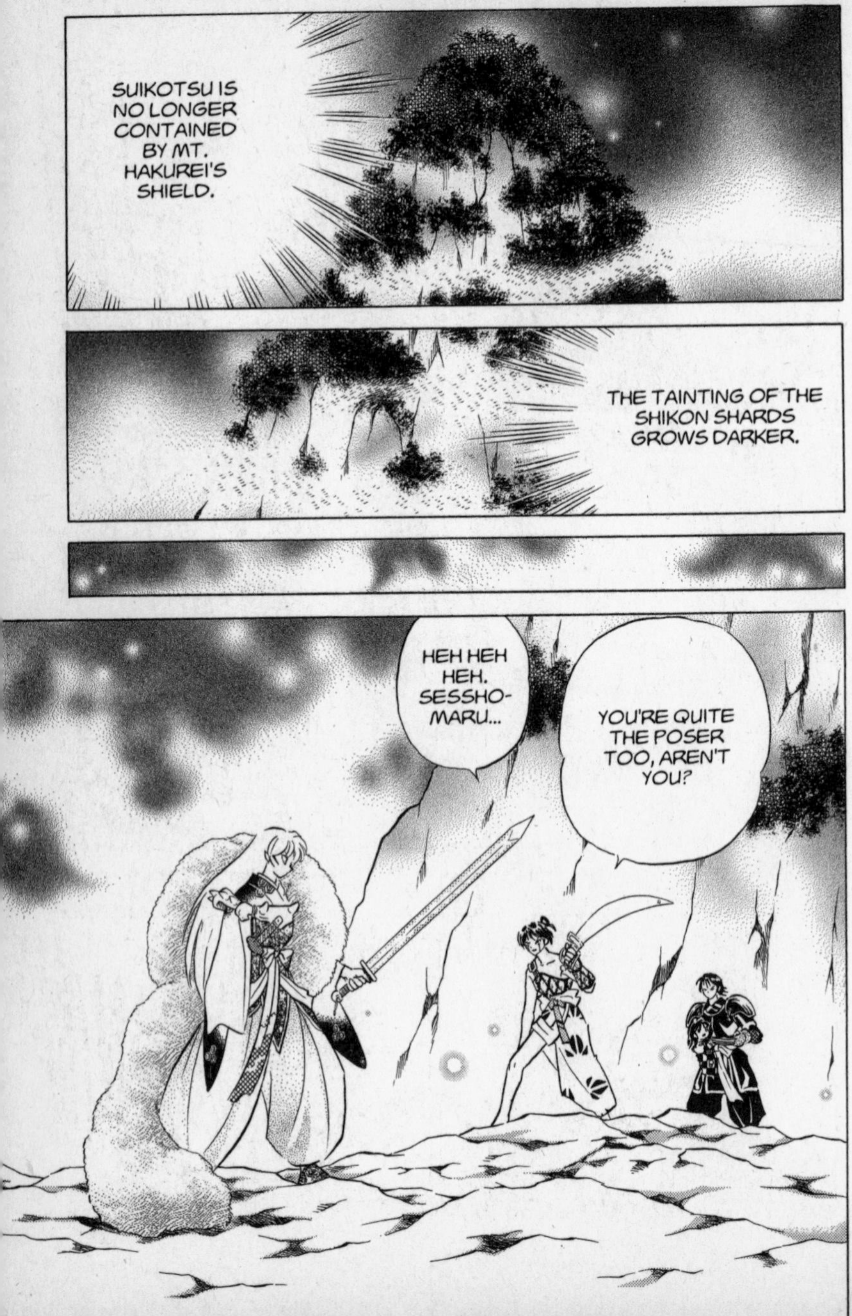
SUIKOTSU IS NO LONGER CONTAINED BY MT. HAKUREI'S SHIELD.
THE TAINTING OF THE SHIKON SHARDS GROWS DARKER.
HEH HEH HEH. SESSHO-MARU...
YOU'RE QUITE THE POSER TOO, AREN'T YOU?

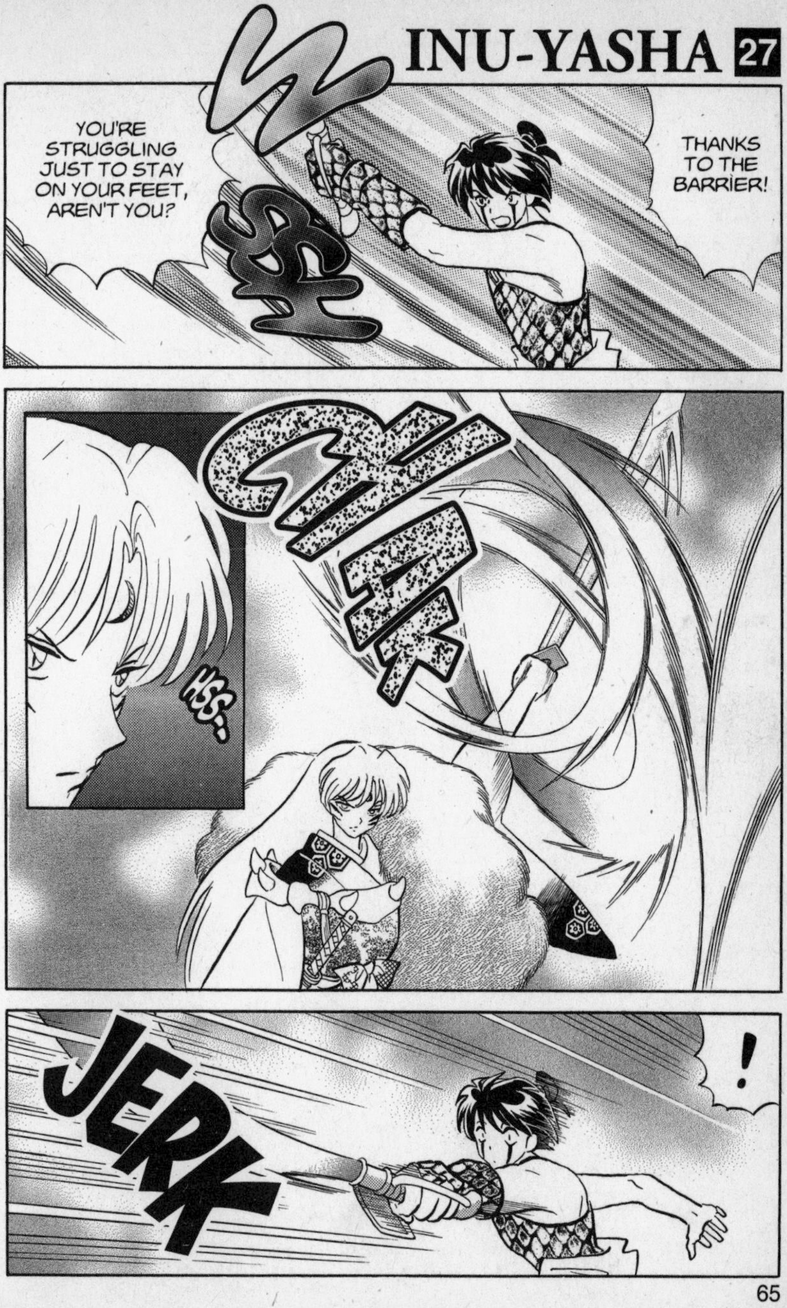
THANKS TO THE BARRIER!
YOU'RE STRUGGLING JUST TO STAY ON YOUR FEET, AREN'T YOU?
WSSH
CHAK
HSS..
!
JERK

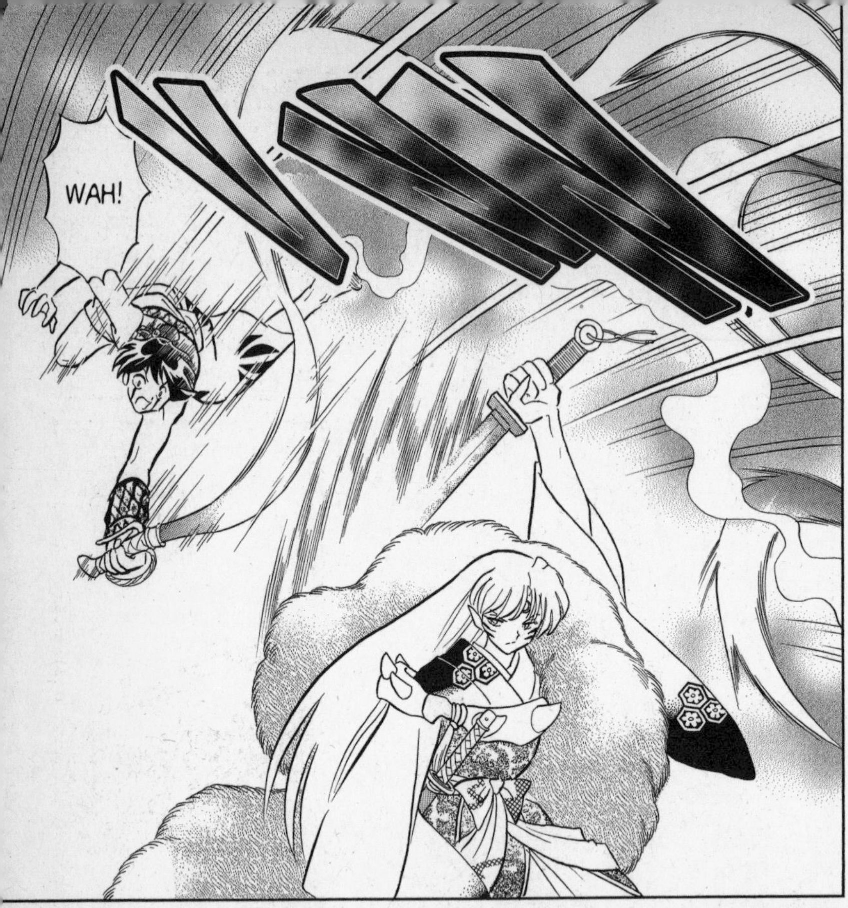
WAH!

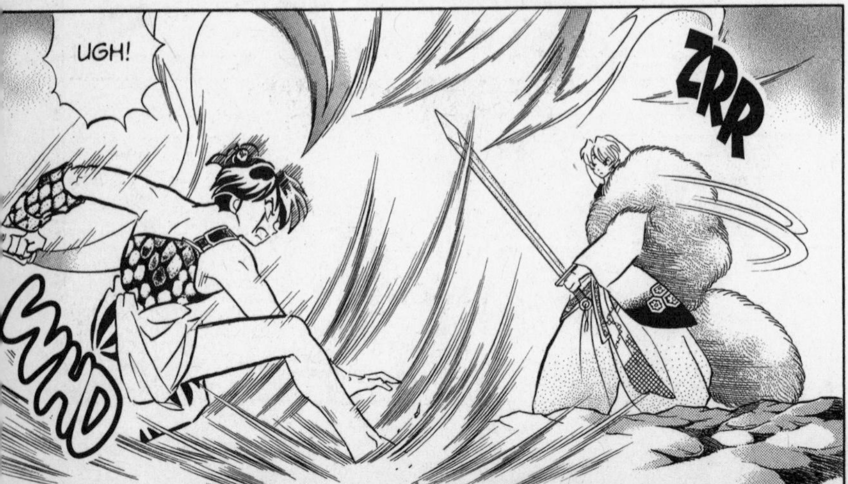
UGH!
ZRR
WHD

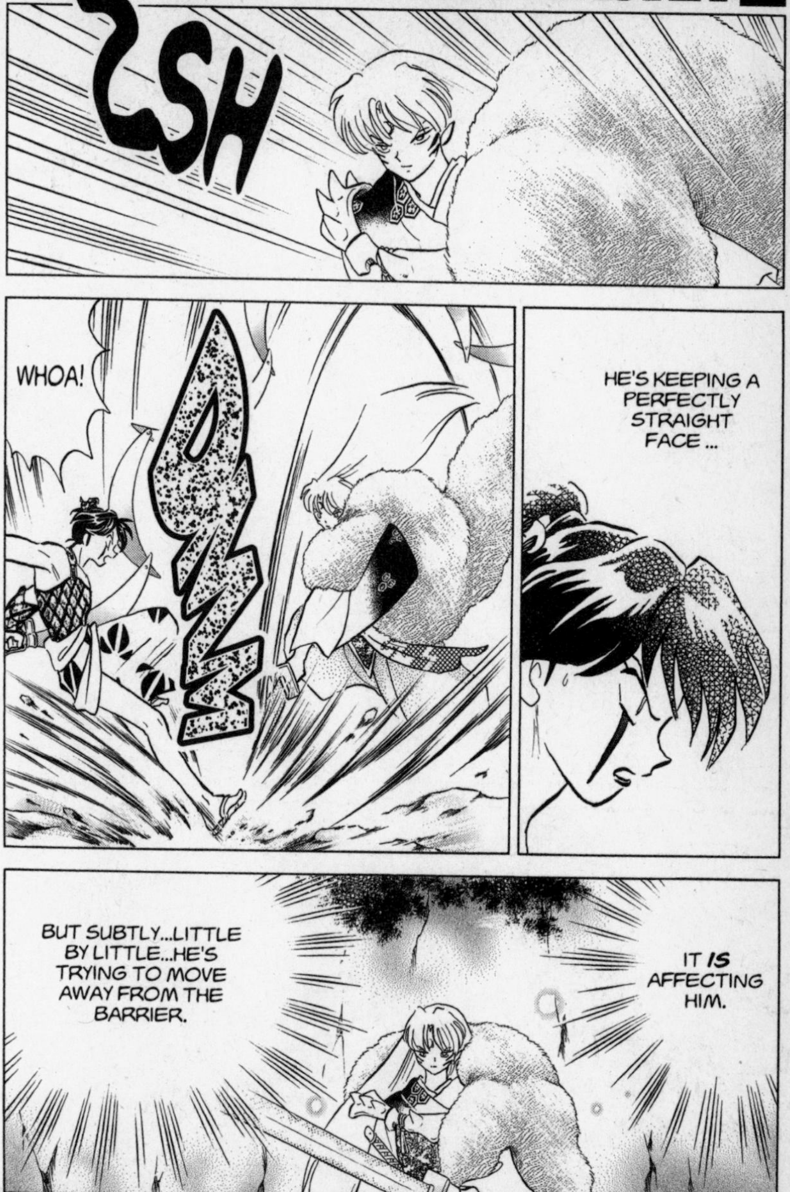
ZSH
HE'S KEEPING A PERFECTLY STRAIGHT FACE ...
WHOA!
IT *IS* AFFECTING HIM.
BUT SUBTLY...LITTLE BY LITTLE...HE'S TRYING TO MOVE AWAY FROM THE BARRIER.

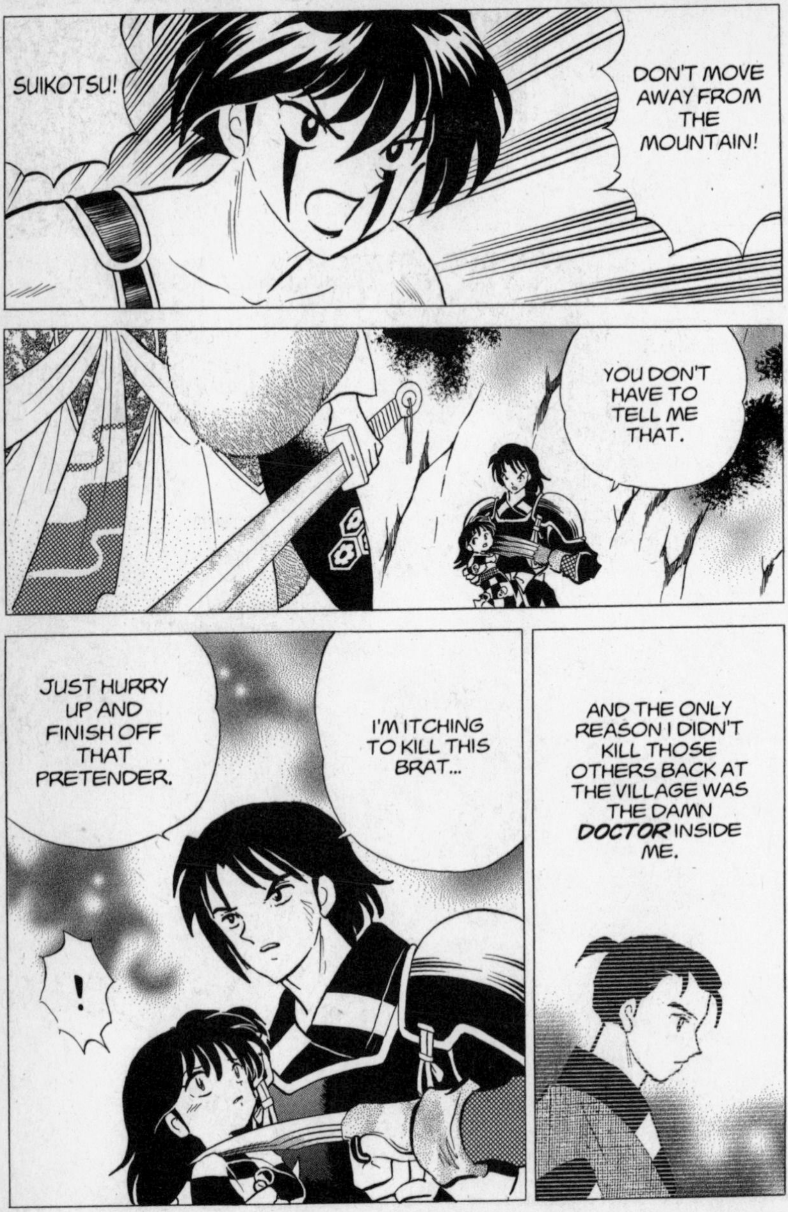
SUIKOTSU!
DON'T MOVE AWAY FROM THE MOUNTAIN!
YOU DON'T HAVE TO TELL ME THAT.
JUST HURRY UP AND FINISH OFF THAT PRETENDER.
I'M ITCHING TO KILL THIS BRAT...
!
AND THE ONLY REASON I DIDN'T KILL THOSE OTHERS BACK AT THE VILLAGE WAS THE DAMN DOCTOR INSIDE ME.

THIS TIME--

LORD SESSHO-MARU...

DO YOU GET IT, FINALLY?

TRY ANYTHING STUPID, AND THIS SHE-WHELP IS A CORPSE.

OF COURSE...IT'S REALLY JUST A MATTER OF *WHEN*!

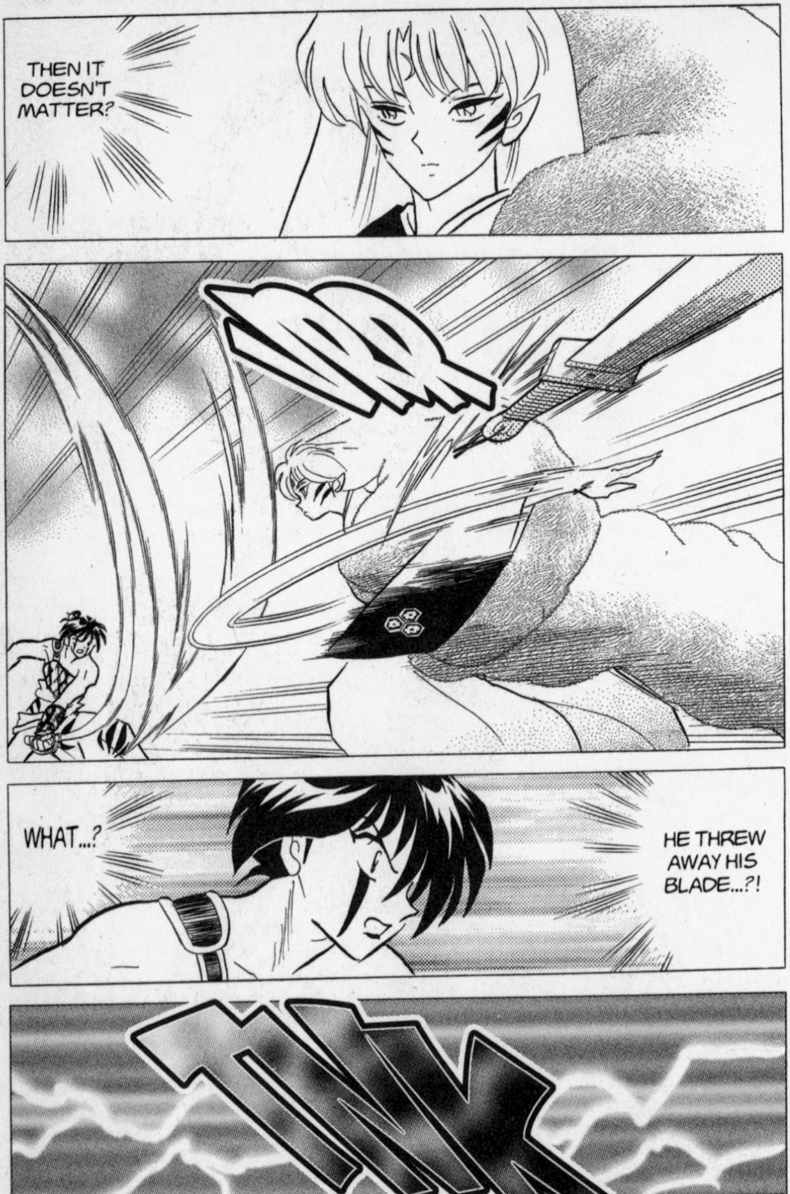
THEN IT DOESN'T MATTER?
WHAT...?
HE THREW AWAY HIS BLADE...?!
TINK

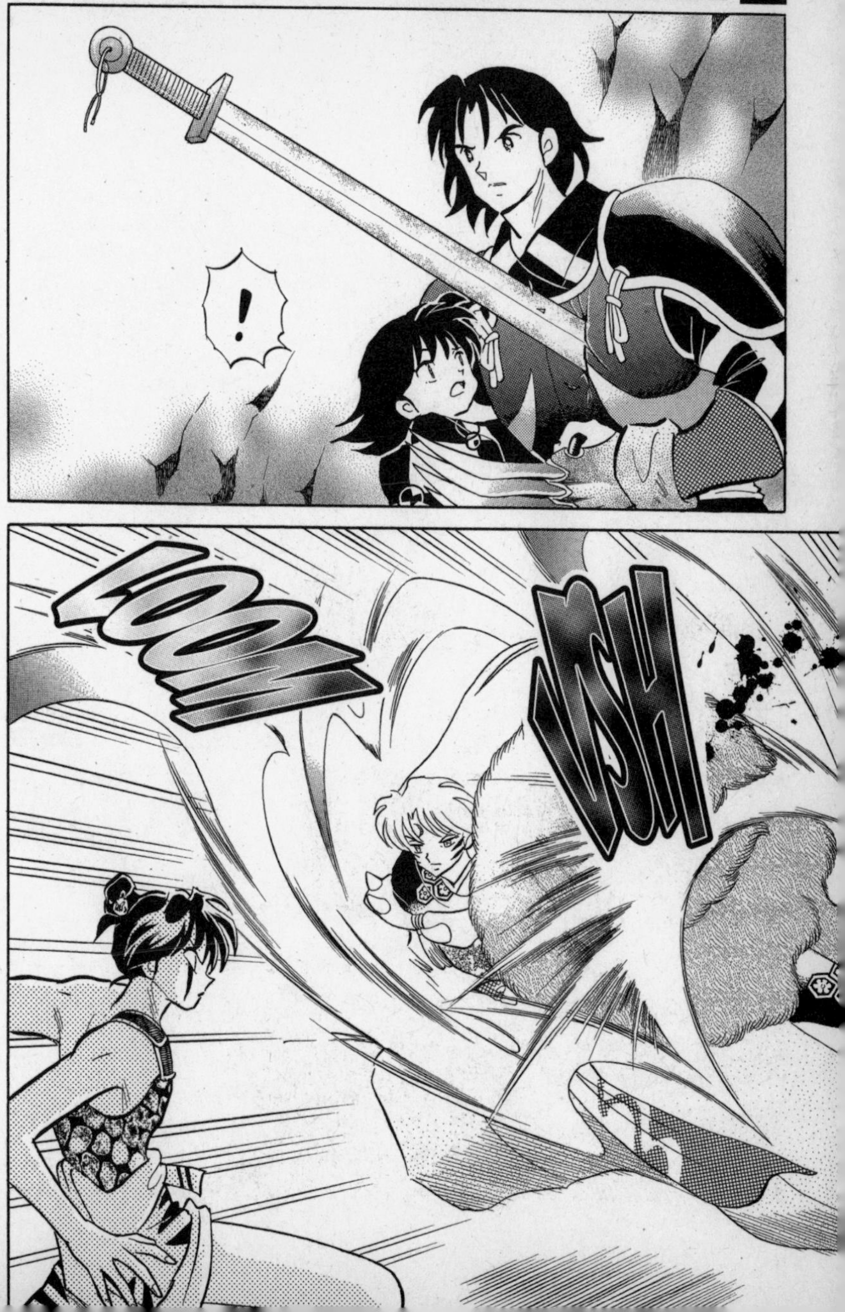
!
VOOM
VSH

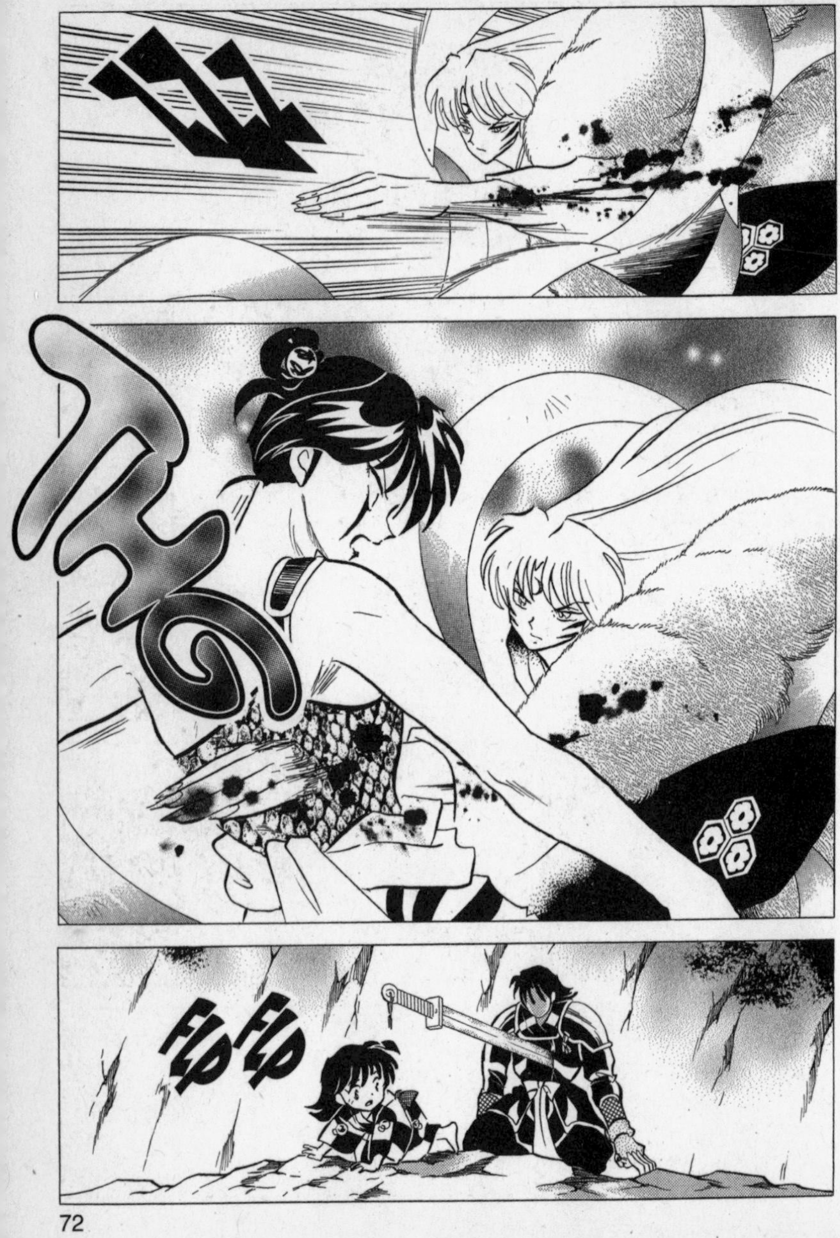
FLIP FLIP

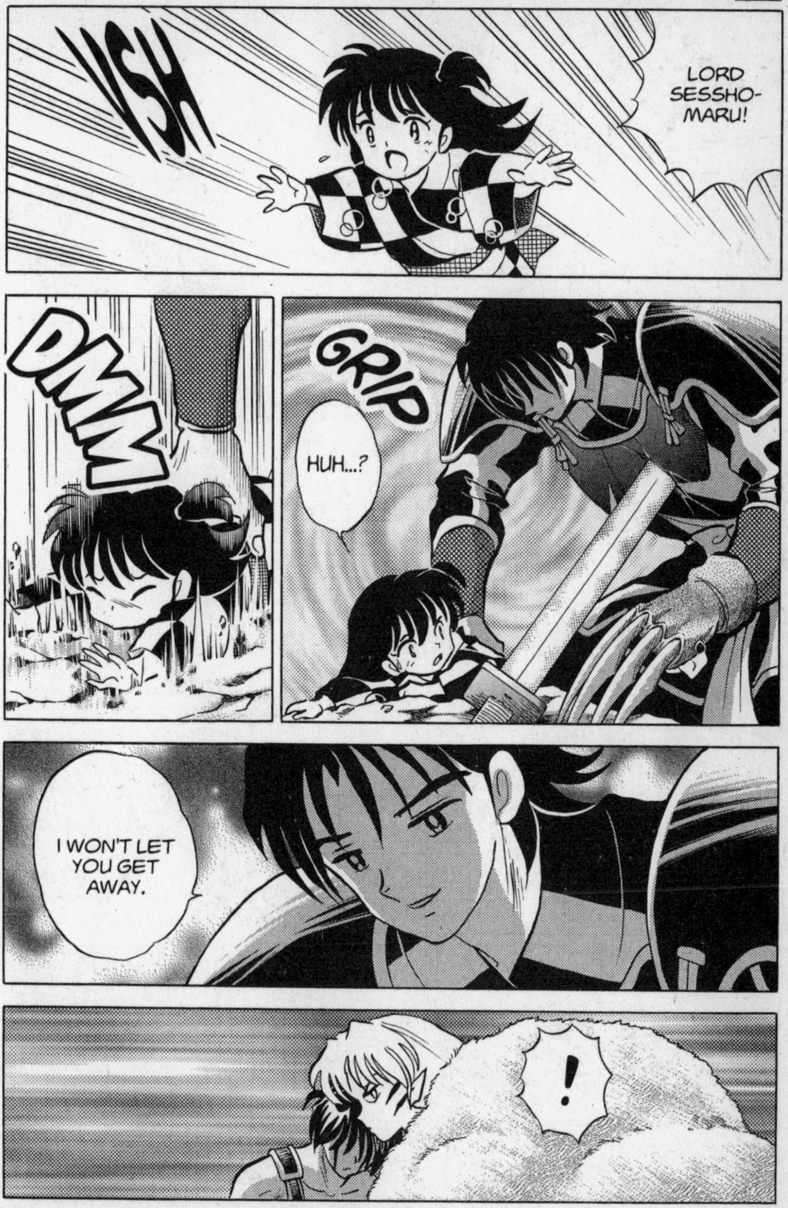
VISH
LORD SESSHO-MARU!
DMM
GRIP
HUH...?
I WON'T LET YOU GET AWAY.
!

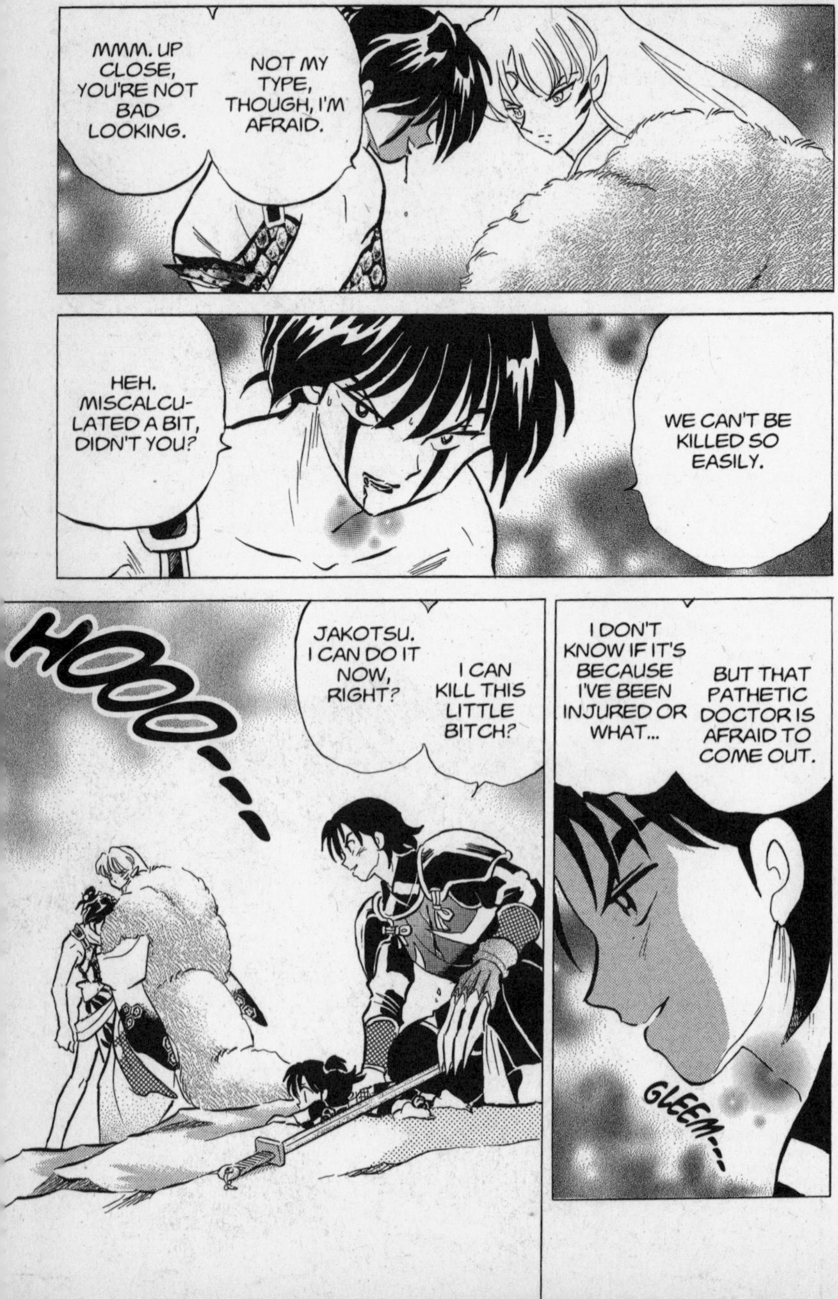
MMM. UP CLOSE, YOU'RE NOT BAD LOOKING.
NOT MY TYPE, THOUGH, I'M AFRAID.
HEH. MISCALCU-LATED A BIT, DIDN'T YOU?
WE CAN'T BE KILLED SO EASILY.
HOOO...
JAKOTSU. I CAN DO IT NOW, RIGHT?
I CAN KILL THIS LITTLE BITCH?
I DON'T KNOW IF IT'S BECAUSE I'VE BEEN INJURED OR WHAT...
BUT THAT PATHETIC DOCTOR IS AFRAID TO COME OUT.
GLEEM...

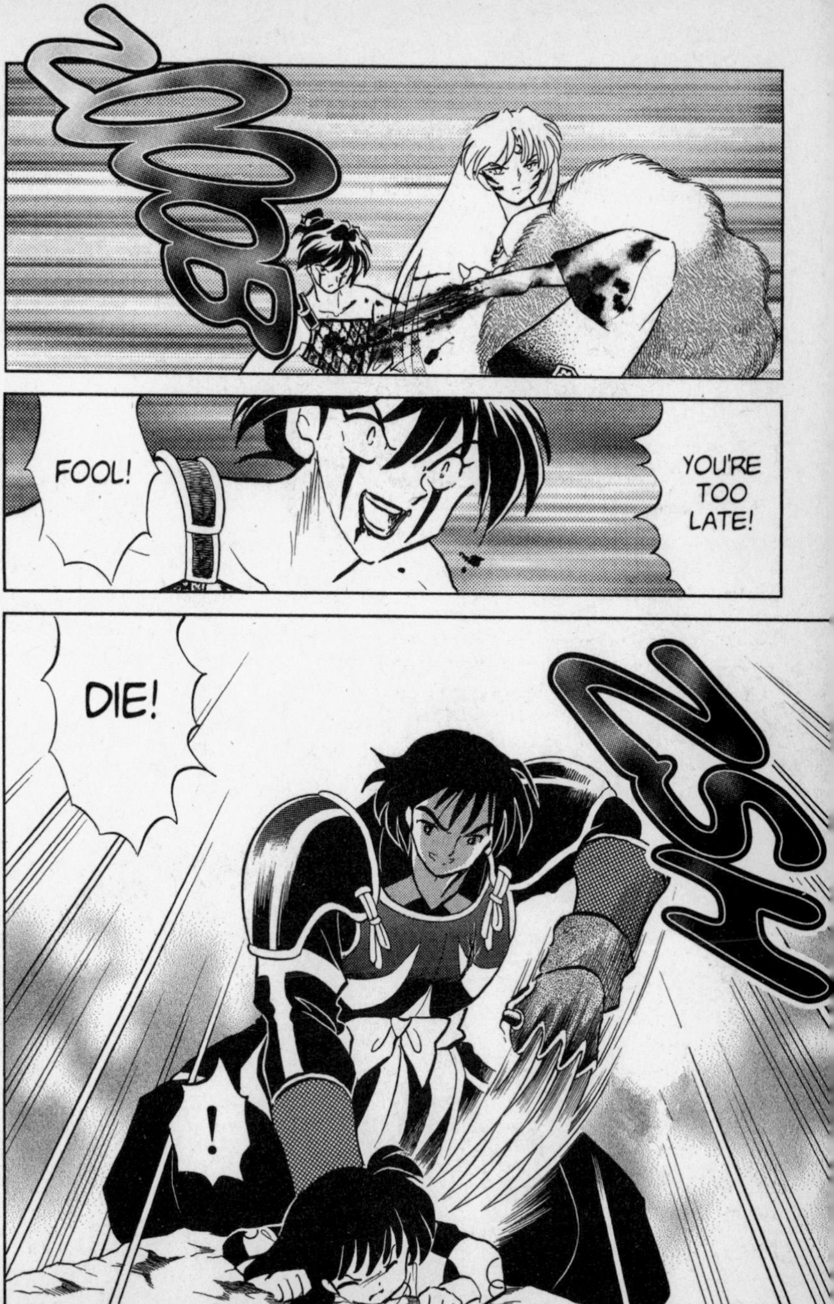
ZOOB
YOU'RE TOO LATE!
FOOL!
ZASH
DIE!
!

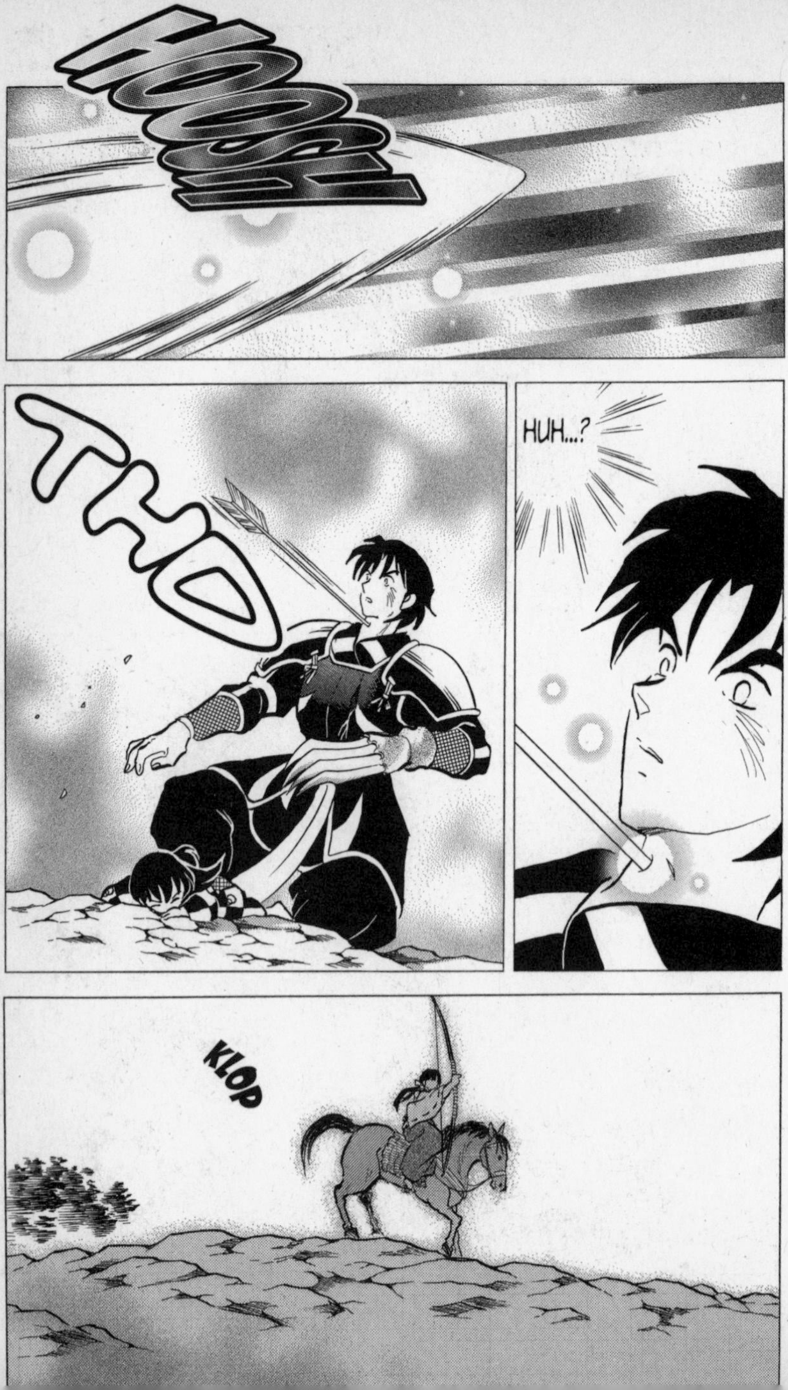
WHOOSH
THD
HUH...?
KLOP

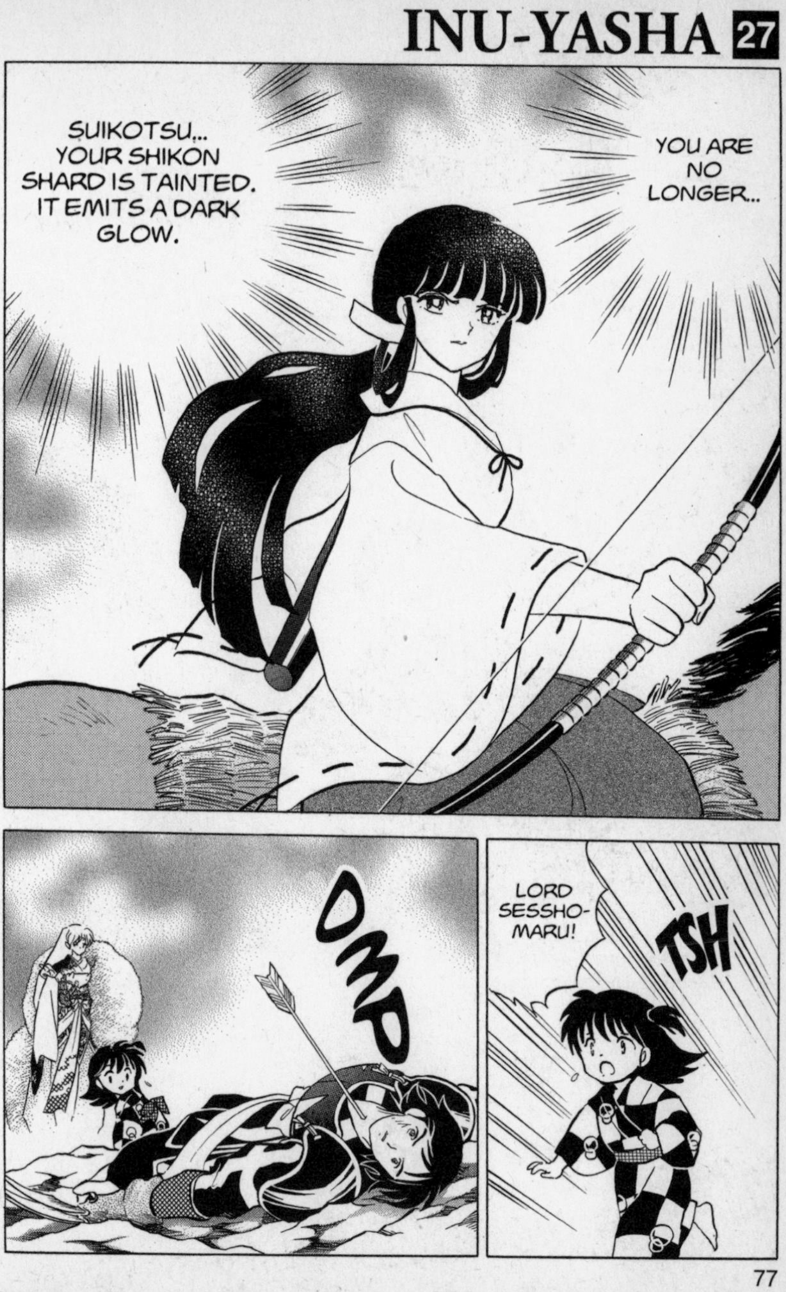
SUIKOTSU... YOUR SHIKON SHARD IS TAINTED. IT EMITS A DARK GLOW.
YOU ARE NO LONGER...
DMP
LORD SESSHO-MARU!
TSH

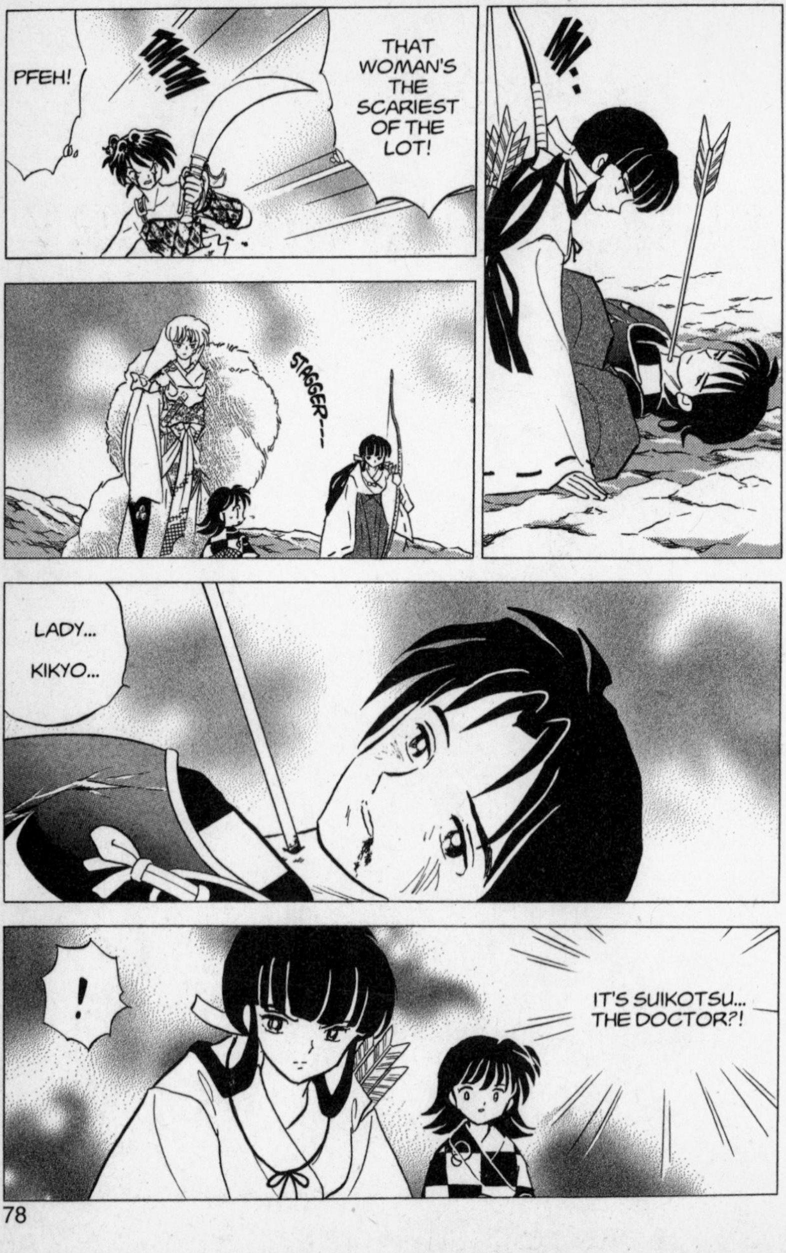
PFEH!
THAT WOMAN'S THE SCARIEST OF THE LOT!
MN..
STAGGER---
LADY...
KIKYO...
!
IT'S SUIKOTSU... THE DOCTOR?!

SCROLL FIVE

SUIKOTSU'S MEMORY

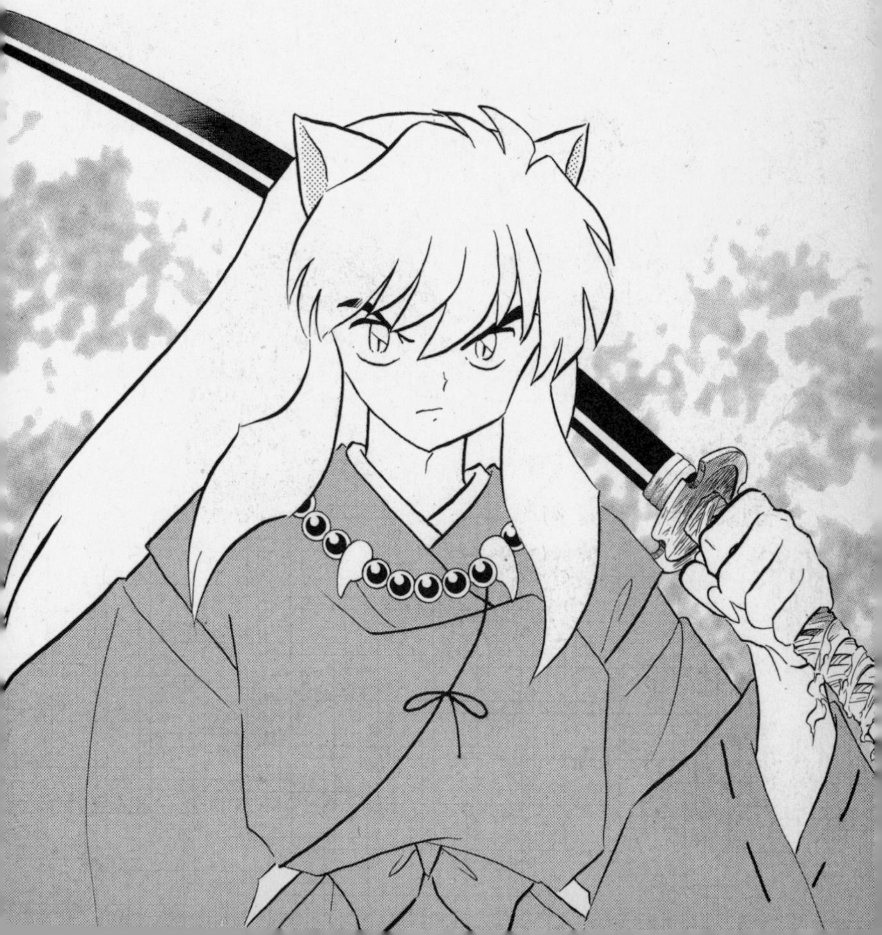

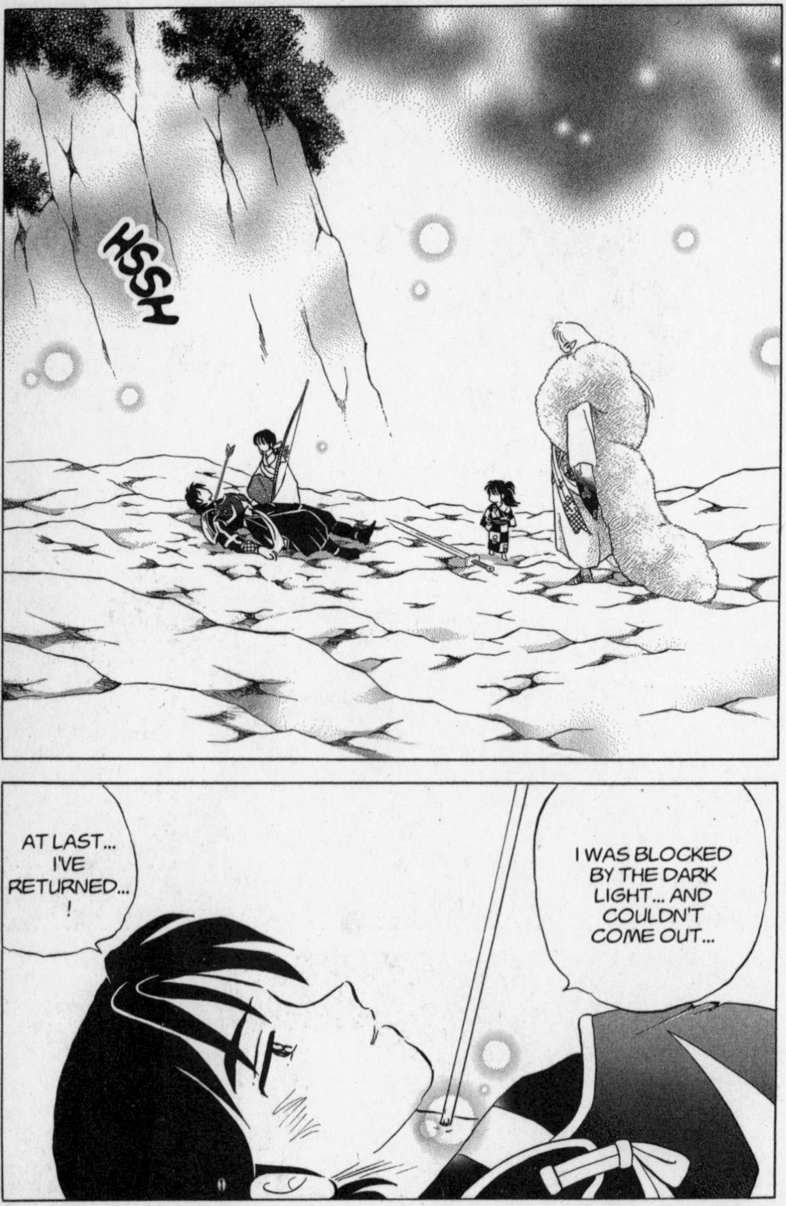
HSSH
I WAS BLOCKED BY THE DARK LIGHT... AND COULDN'T COME OUT...
AT LAST... I'VE RETURNED... !

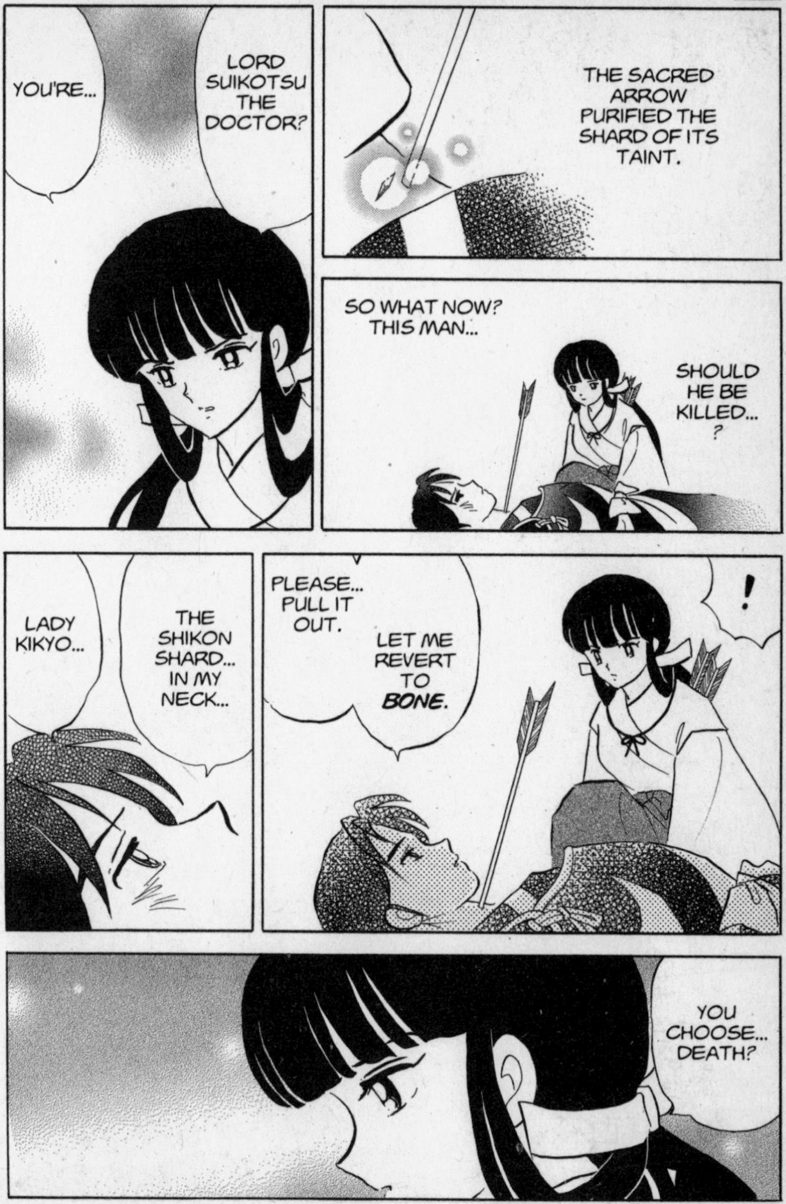
YOU'RE...
LORD SUIKOTSU THE DOCTOR?
THE SACRED ARROW PURIFIED THE SHARD OF ITS TAINT.
SO WHAT NOW? THIS MAN...
SHOULD HE BE KILLED... ?
LADY KIKYO...
THE SHIKON SHARD... IN MY NECK...
PLEASE... PULL IT OUT.
LET ME REVERT TO BONE.
!
YOU CHOOSE... DEATH?

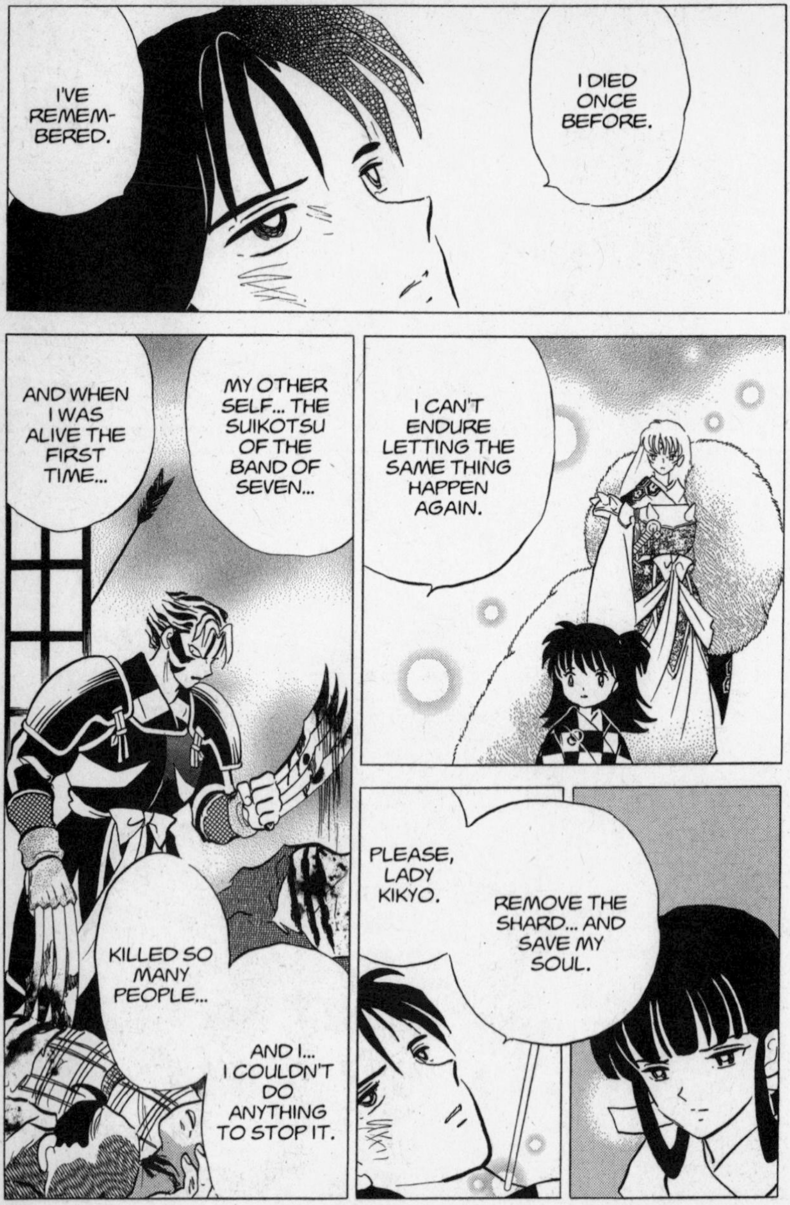

I'VE REMEMBERED.
I DIED ONCE BEFORE.
AND WHEN I WAS ALIVE THE FIRST TIME...
MY OTHER SELF... THE SUIKOTSU OF THE BAND OF SEVEN...
KILLED SO MANY PEOPLE...
AND I... I COULDN'T DO ANYTHING TO STOP IT.
I CAN'T ENDURE LETTING THE SAME THING HAPPEN AGAIN.
PLEASE, LADY KIKYO.
REMOVE THE SHARD... AND SAVE MY SOUL.

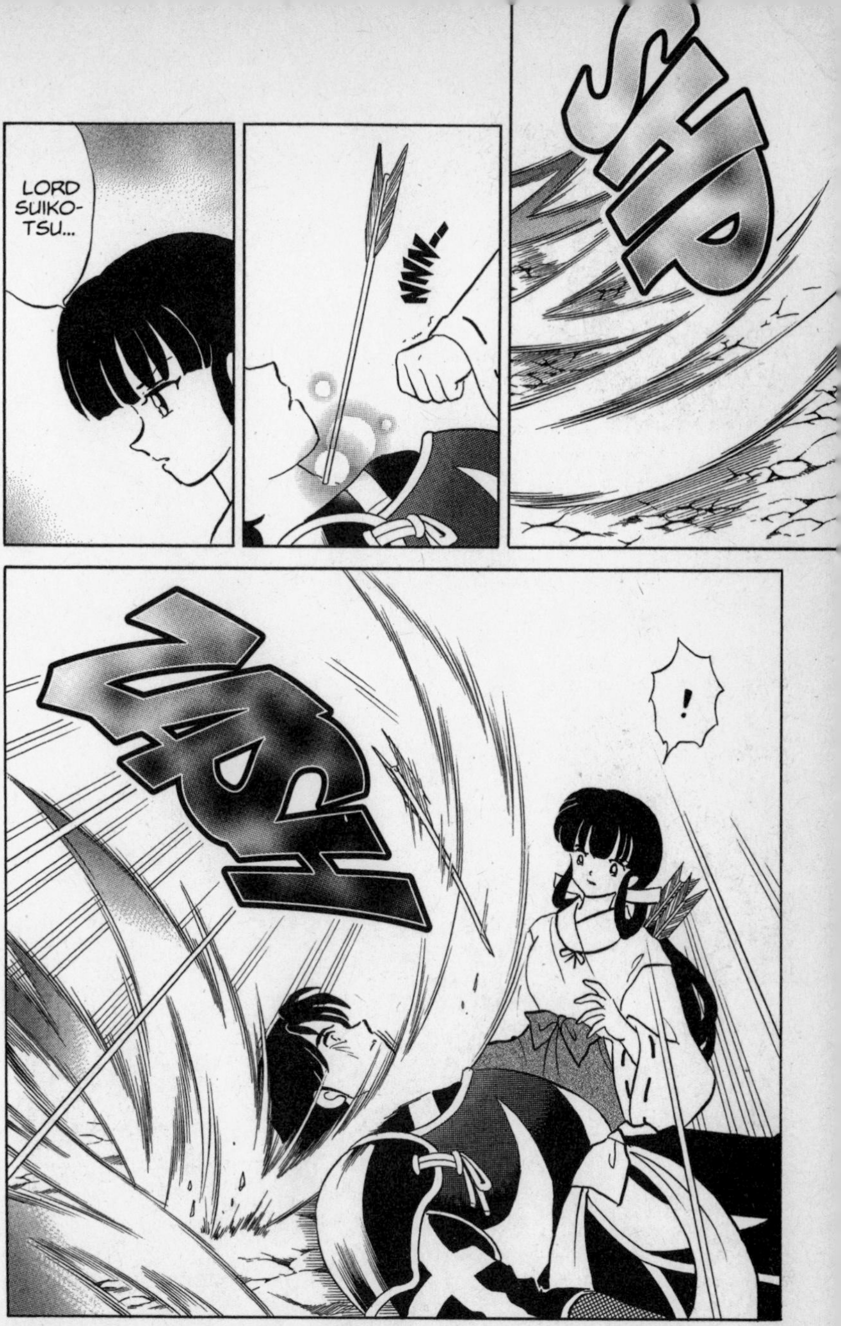
SHIP
NNN...
LORD SUIKOTSU...
ZASH
!

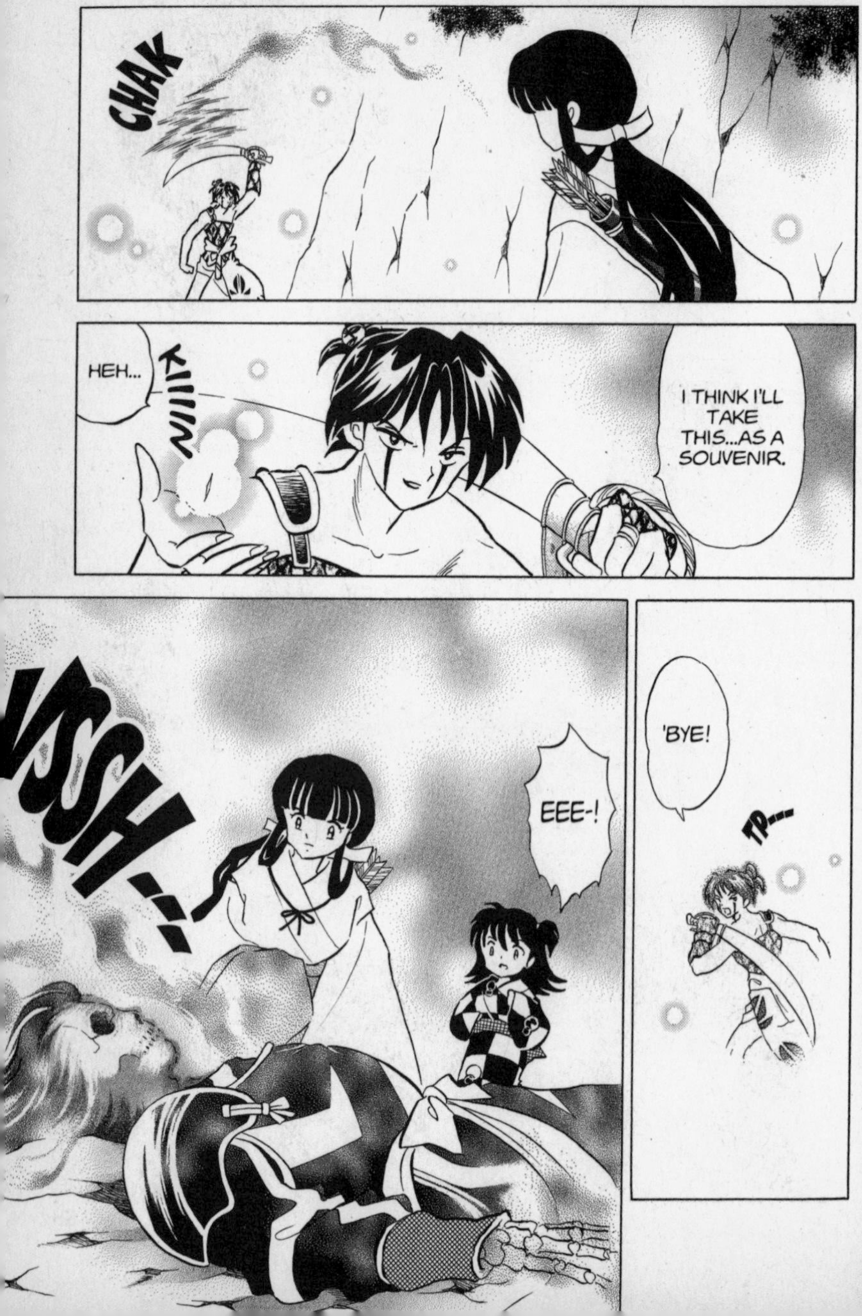
CHAK
I THINK I'LL TAKE THIS...AS A SOUVENIR.
KIIIIN
HEH...
'BYE!
TP...
EEE-!
VSSH...

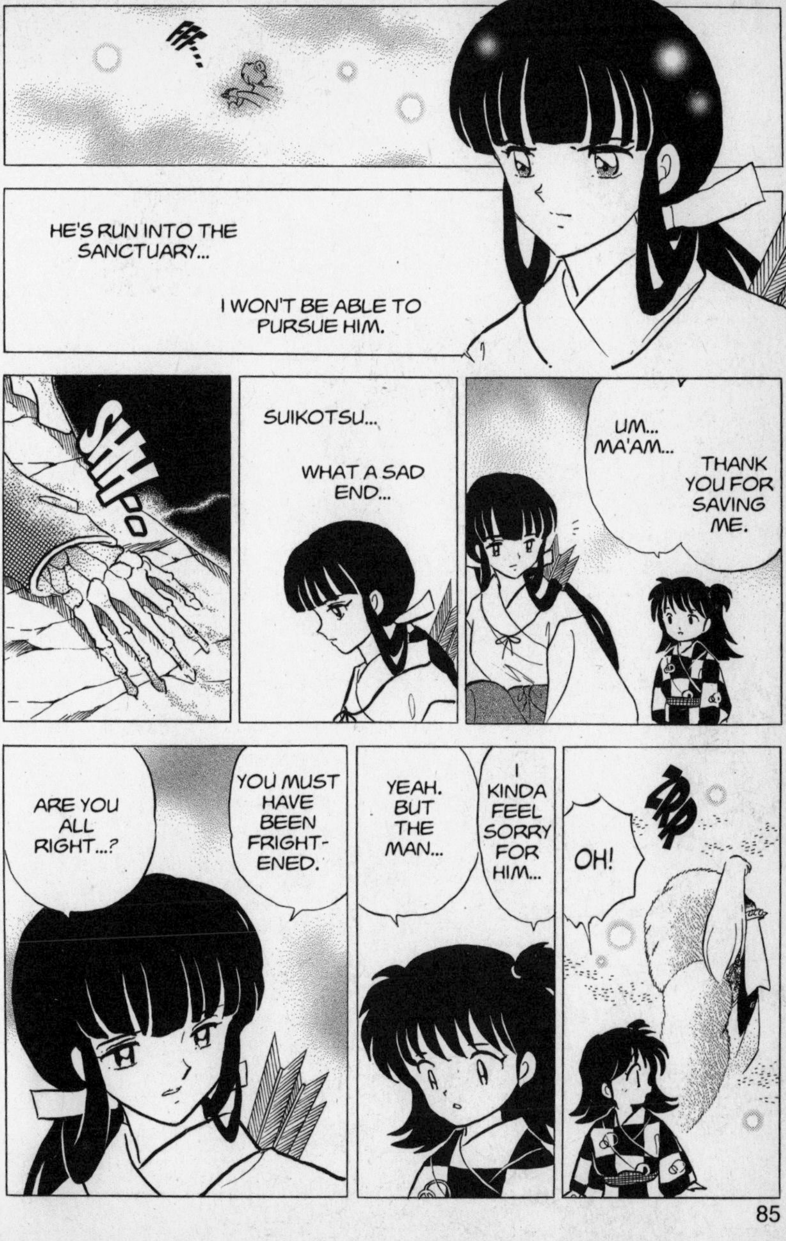
FFF...
HE'S RUN INTO THE SANCTUARY...
I WON'T BE ABLE TO PURSUE HIM.
SHHPO
SUIKOTSU...
WHAT A SAD END...
UM... MA'AM...
THANK YOU FOR SAVING ME.
ARE YOU ALL RIGHT...?
YOU MUST HAVE BEEN FRIGHT-ENED.
YEAH. BUT THE MAN...
I KINDA FEEL SORRY FOR HIM...
ZRR
OH!

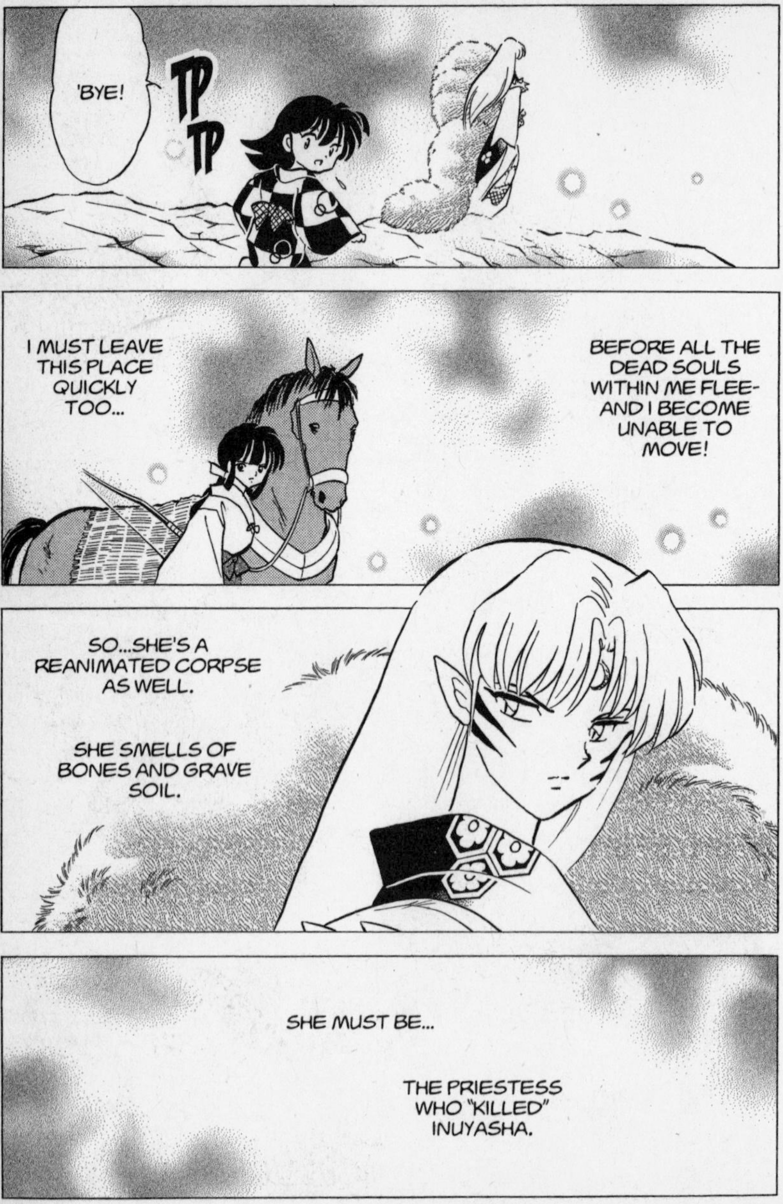
'BYE!
TP TP
I MUST LEAVE THIS PLACE QUICKLY TOO...
BEFORE ALL THE DEAD SOULS WITHIN ME FLEE- AND I BECOME UNABLE TO MOVE!
SO...SHE'S A REANIMATED CORPSE AS WELL.
SHE SMELLS OF BONES AND GRAVE SOIL.
SHE MUST BE...
THE PRIESTESS WHO "KILLED" INUYASHA.

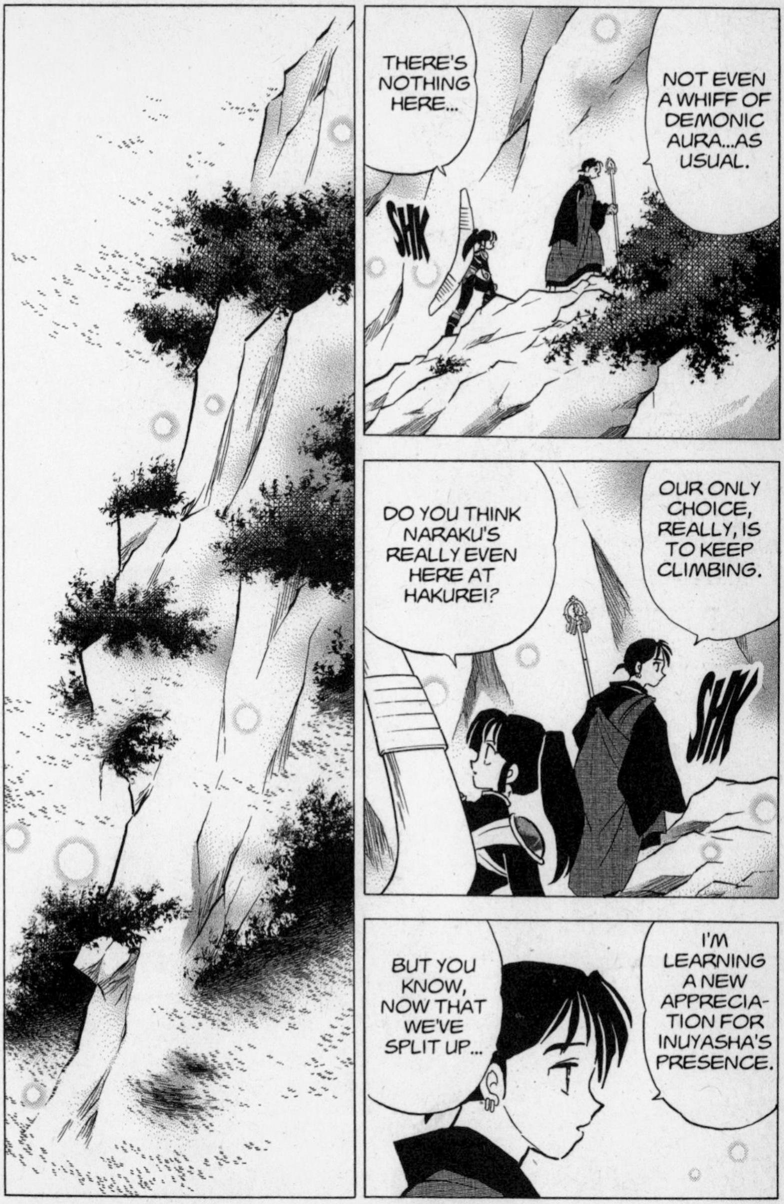
THERE'S NOTHING HERE...
NOT EVEN A WHIFF OF DEMONIC AURA...AS USUAL.
SHK
DO YOU THINK NARAKU'S REALLY EVEN HERE AT HAKUREI?
OUR ONLY CHOICE, REALLY, IS TO KEEP CLIMBING.
SHK
BUT YOU KNOW, NOW THAT WE'VE SPLIT UP...
I'M LEARNING A NEW APPRECIATION FOR INUYASHA'S PRESENCE.

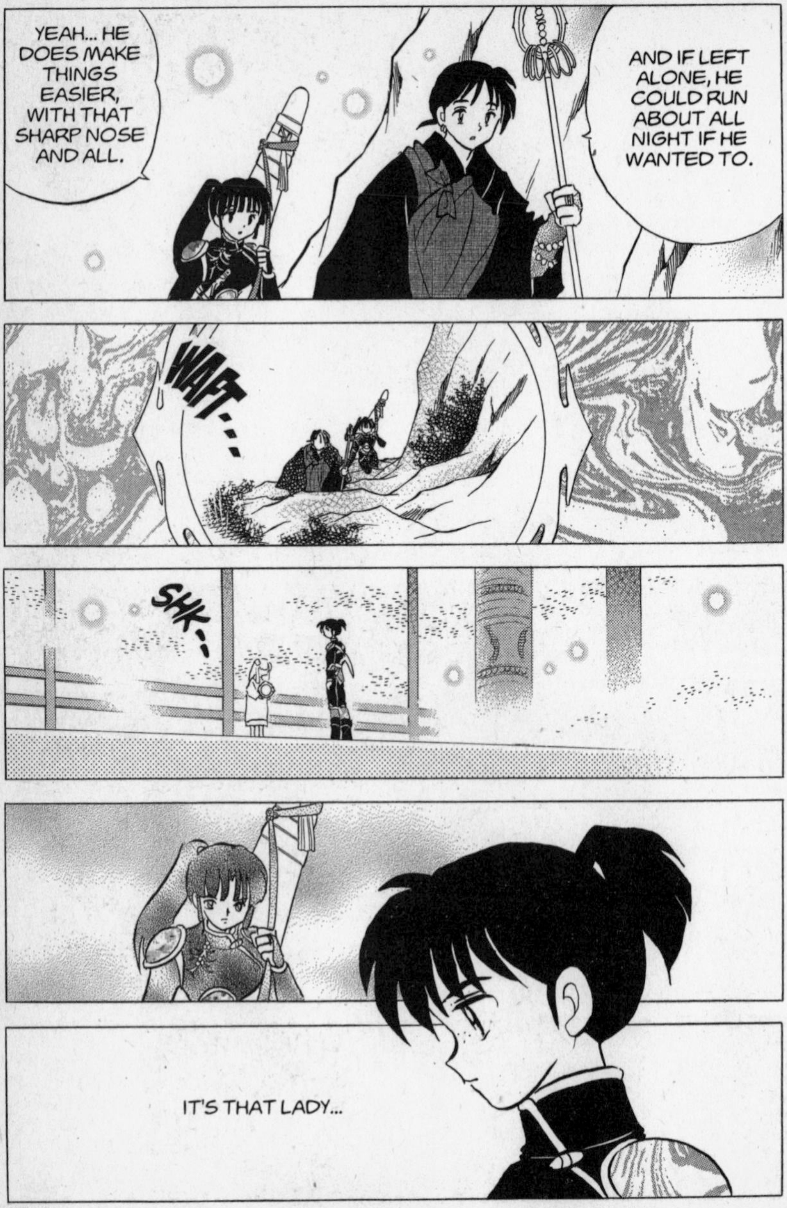
AND IF LEFT ALONE, HE COULD RUN ABOUT ALL NIGHT IF HE WANTED TO.
YEAH... HE DOES MAKE THINGS EASIER, WITH THAT SHARP NOSE AND ALL.
WAFT...
SHK...
IT'S THAT LADY...

I WISH SHE'D TURN BACK...

I WISH SHE WOULDN'T FIND ANYTHING...

I DON'T WANT TO HAVE TO FIGHT HER...

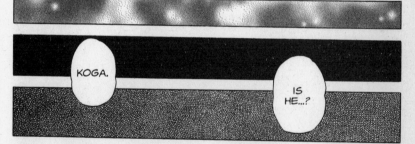

KOGA.

IS HE...?

NNN...

KOGA!

HE'S COME TO!

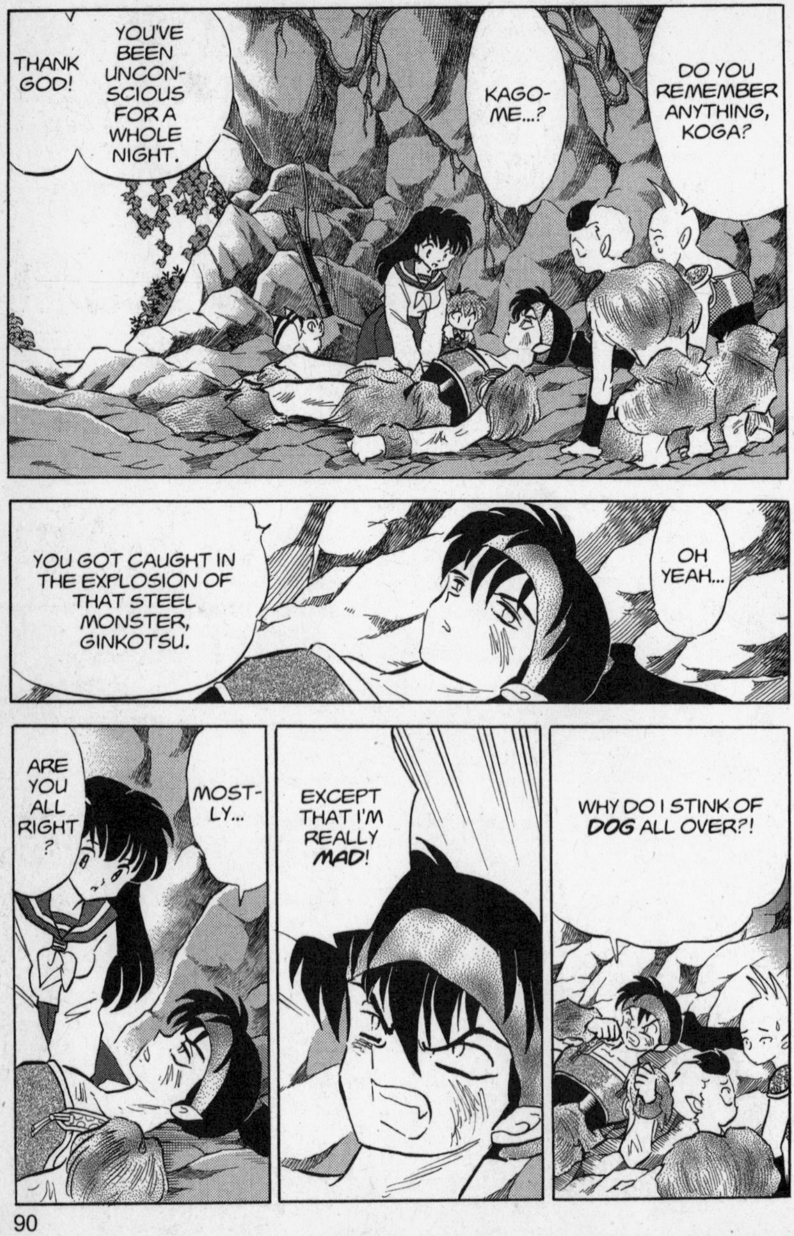
THANK GOD!
YOU'VE BEEN UNCONSCIOUS FOR A WHOLE NIGHT.
KAGO-ME...?
DO YOU REMEMBER ANYTHING, KOGA?
YOU GOT CAUGHT IN THE EXPLOSION OF THAT STEEL MONSTER, GINKOTSU.
OH YEAH...
ARE YOU ALL RIGHT?
MOSTLY...
EXCEPT THAT I'M REALLY *MAD*!
WHY DO I STINK OF *DOG* ALL OVER?!

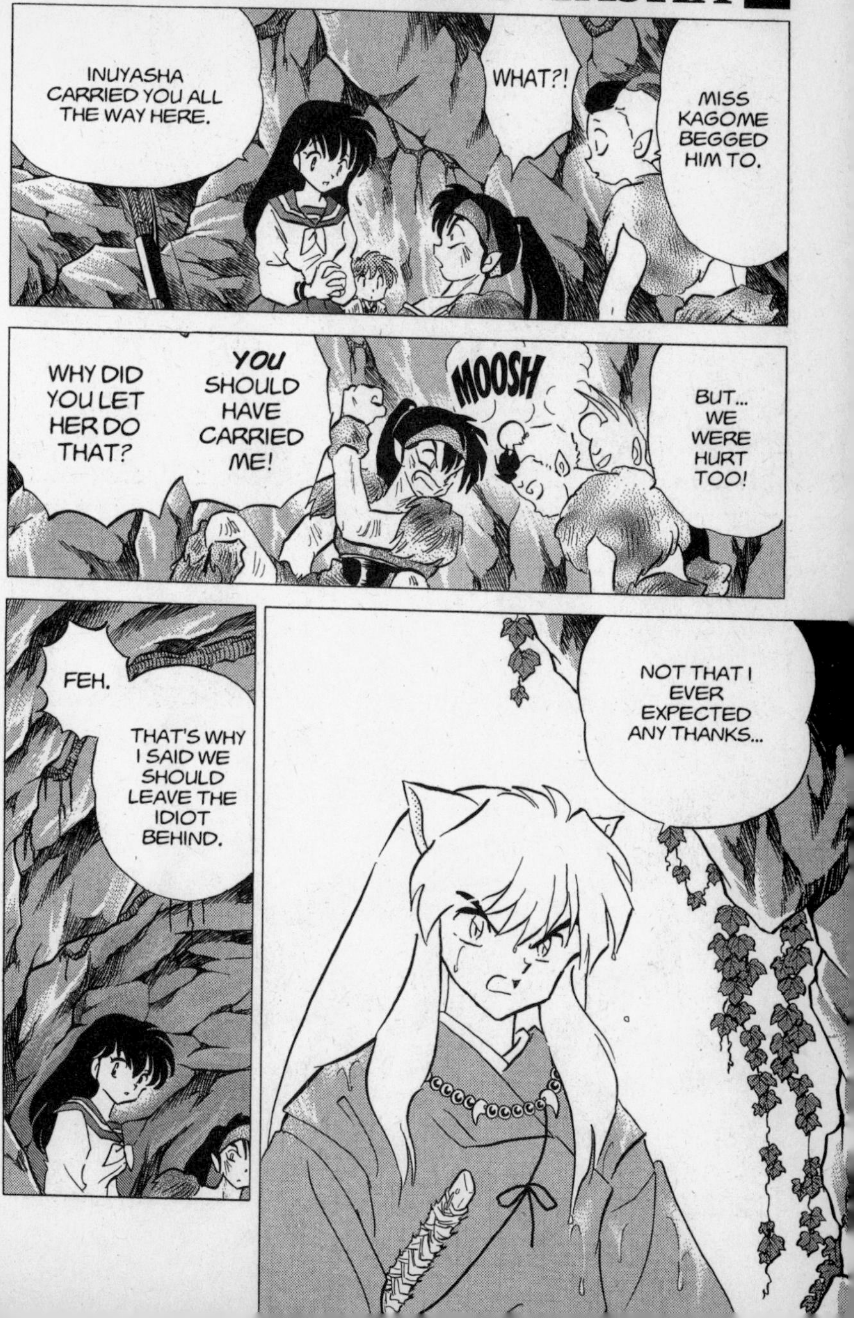
INUYASHA CARRIED YOU ALL THE WAY HERE.
WHAT?!
MISS KAGOME BEGGED HIM TO.
WHY DID YOU LET HER DO THAT?
YOU SHOULD HAVE CARRIED ME!
MOOSH
BUT... WE WERE HURT TOO!
FEH.
THAT'S WHY I SAID WE SHOULD LEAVE THE IDIOT BEHIND.
NOT THAT I EVER EXPECTED ANY THANKS...

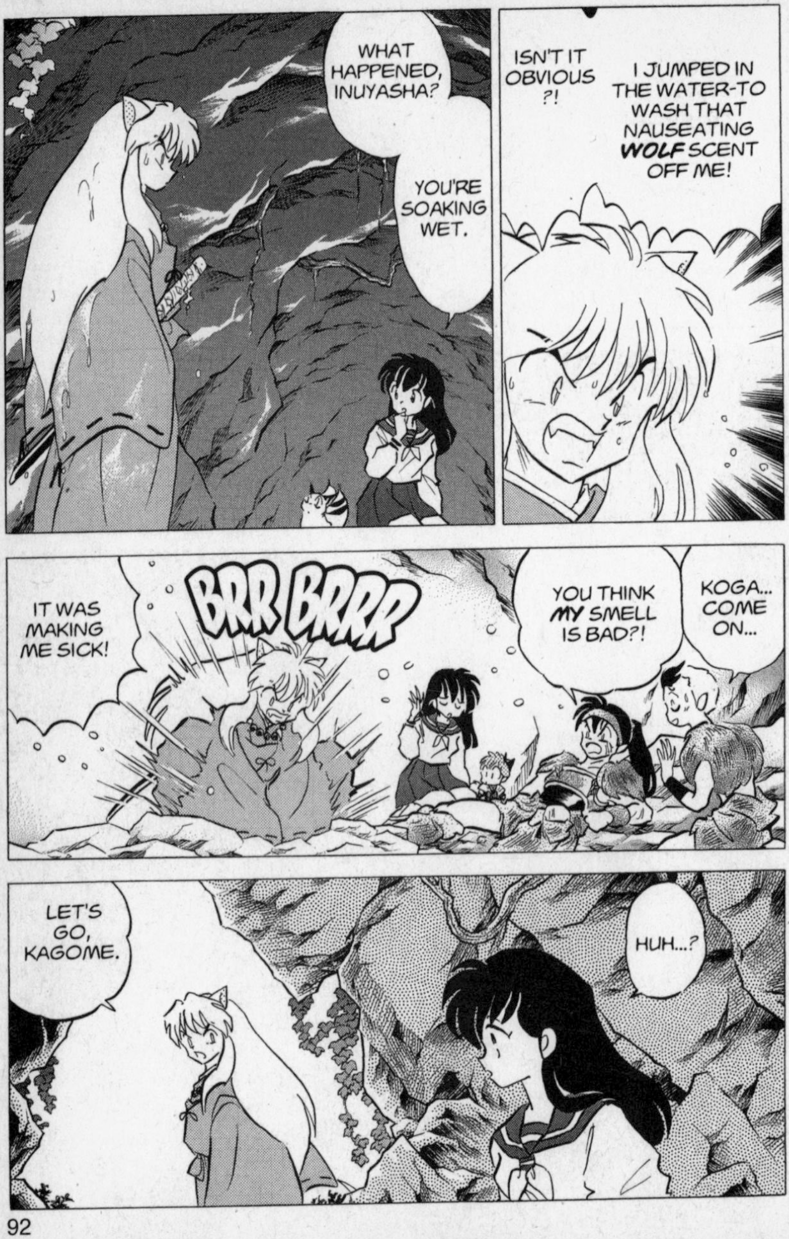
WHAT HAPPENED, INUYASHA?
YOU'RE SOAKING WET.
ISN'T IT OBVIOUS ?!
I JUMPED IN THE WATER-TO WASH THAT NAUSEATING WOLF SCENT OFF ME!
IT WAS MAKING ME SICK!
BRR BRRR
YOU THINK MY SMELL IS BAD?!
KOGA... COME ON...
LET'S GO, KAGOME.
HUH...?

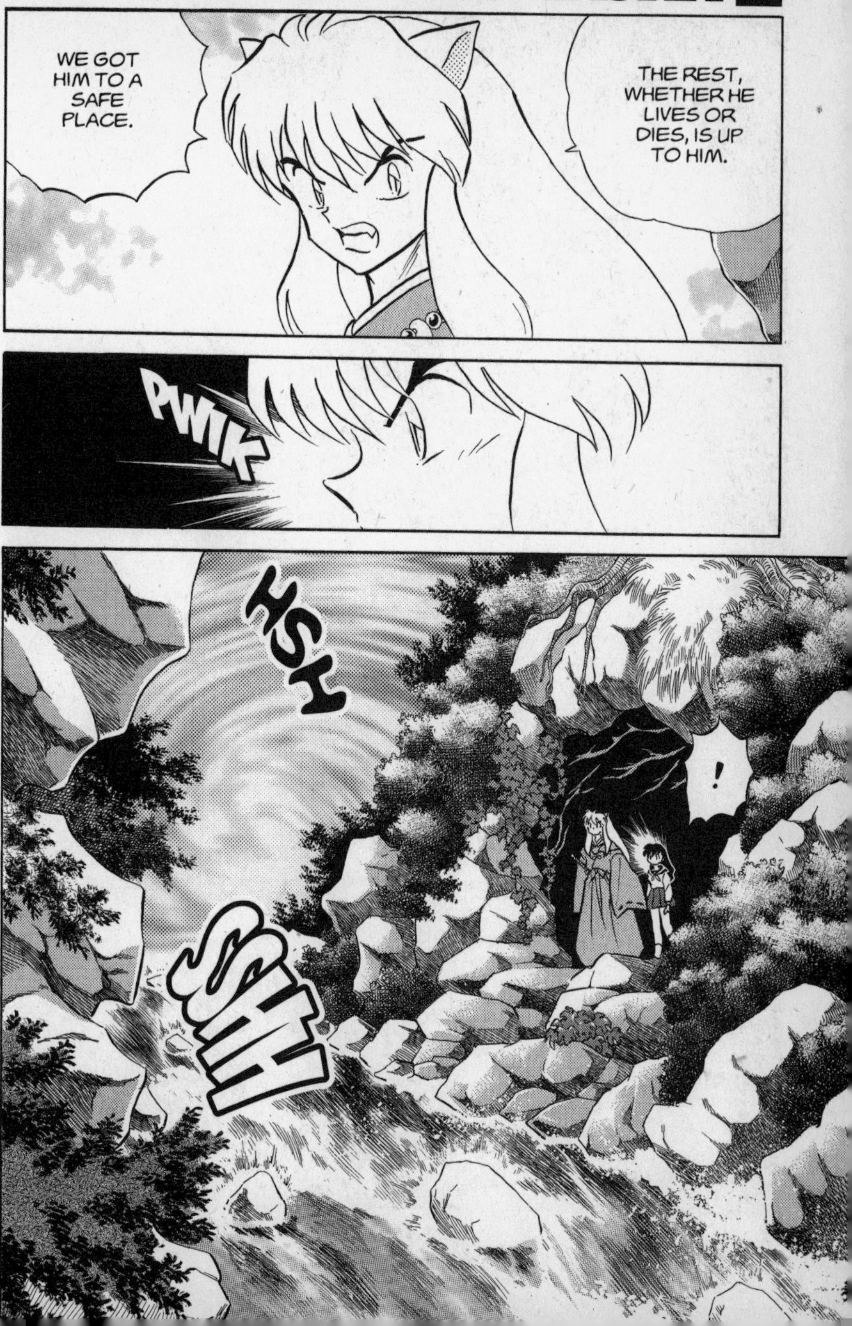
WE GOT HIM TO A SAFE PLACE.
THE REST, WHETHER HE LIVES OR DIES, IS UP TO HIM.
PWIK
HSH
!
SSHH

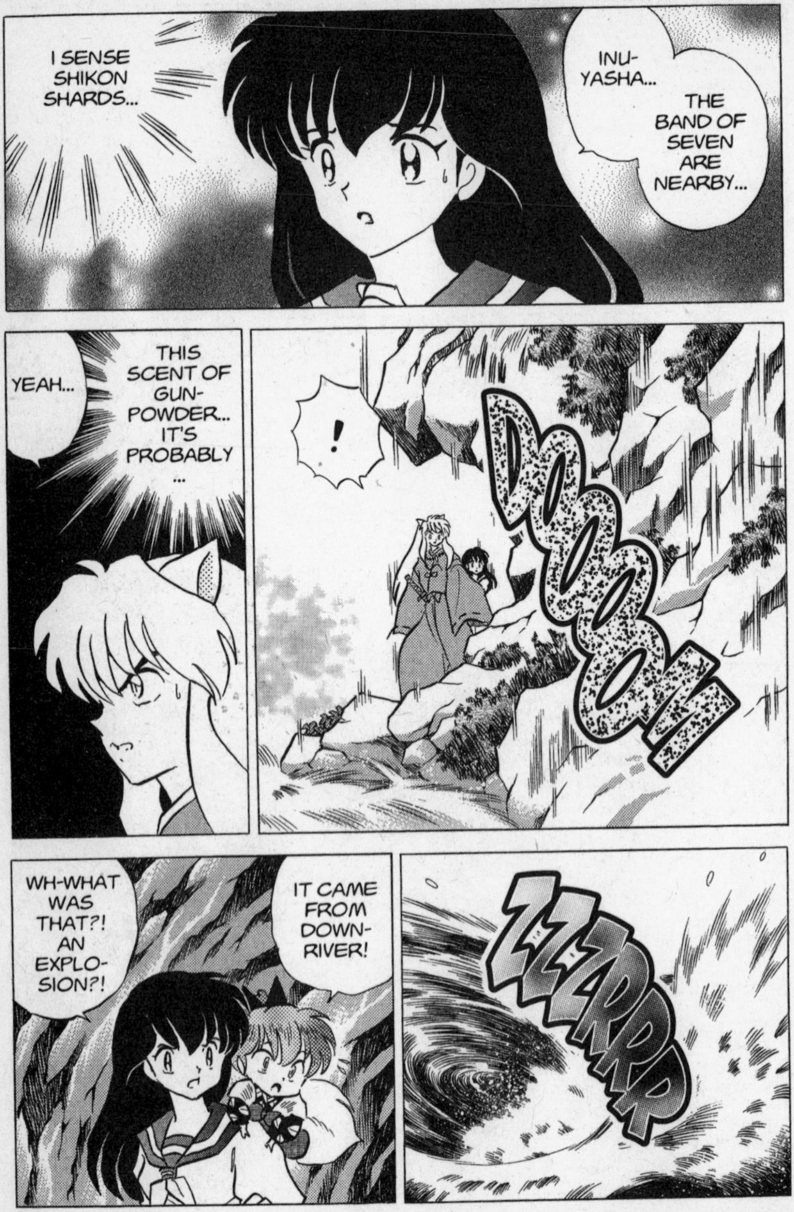

I SENSE SHIKON SHARDS...
INU-YASHA...
THE BAND OF SEVEN ARE NEARBY...
YEAH...
THIS SCENT OF GUN-POWDER... IT'S PROBABLY ...
!
DOOOOM
WH-WHAT WAS THAT?! AN EXPLO-SION?!
IT CAME FROM DOWN-RIVER!
ZZZRRR

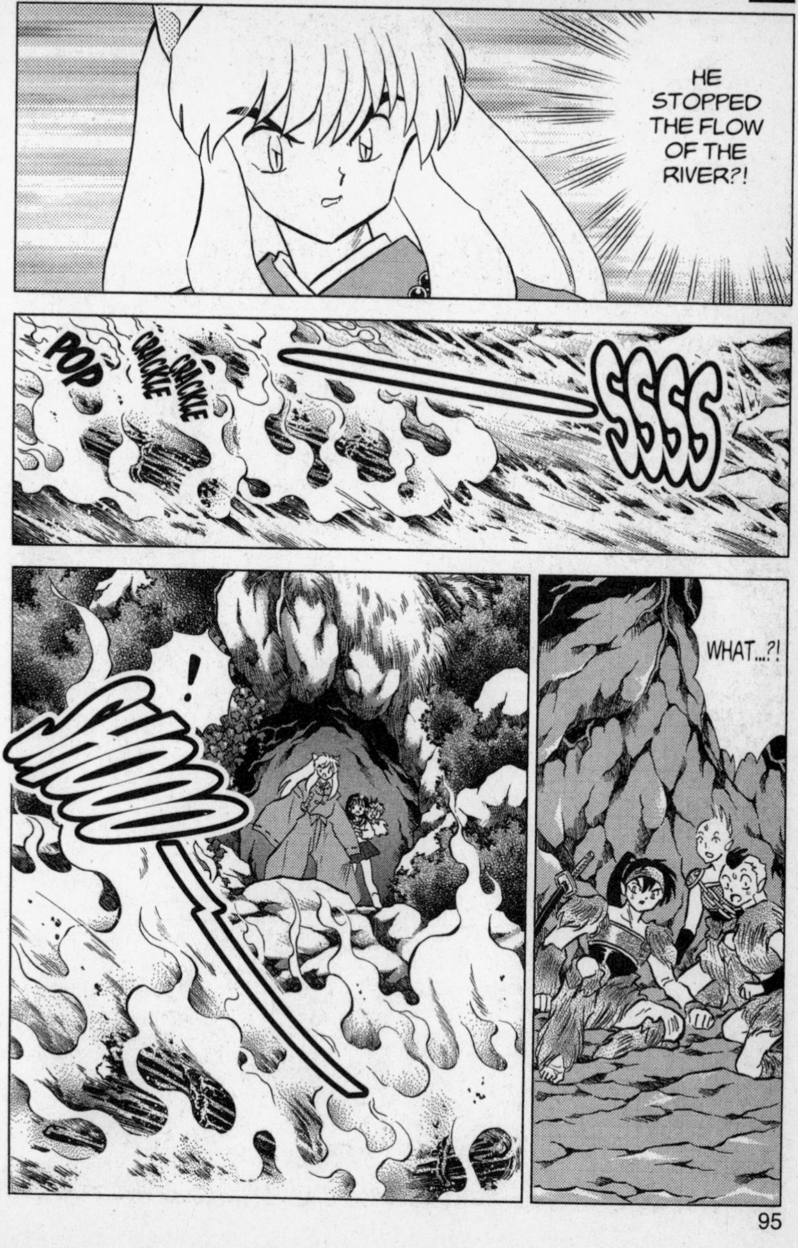
HE STOPPED THE FLOW OF THE RIVER?!
SSSS
CRACKLE CRACKLE
POP
WHAT...?!
!
SHOOO

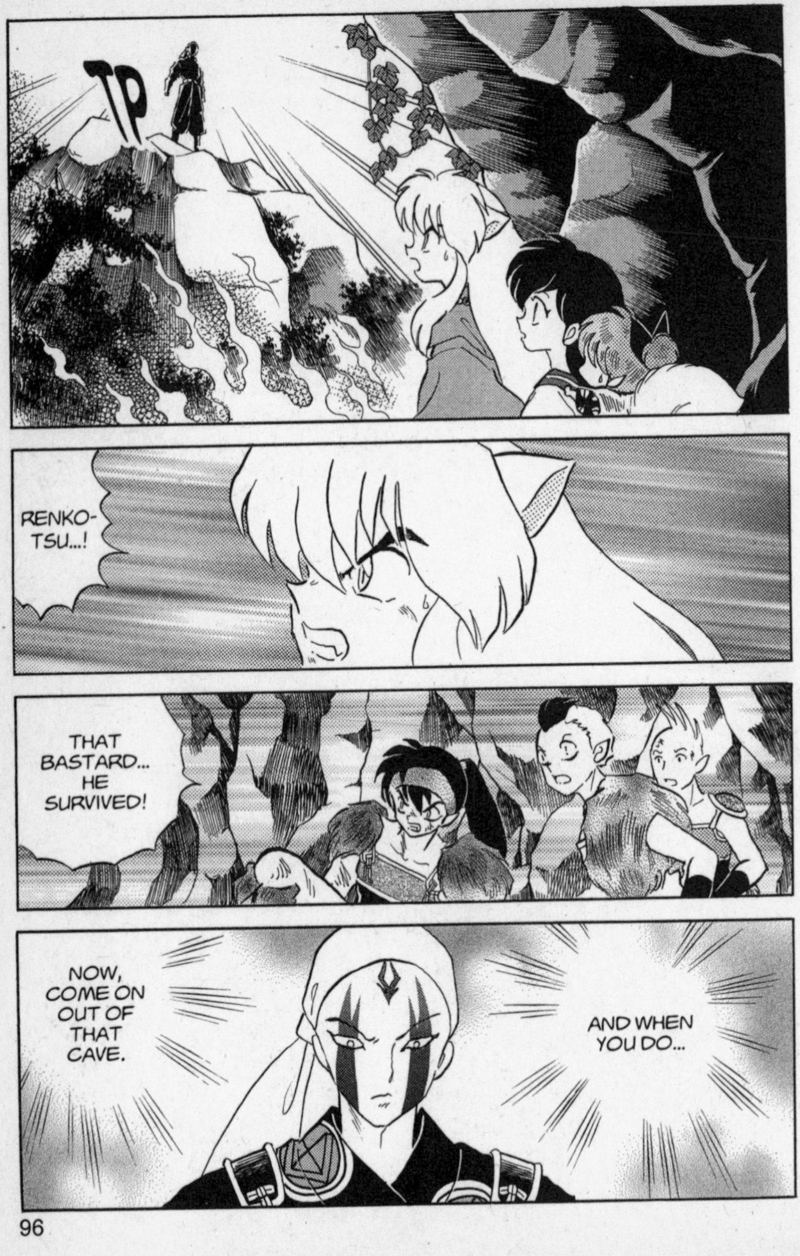
TP
RENKO-
TSU...!
THAT
BASTARD...
HE
SURVIVED!
NOW,
COME ON
OUT OF
THAT
CAVE.
AND WHEN
YOU DO...

SCROLL 6
THE RIVER OF FIRE

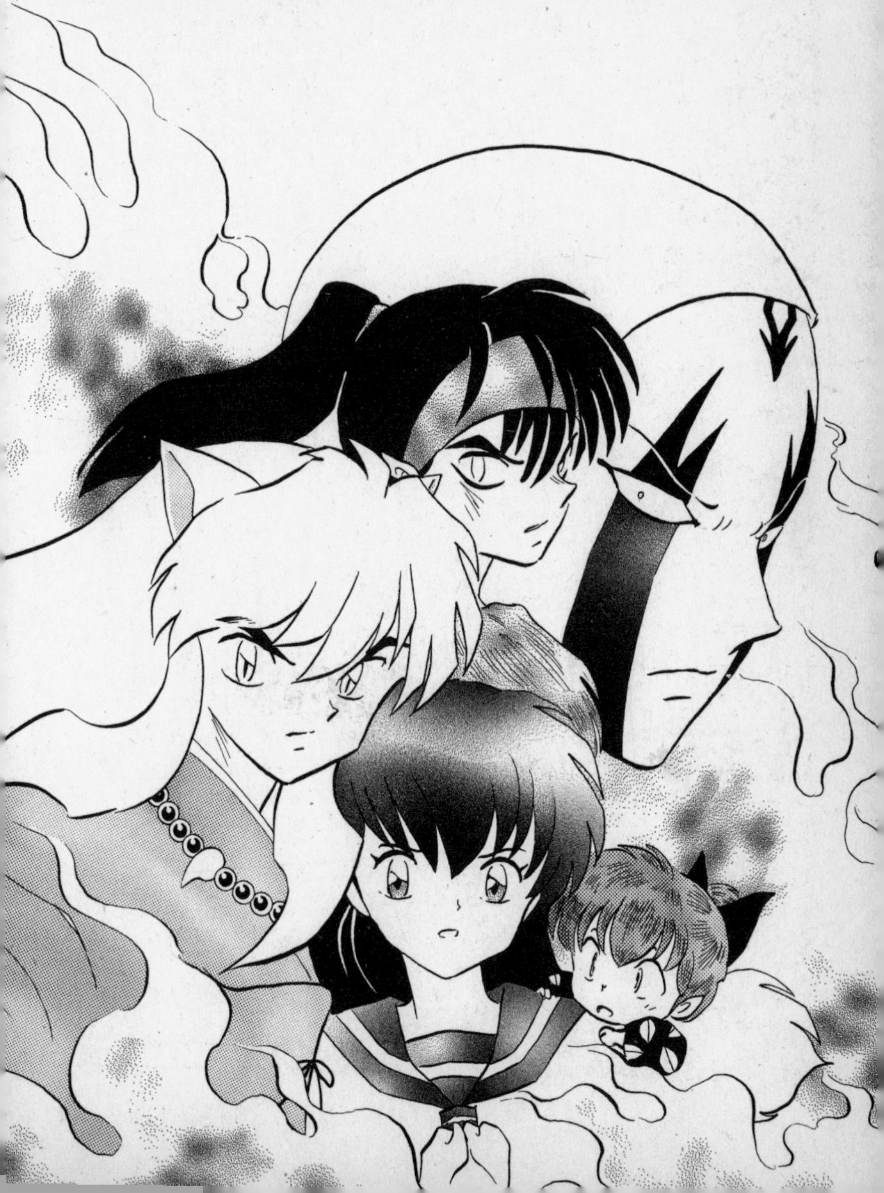

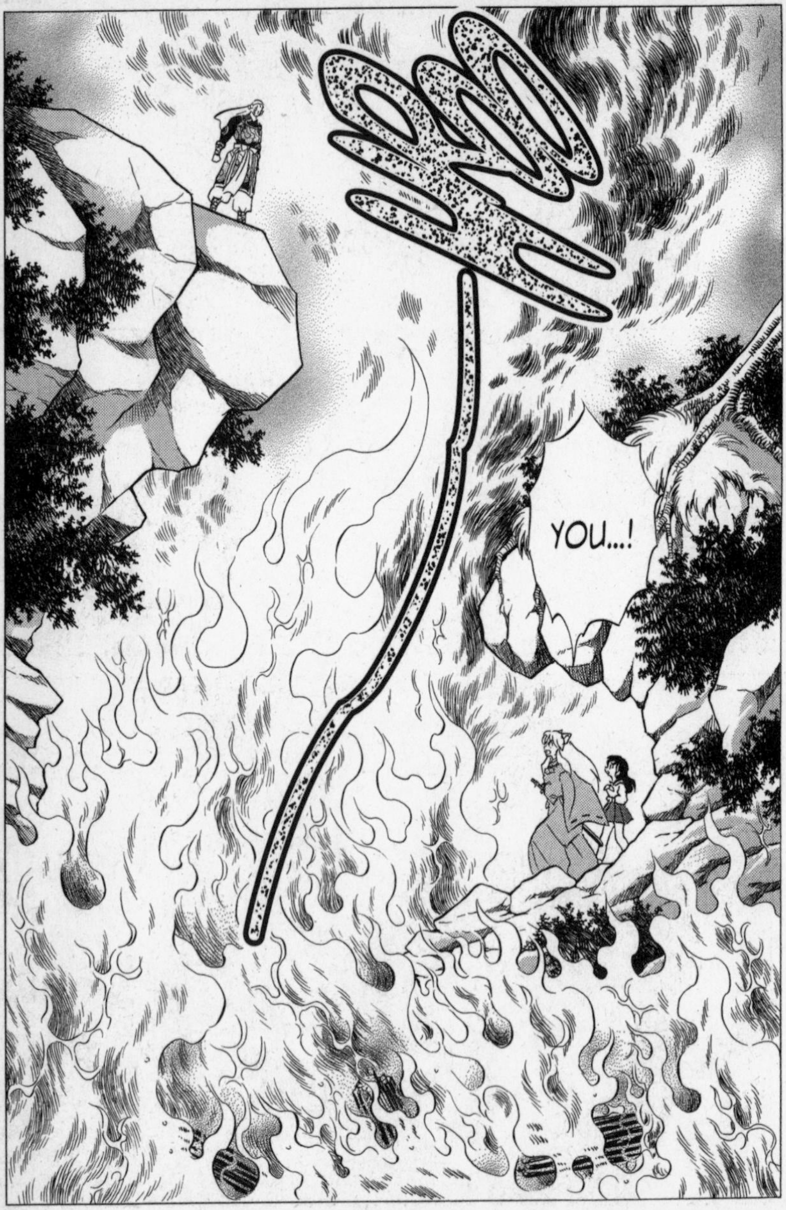
YOU...!

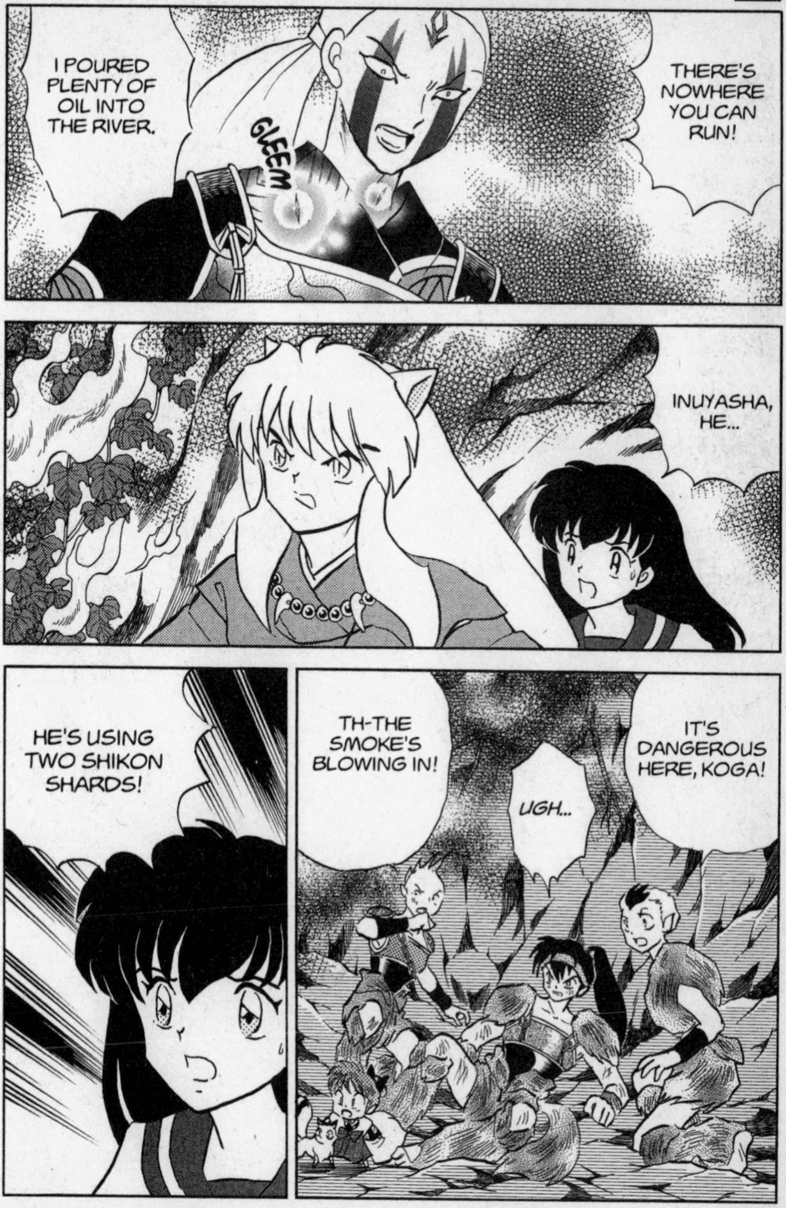
I POURED PLENTY OF OIL INTO THE RIVER.
GLEEM
THERE'S NOWHERE YOU CAN RUN!
INUYASHA, HE...
HE'S USING TWO SHIKON SHARDS!
TH-THE SMOKE'S BLOWING IN!
UGH...
IT'S DANGEROUS HERE, KOGA!

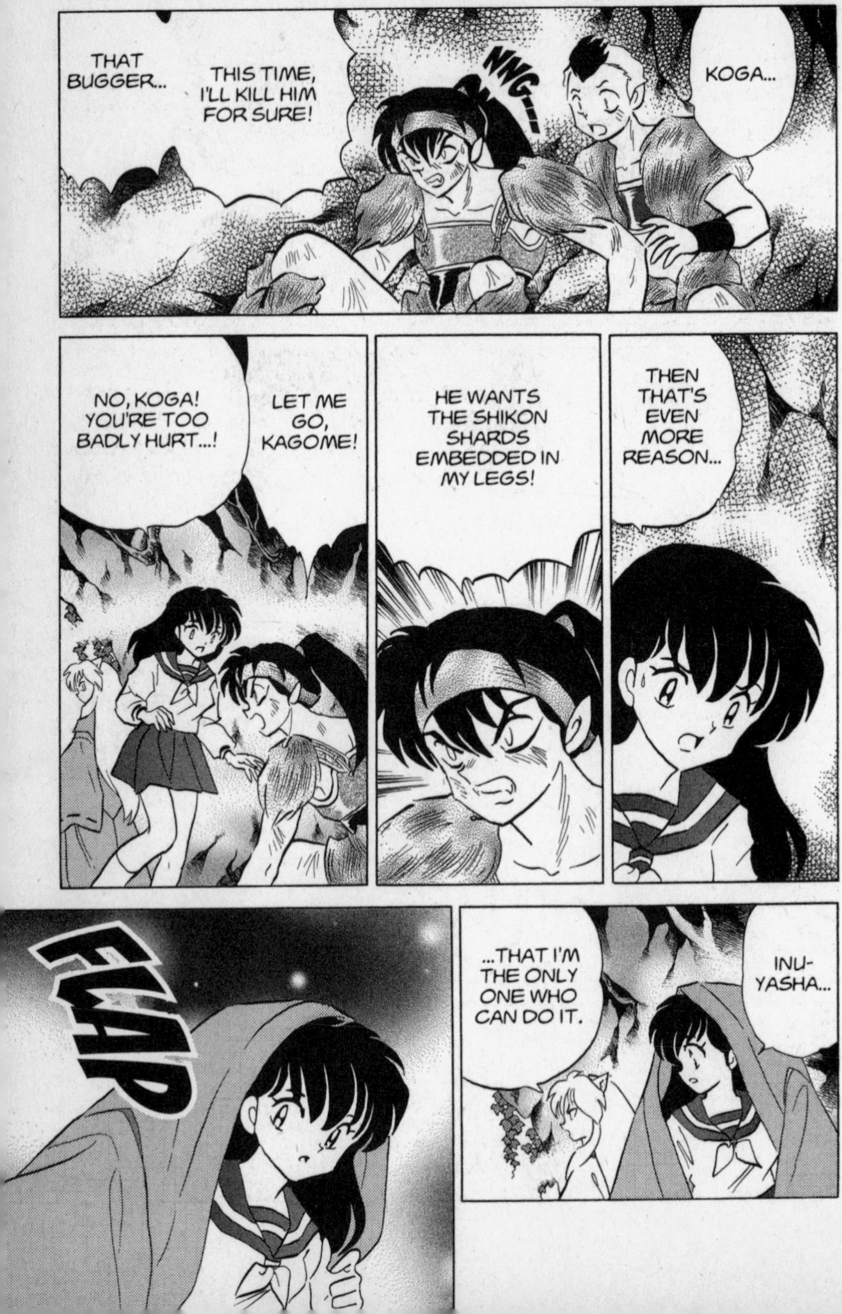
THAT BUGGER...
THIS TIME, I'LL KILL HIM FOR SURE!
NNG...
KOGA...
NO, KOGA! YOU'RE TOO BADLY HURT...!
LET ME GO, KAGOME!
HE WANTS THE SHIKON SHARDS EMBEDDED IN MY LEGS!
THEN THAT'S EVEN MORE REASON...
FLAP
...THAT I'M THE ONLY ONE WHO CAN DO IT.
INU-YASHA...

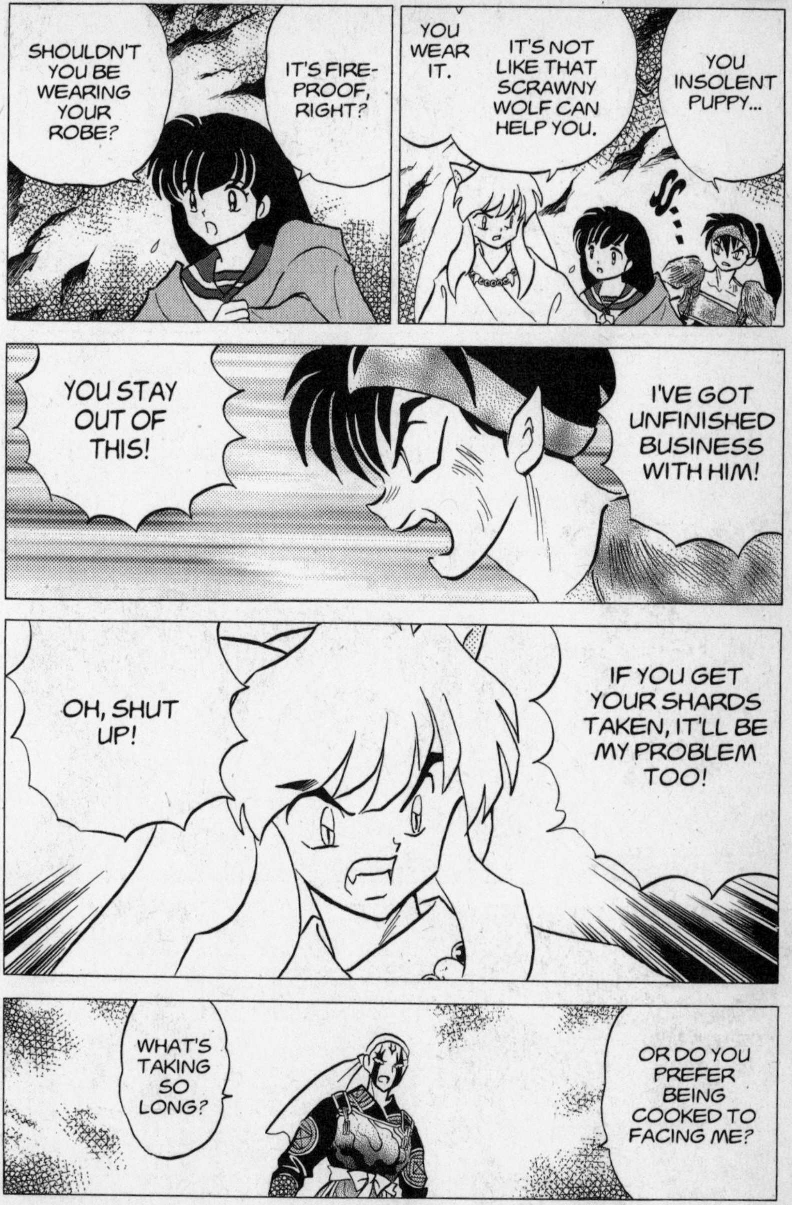
SHOULDN'T YOU BE WEARING YOUR ROBE?
IT'S FIRE-PROOF, RIGHT?
YOU WEAR IT.
IT'S NOT LIKE THAT SCRAWNY WOLF CAN HELP YOU.
YOU INSOLENT PUPPY...
YOU STAY OUT OF THIS!
I'VE GOT UNFINISHED BUSINESS WITH HIM!
OH, SHUT UP!
IF YOU GET YOUR SHARDS TAKEN, IT'LL BE MY PROBLEM TOO!
WHAT'S TAKING SO LONG?
OR DO YOU PREFER BEING COOKED TO FACING ME?

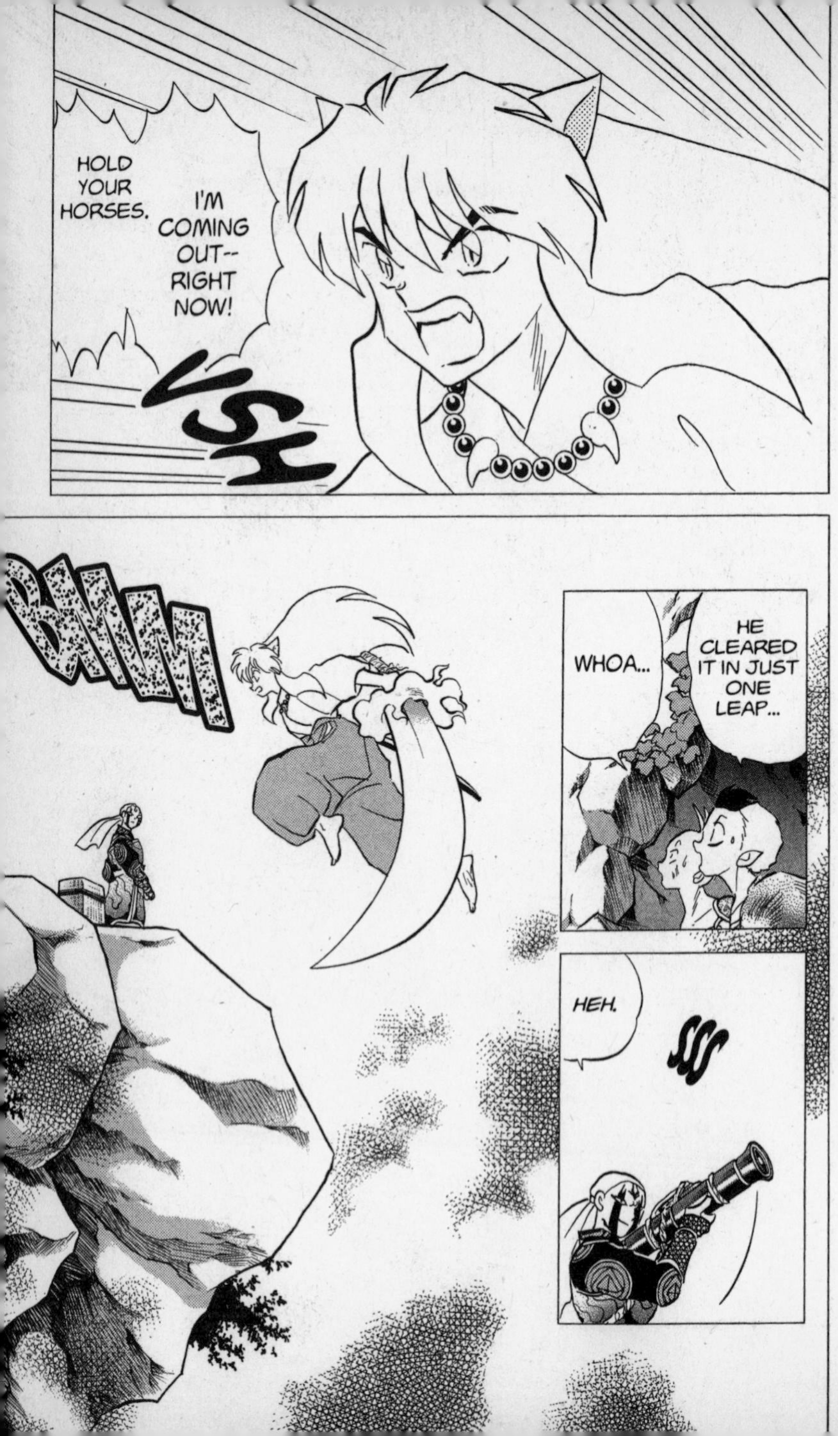
HOLD YOUR HORSES.
I'M COMING OUT-- RIGHT NOW!
VSH
BMM
WHOA...
HE CLEARED IT IN JUST ONE LEAP...
HEH.
SSS

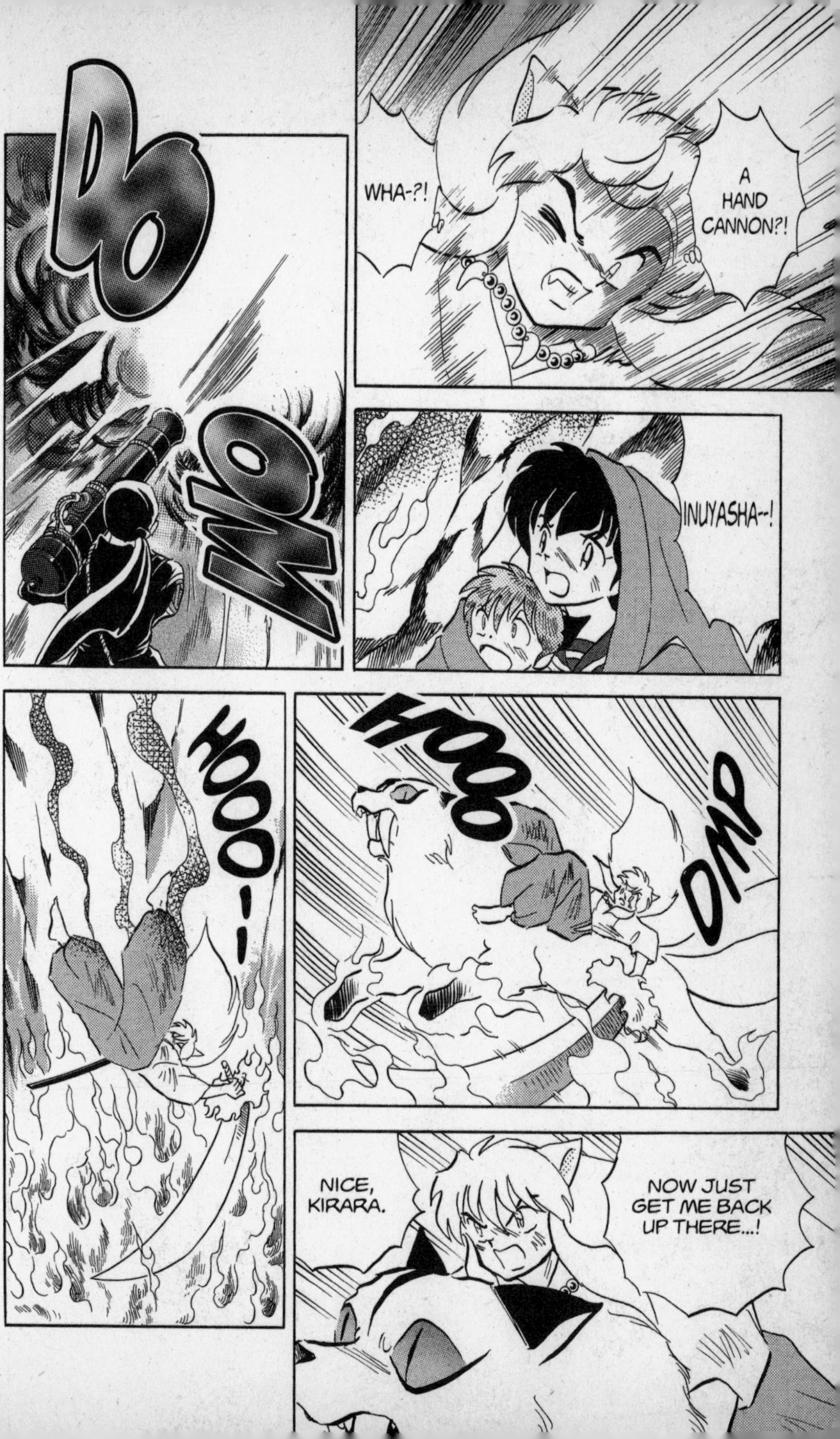
WHA-?!
A HAND CANNON?!
DOOM
INUYASHA--!
FOOO
DMP
HOOO!!
NICE, KIRARA.
NOW JUST GET ME BACK UP THERE...!

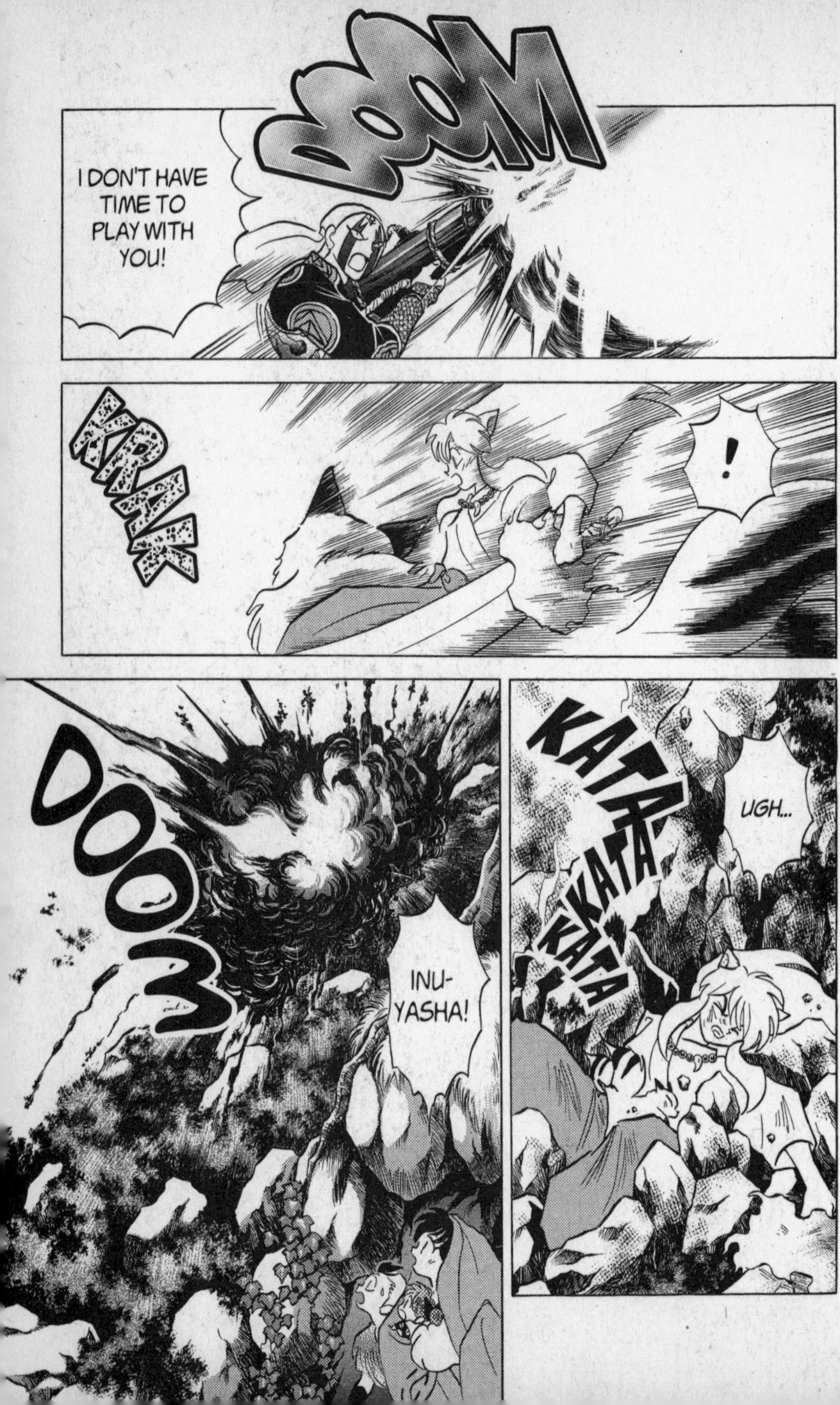
BOOM
I DON'T HAVE TIME TO PLAY WITH YOU!
KRANK
!
DOOOM
INU-YASHA!
KATA KATA KATA KATA
UGH...

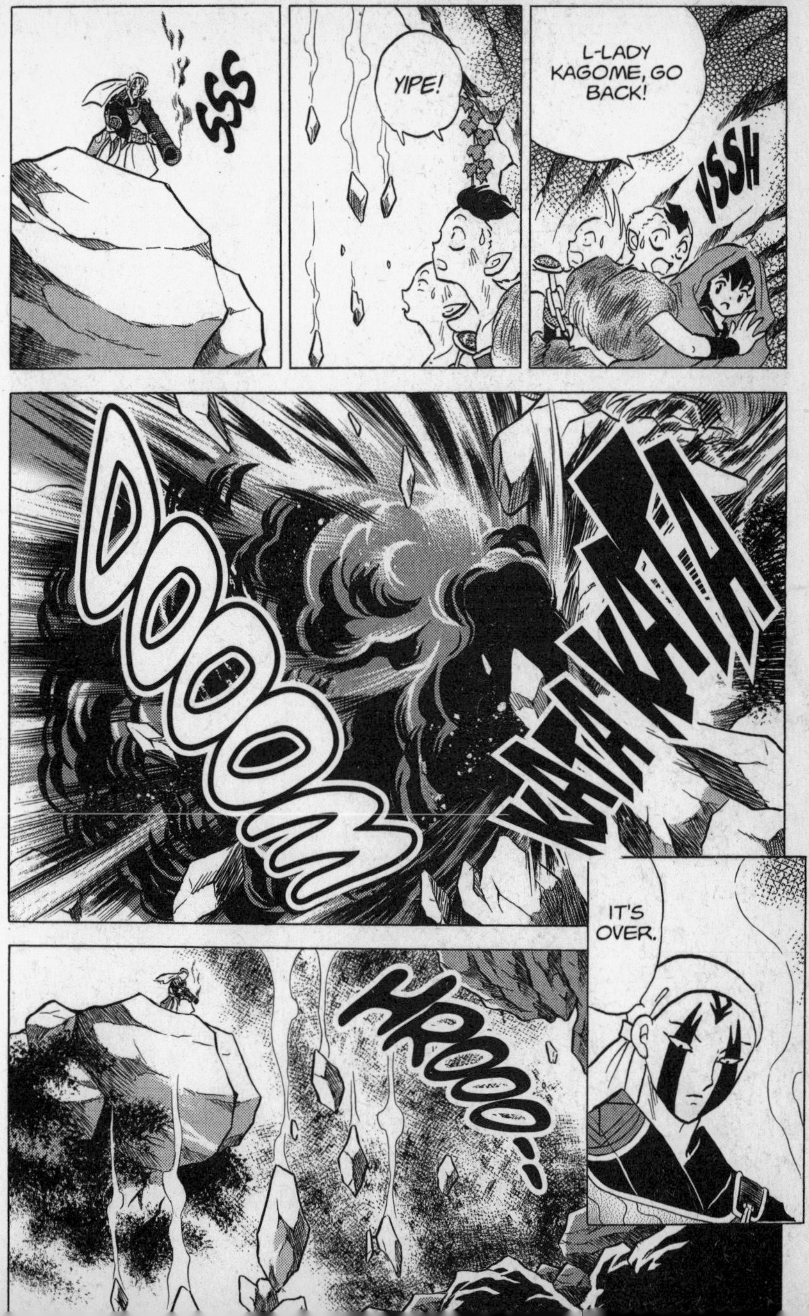
SSS
YIPE!
L-LADY KAGOME, GO BACK!
VSSH
KAKAKAKA
DOOOOOM
IT'S OVER.
HROOO...

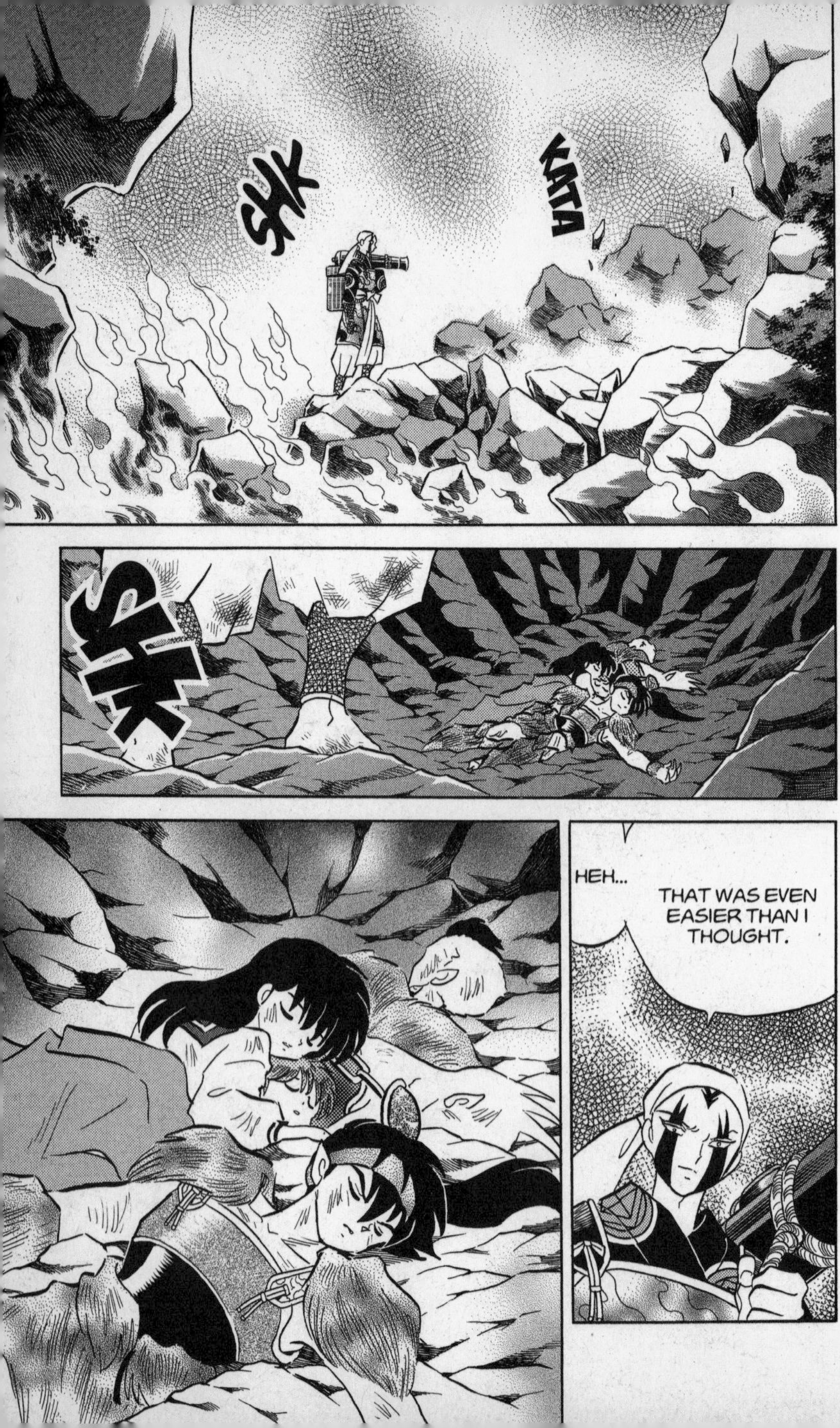
KATA
SHK
SHK
HEH...
THAT WAS EVEN EASIER THAN I THOUGHT.

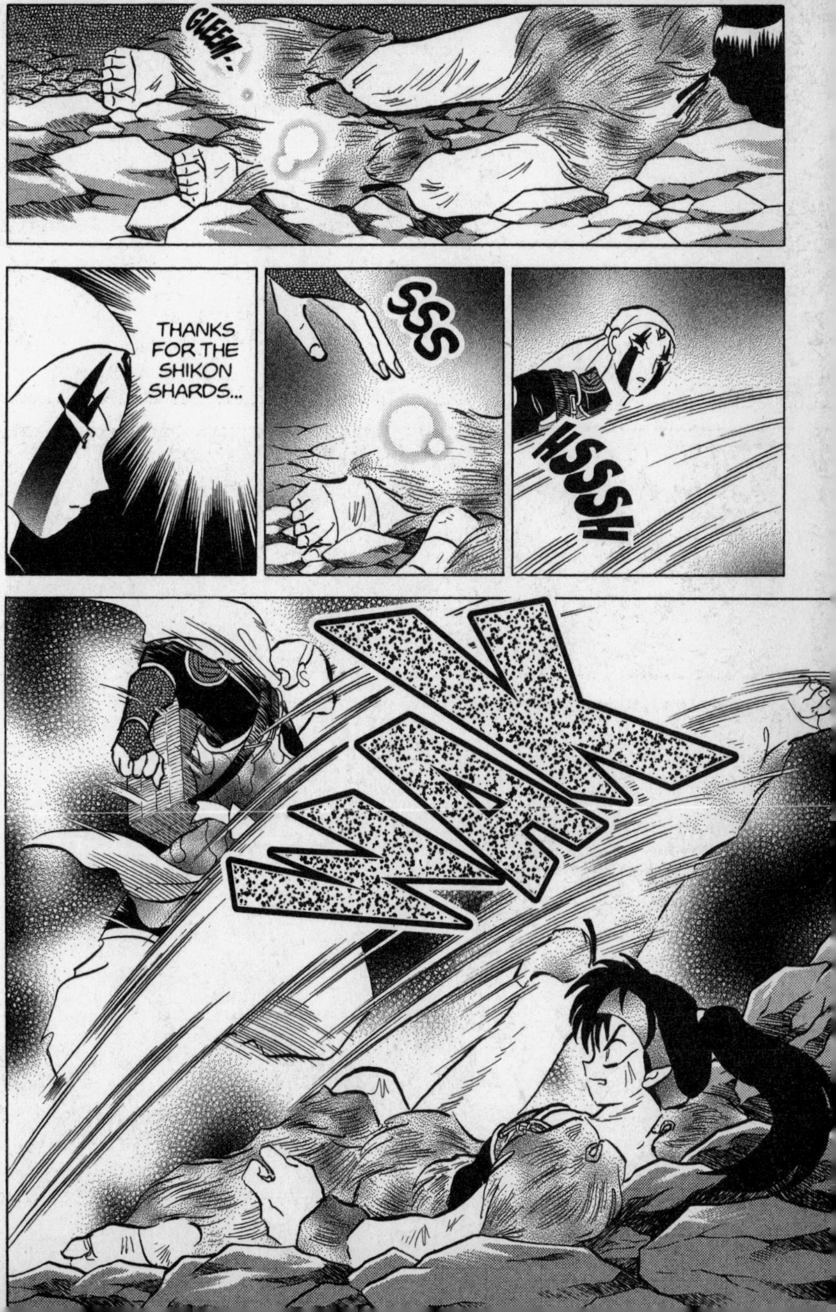
GLEEM...
THANKS FOR THE SHIKON SHARDS...
SSS
HSSSH
WAK

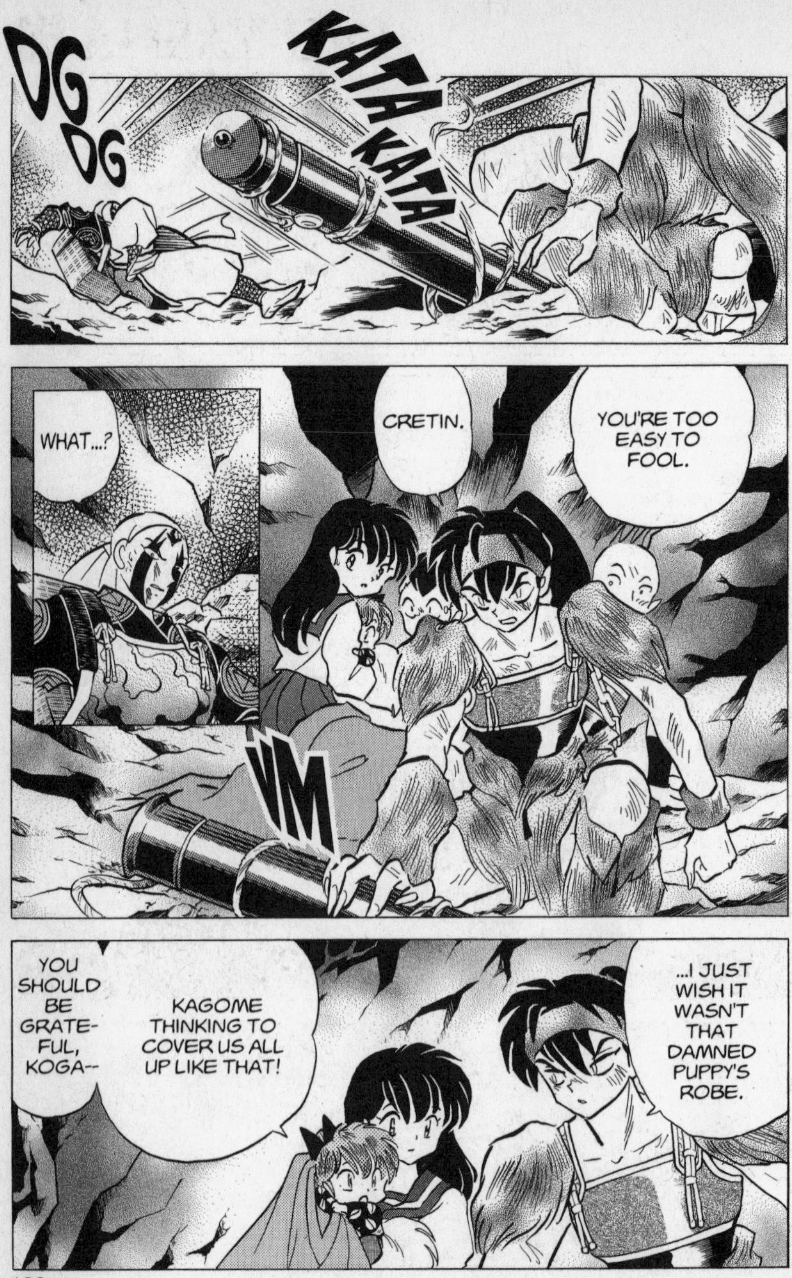
DG DG
KATA KATA KATA
WHAT...?
CRETIN.
YOU'RE TOO EASY TO FOOL.
VM
YOU SHOULD BE GRATE-FUL, KOGA--
KAGOME THINKING TO COVER US ALL UP LIKE THAT!
...I JUST WISH IT WASN'T THAT DAMNED PUPPY'S ROBE.

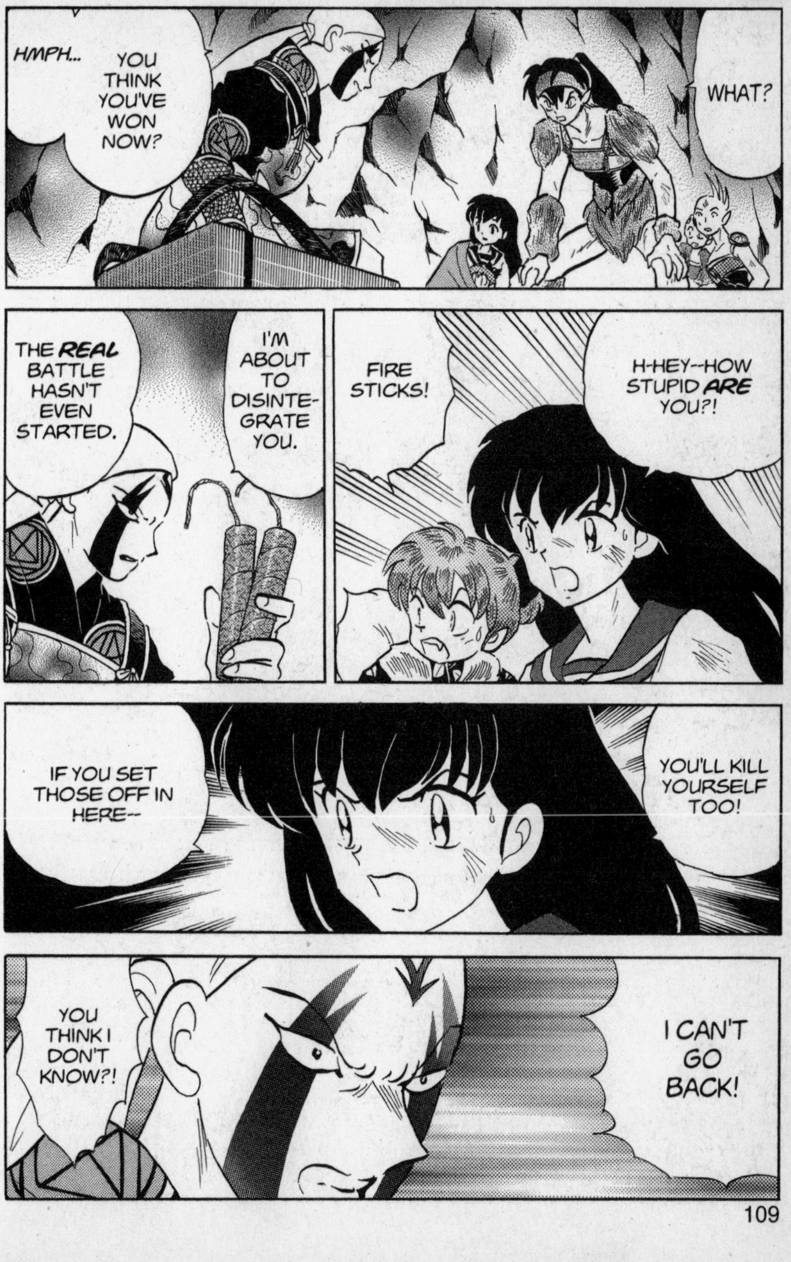
HMPH...
YOU THINK YOU'VE WON NOW?
WHAT?
THE REAL BATTLE HASN'T EVEN STARTED.
I'M ABOUT TO DISINTEGRATE YOU.
FIRE STICKS!
H-HEY--HOW STUPID ARE YOU?!
IF YOU SET THOSE OFF IN HERE--
YOU'LL KILL YOURSELF TOO!
YOU THINK I DON'T KNOW?!
I CAN'T GO BACK!

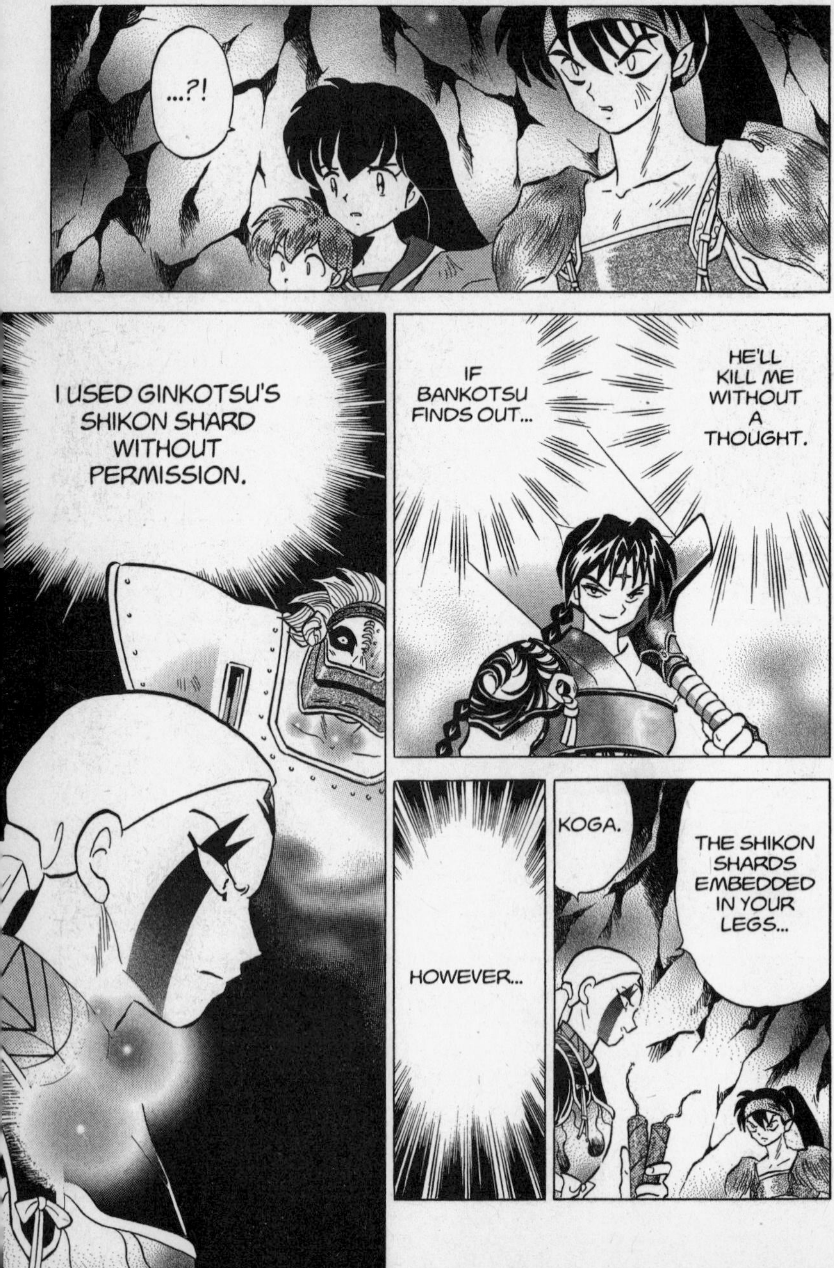
...?!
I USED GINKOTSU'S SHIKON SHARD WITHOUT PERMISSION.
IF BANKOTSU FINDS OUT...
HE'LL KILL ME WITHOUT A THOUGHT.
HOWEVER...
KOGA.
THE SHIKON SHARDS EMBEDDED IN YOUR LEGS...

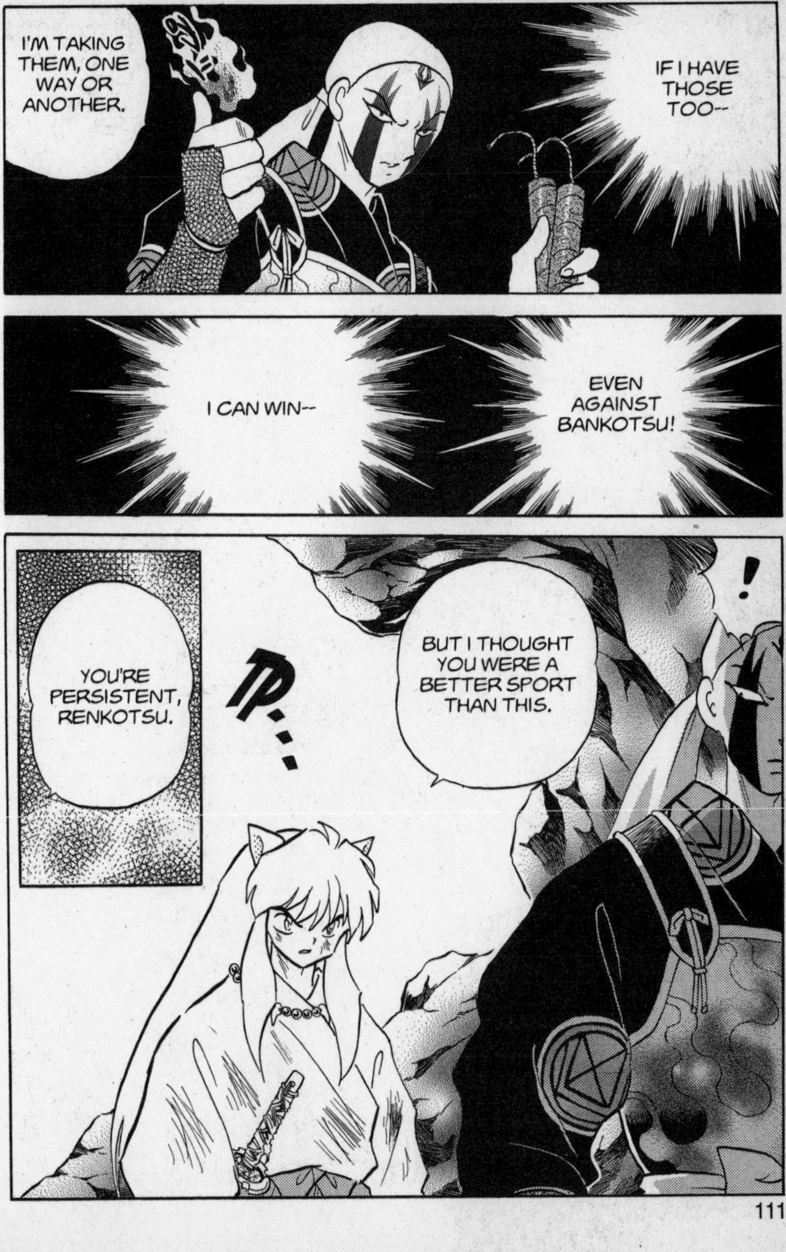
I'M TAKING THEM, ONE WAY OR ANOTHER.
IF I HAVE THOSE TOO--
I CAN WIN--
EVEN AGAINST BANKOTSU!
YOU'RE PERSISTENT, RENKOTSU.
TP...
BUT I THOUGHT YOU WERE A BETTER SPORT THAN THIS.
!

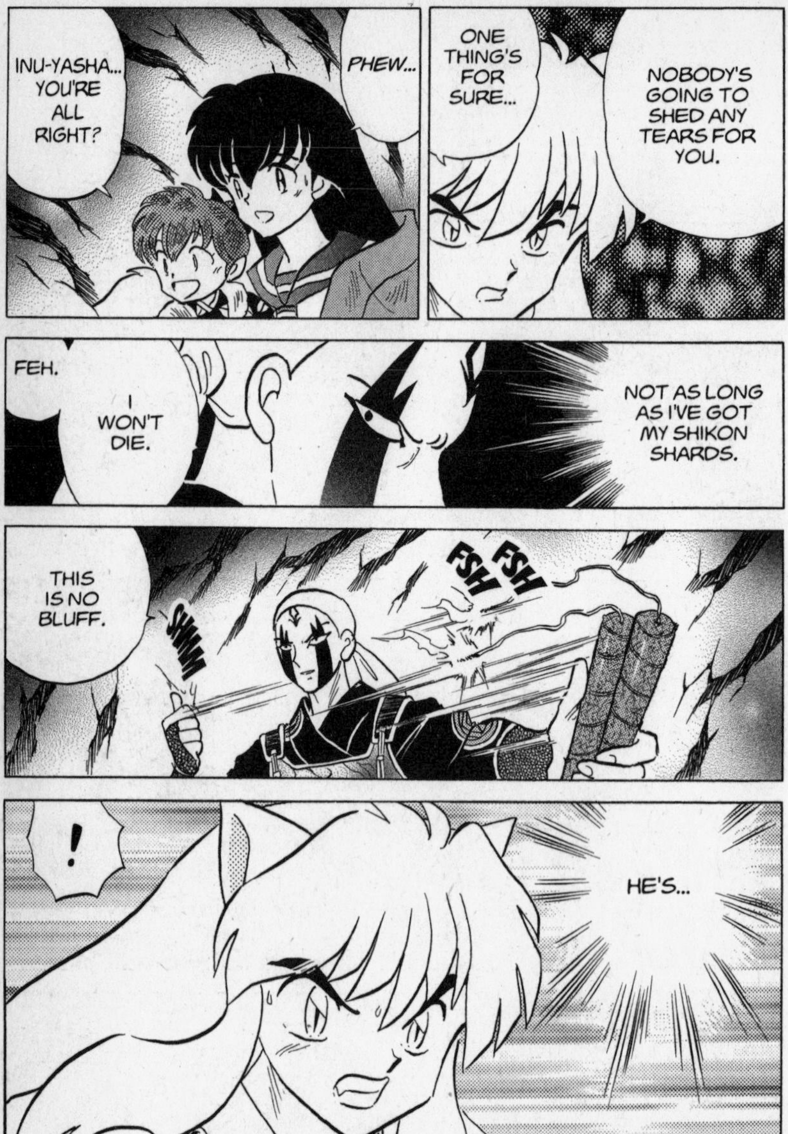
INU-YASHA... YOU'RE ALL RIGHT?
PHEW...
ONE THING'S FOR SURE...
NOBODY'S GOING TO SHED ANY TEARS FOR YOU.
FEH.
I WON'T DIE.
NOT AS LONG AS I'VE GOT MY SHIKON SHARDS.
THIS IS NO BLUFF.
FSH
FSH
!
HE'S...

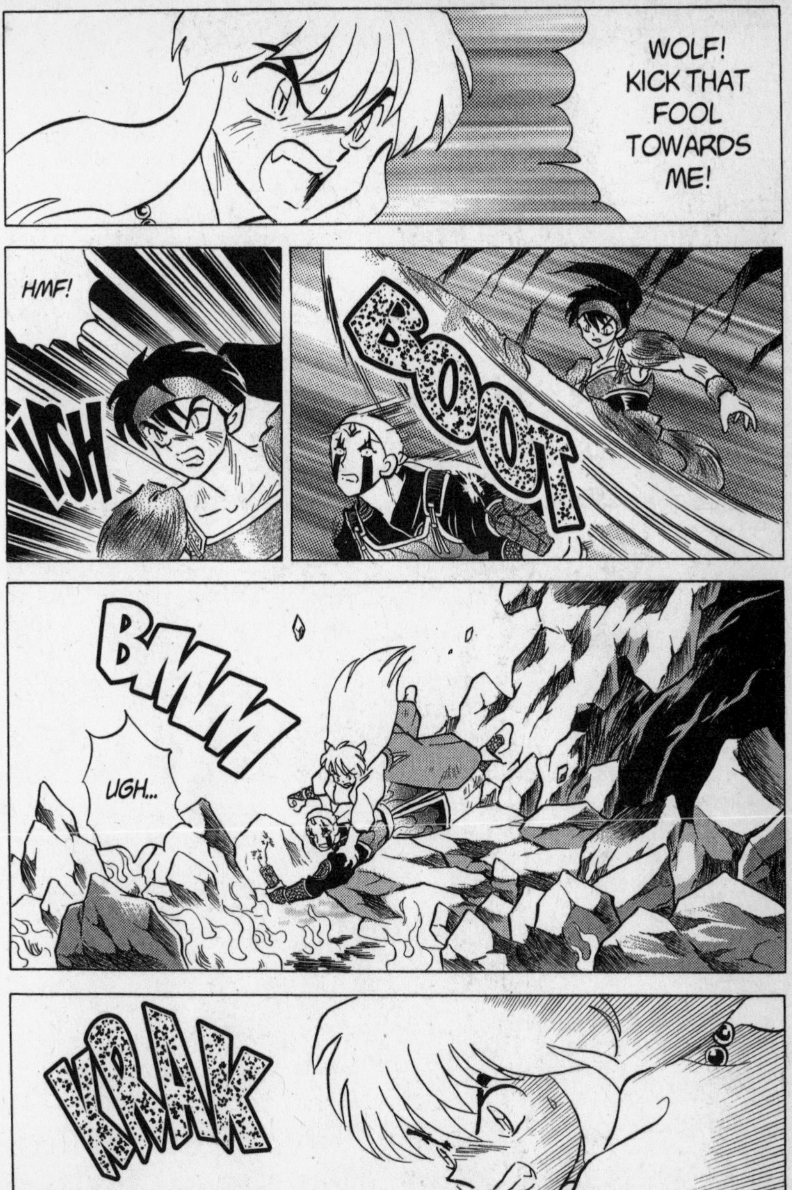
WOLF! KICK THAT FOOL TOWARDS ME!
BOOT
HMF!
BMM
UGH...
KRAK

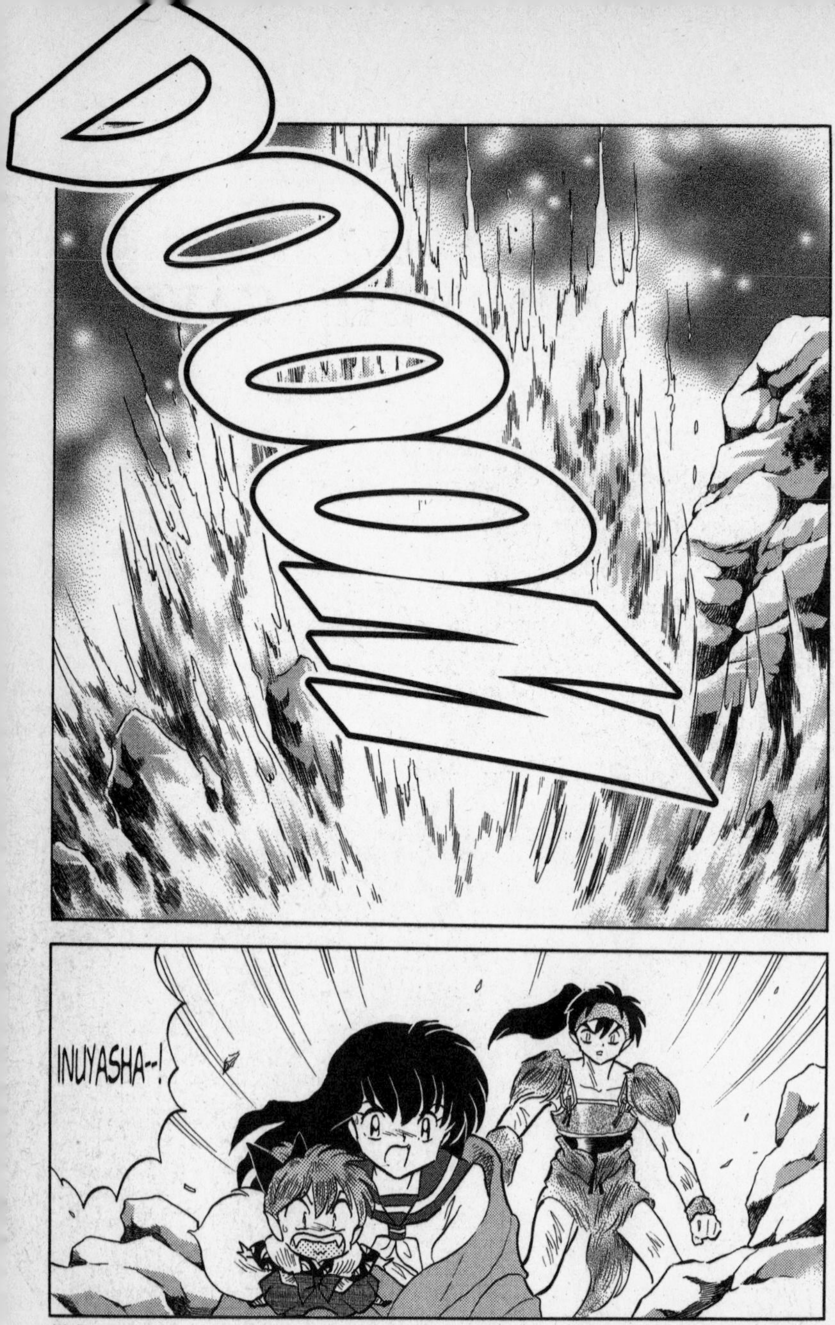
DOOOON
INUYASHA--!

SCROLL 7

THE MOUNTAIN CAVE

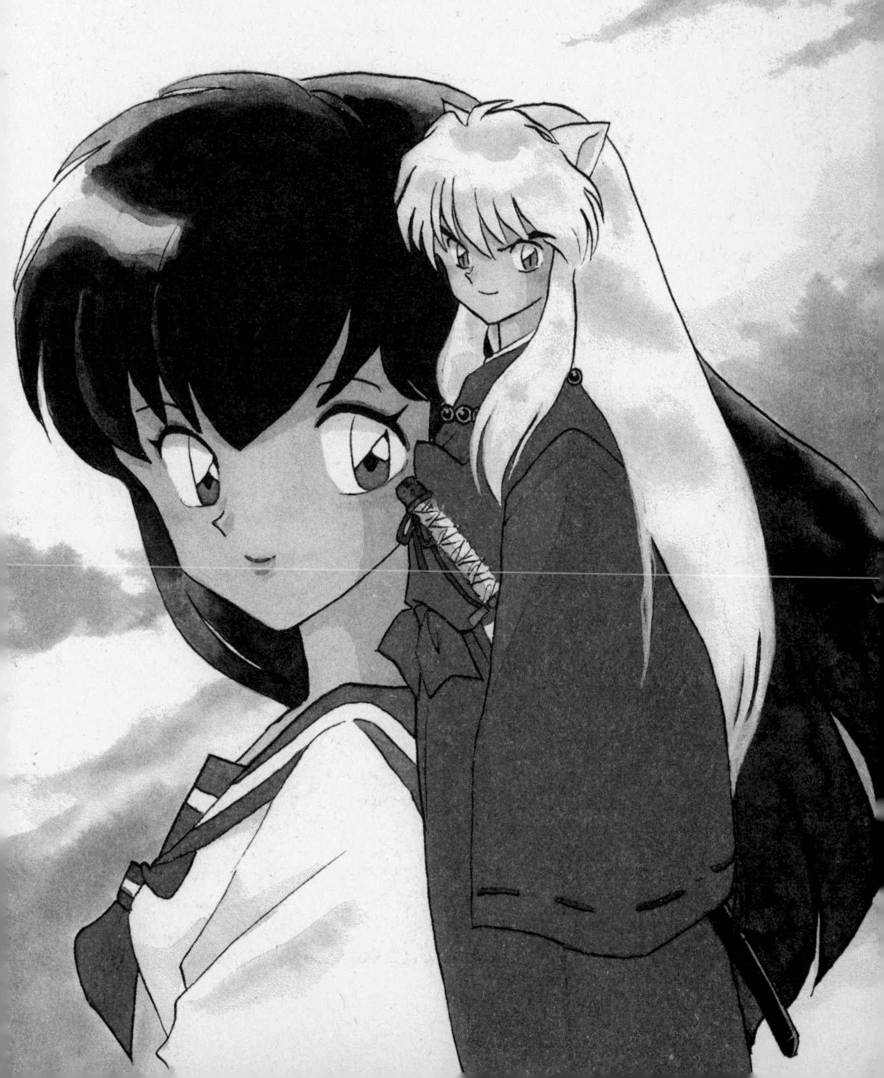

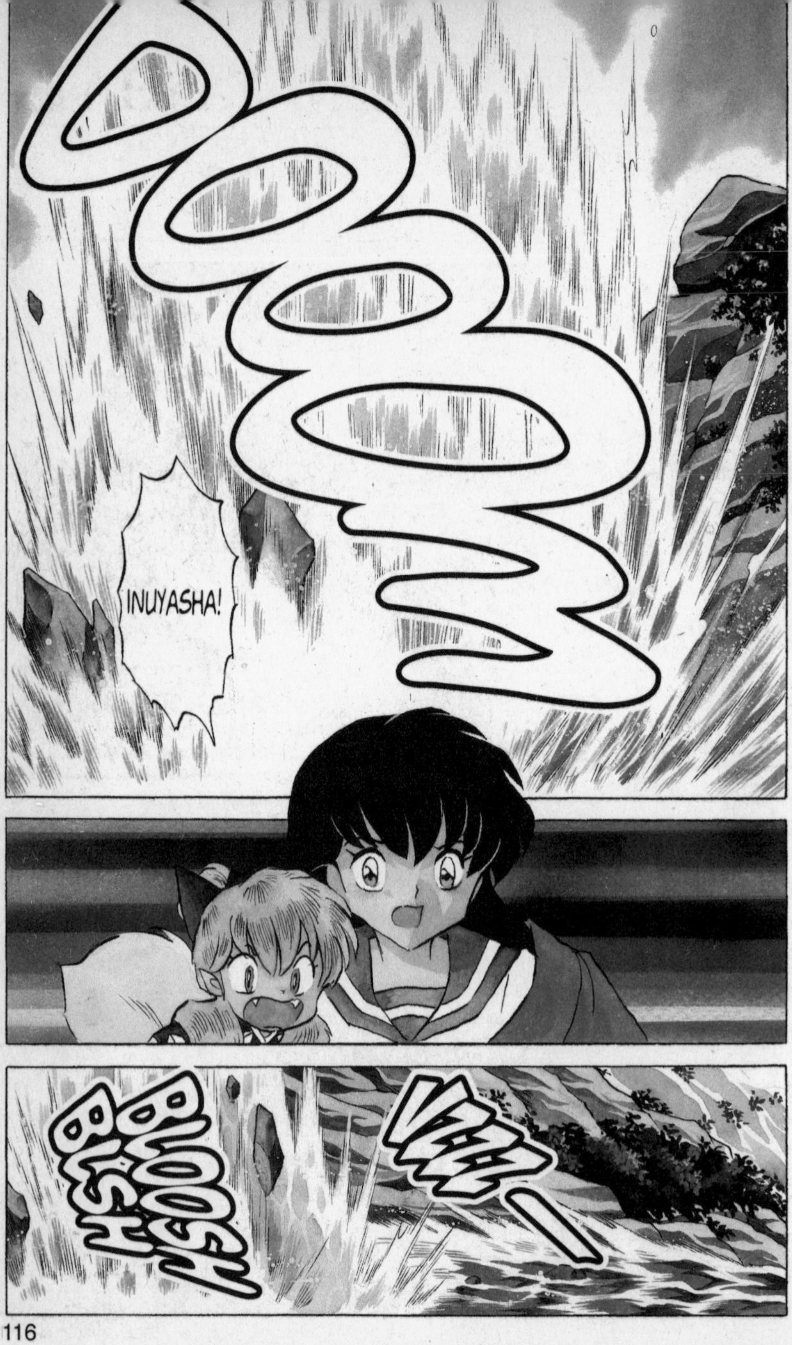
DOOOOM
INUYASHA!
VWM!
BLOOSH BLOOSH

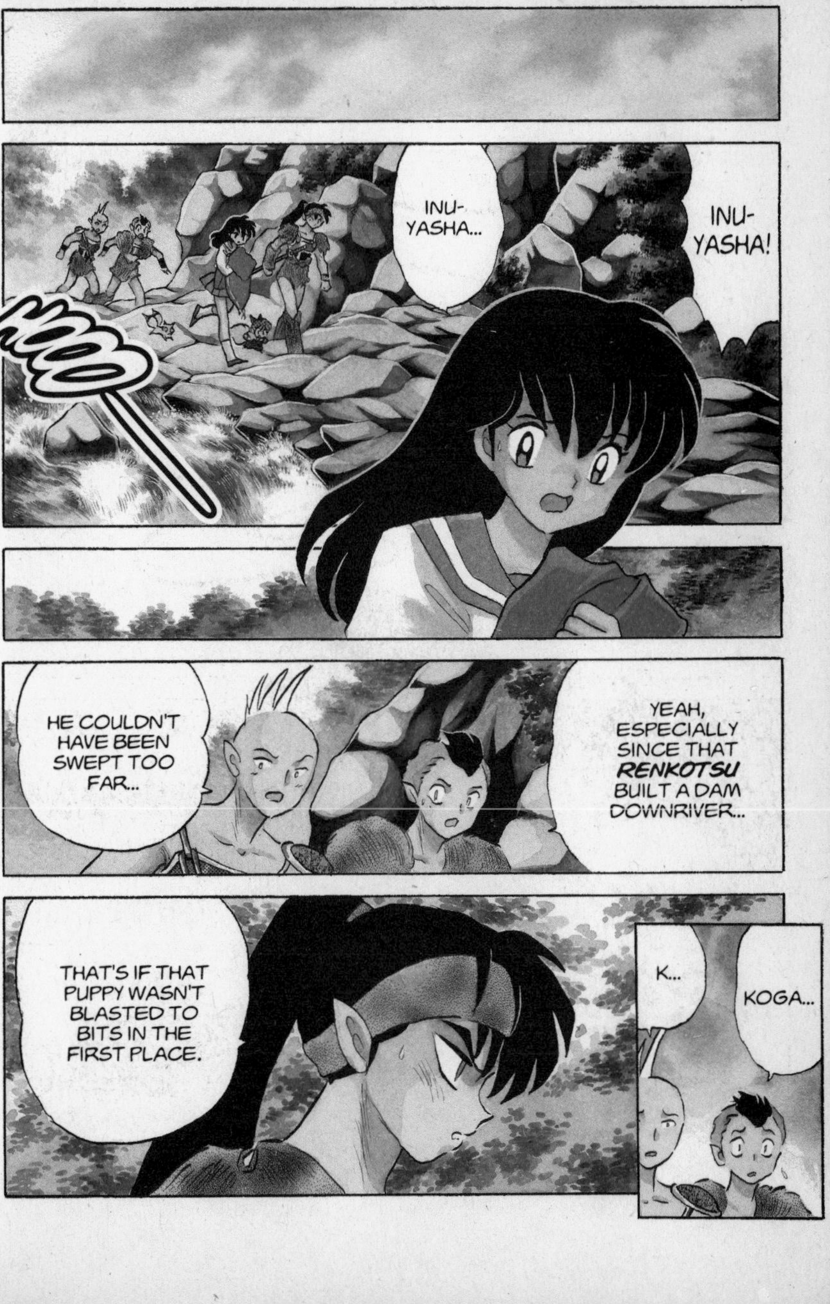
INU-YASHA...
INU-YASHA!
HOOO
HE COULDN'T HAVE BEEN SWEPT TOO FAR...
YEAH, ESPECIALLY SINCE THAT ***RENKOTSU*** BUILT A DAM DOWNRIVER...
THAT'S IF THAT PUPPY WASN'T BLASTED TO BITS IN THE FIRST PLACE.
K...
KOGA...

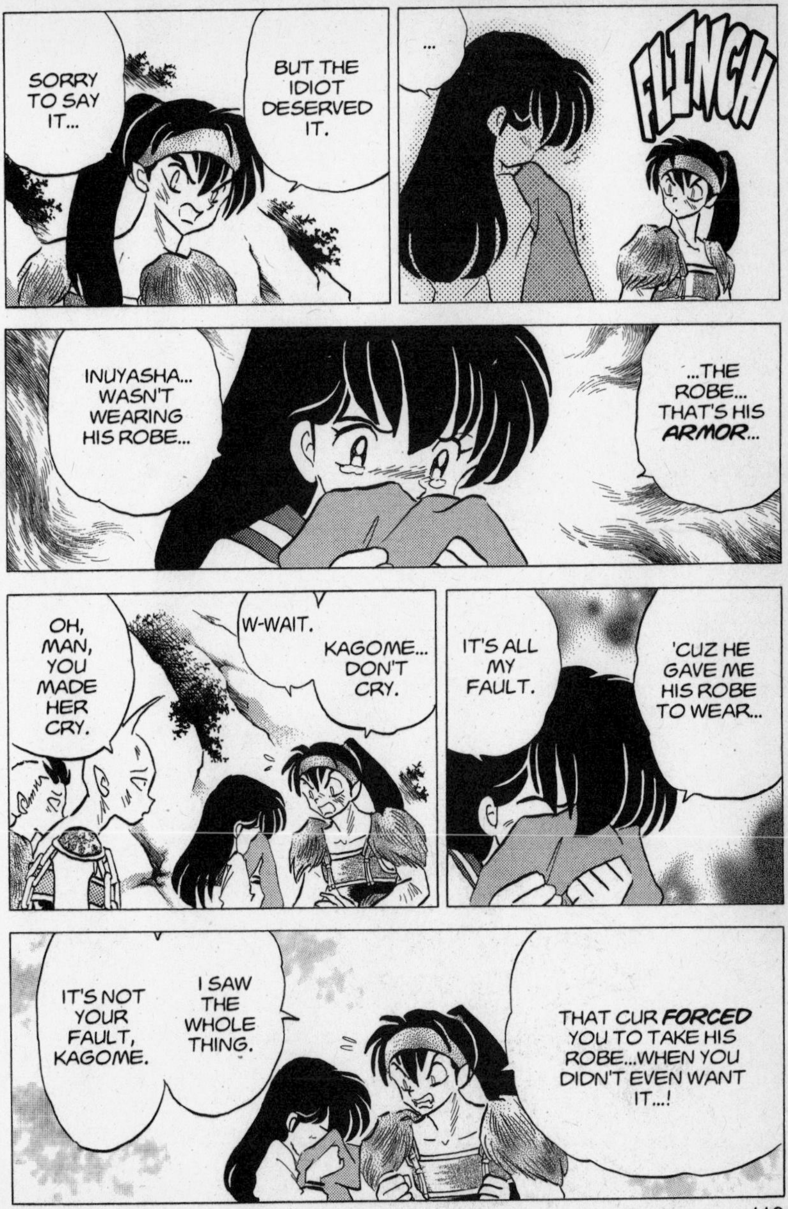
SORRY TO SAY IT...
BUT THE IDIOT DESERVED IT.
...
FLINCH
INUYASHA... WASN'T WEARING HIS ROBE...
...THE ROBE... THAT'S HIS ARMOR...
OH, MAN, YOU MADE HER CRY.
W-WAIT.
KAGOME... DON'T CRY.
IT'S ALL MY FAULT.
'CUZ HE GAVE ME HIS ROBE TO WEAR...
IT'S NOT YOUR FAULT, KAGOME.
I SAW THE WHOLE THING.
THAT CUR FORCED YOU TO TAKE HIS ROBE...WHEN YOU DIDN'T EVEN WANT IT...!

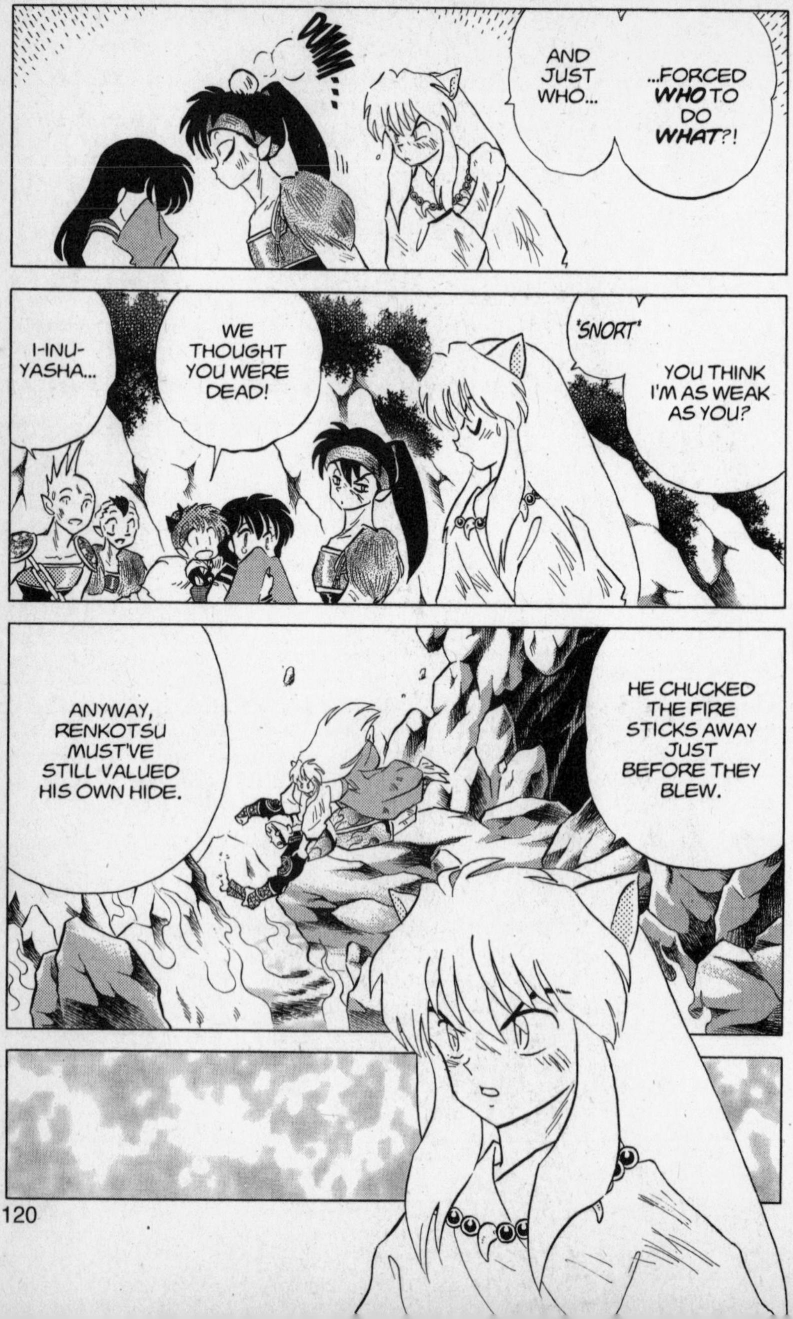
DUMM
AND JUST WHO...
...FORCED WHO TO DO WHAT?!
I-INU-YASHA...
WE THOUGHT YOU WERE DEAD!
SNORT
YOU THINK I'M AS WEAK AS YOU?
ANYWAY, RENKOTSU MUST'VE STILL VALUED HIS OWN HIDE.
HE CHUCKED THE FIRE STICKS AWAY JUST BEFORE THEY BLEW.

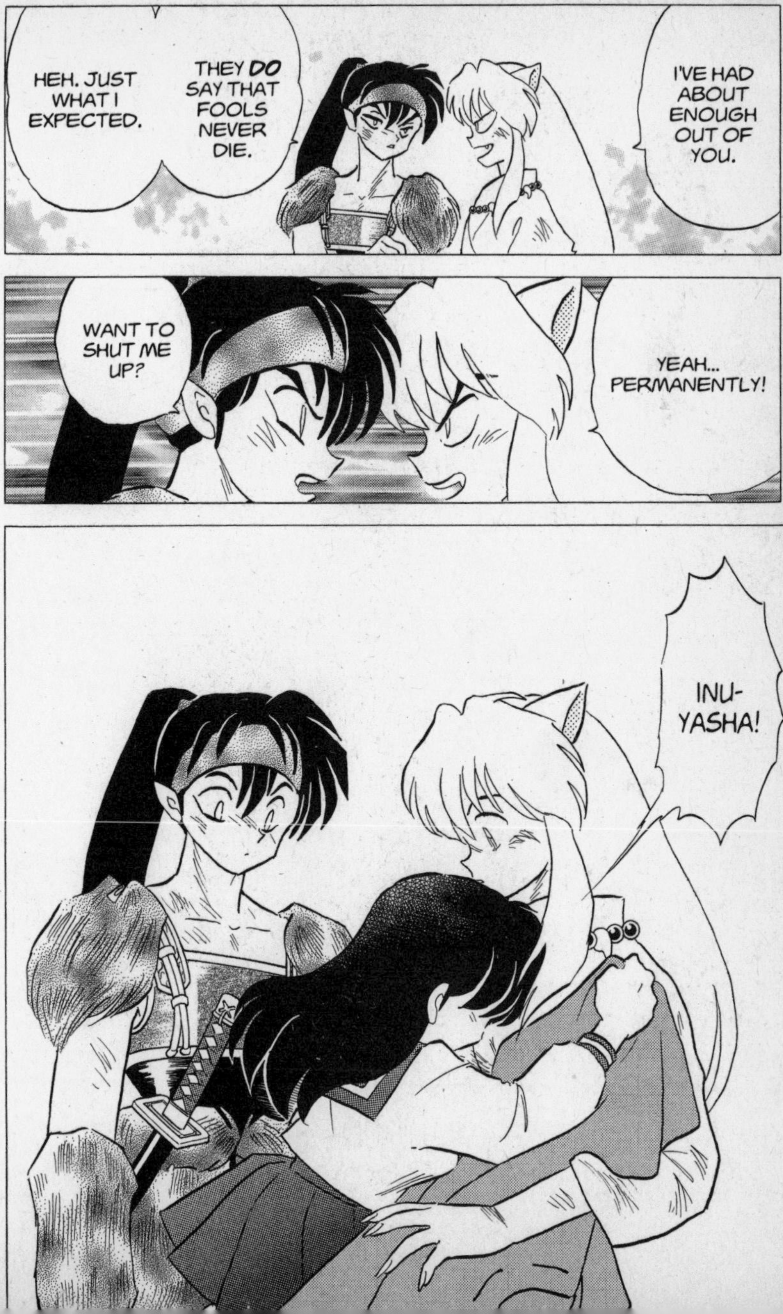
HEH. JUST WHAT I EXPECTED.
THEY DO SAY THAT FOOLS NEVER DIE.
I'VE HAD ABOUT ENOUGH OUT OF YOU.
WANT TO SHUT ME UP?
YEAH... PERMANENTLY!
INU-YASHA!

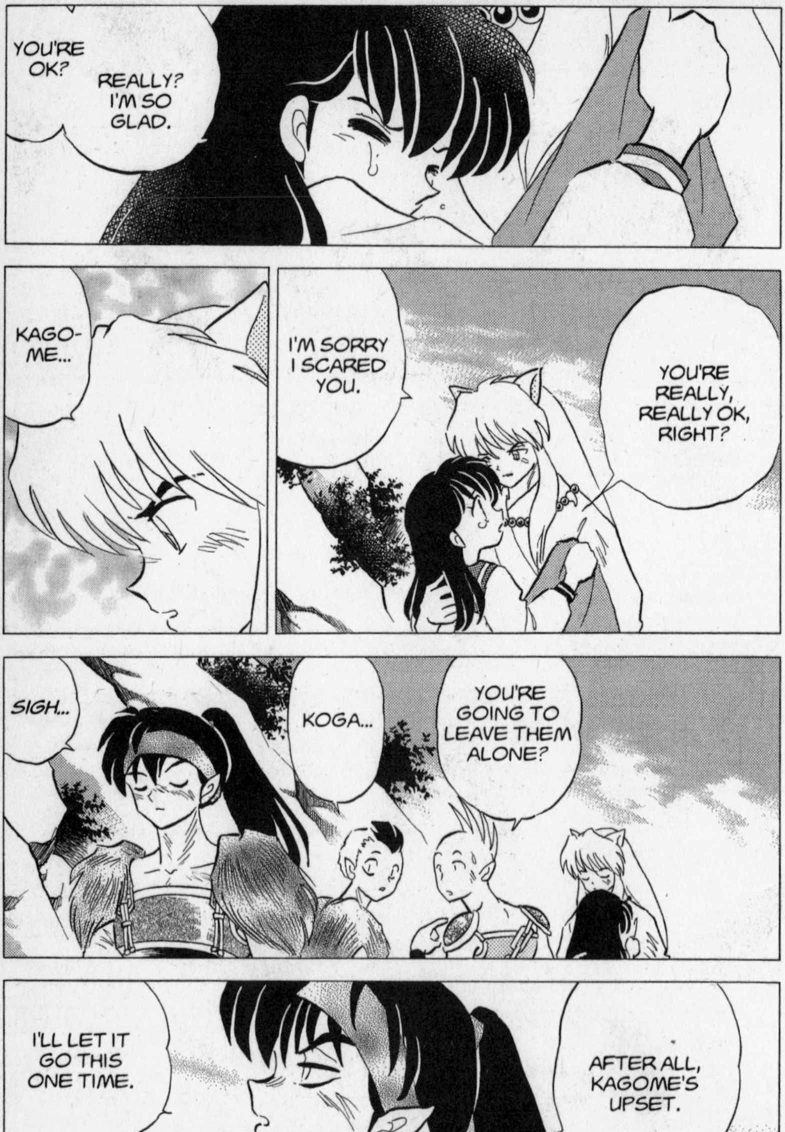
YOU'RE OK?
REALLY? I'M SO GLAD.
KAGOME...
I'M SORRY I SCARED YOU.
YOU'RE REALLY, REALLY OK, RIGHT?
SIGH...
KOGA...
YOU'RE GOING TO LEAVE THEM ALONE?
I'LL LET IT GO THIS ONE TIME.
AFTER ALL, KAGOME'S UPSET.

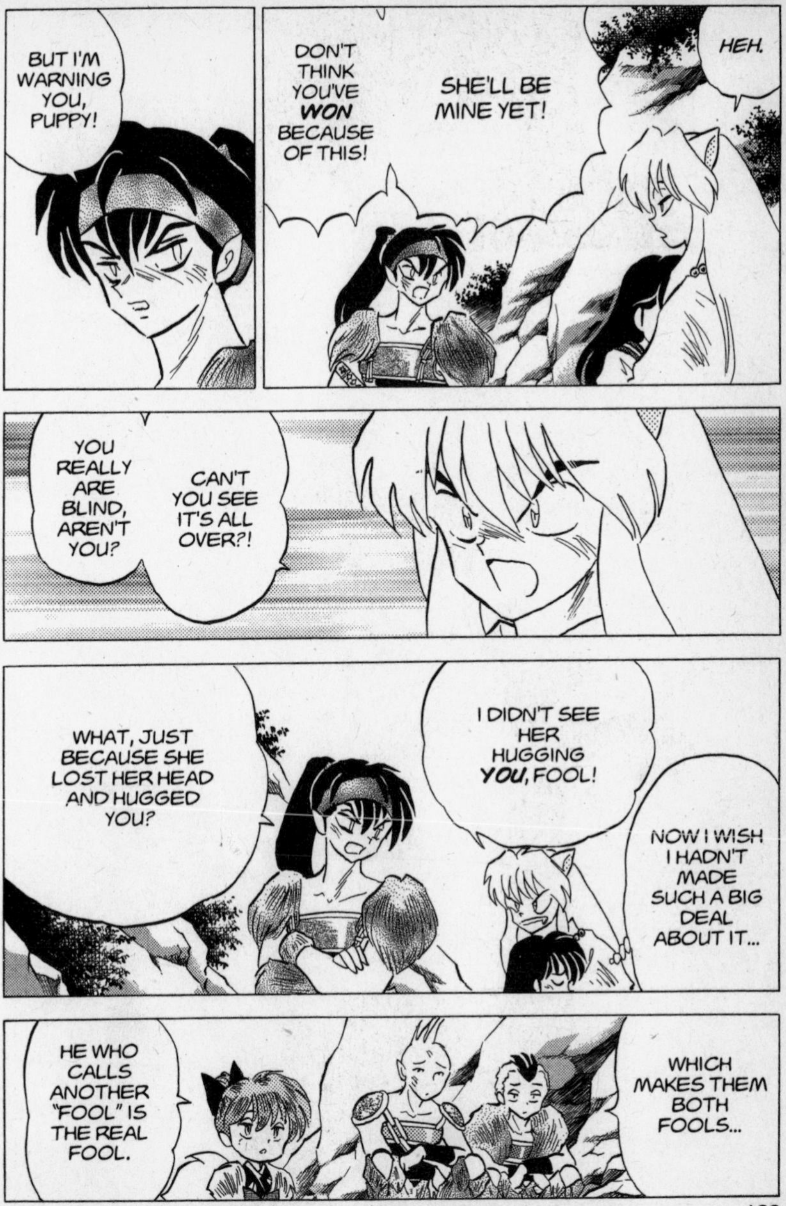
BUT I'M WARNING YOU, PUPPY!
DON'T THINK YOU'VE WON BECAUSE OF THIS!
SHE'LL BE MINE YET!
HEH.
YOU REALLY ARE BLIND, AREN'T YOU?
CAN'T YOU SEE IT'S ALL OVER?!
WHAT, JUST BECAUSE SHE LOST HER HEAD AND HUGGED YOU?
I DIDN'T SEE HER HUGGING YOU, FOOL!
NOW I WISH I HADN'T MADE SUCH A BIG DEAL ABOUT IT...
HE WHO CALLS ANOTHER "FOOL" IS THE REAL FOOL.
WHICH MAKES THEM BOTH FOOLS...

HSSH...

SHK SHK

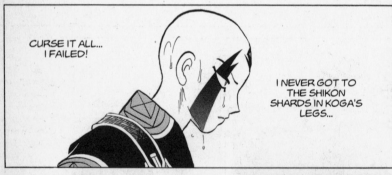

CURSE IT ALL...
I FAILED!

I NEVER GOT TO
THE SHIKON
SHARDS IN KOGA'S
LEGS...

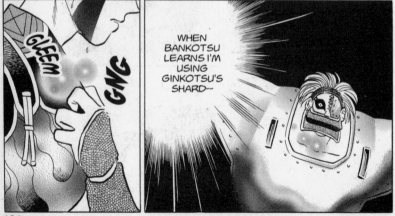

GLEEM

GING

WHEN
BANKOTSU
LEARNS I'M
USING
GINKOTSU'S
SHARD--

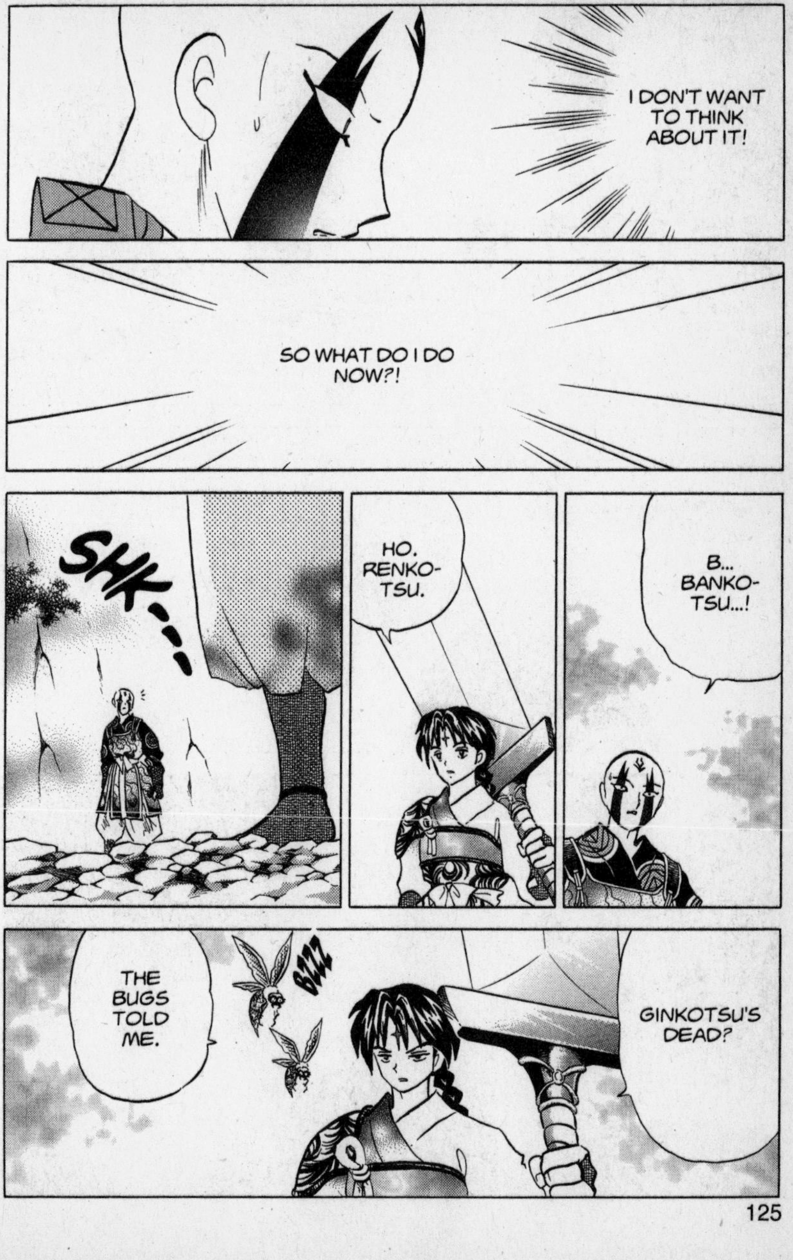
I DON'T WANT TO THINK ABOUT IT!
SO WHAT DO I DO NOW?!
B... BANKO-TSU...!
HO. RENKO-TSU.
SHK...
GINKOTSU'S DEAD?
THE BUGS TOLD ME.
BZZZ

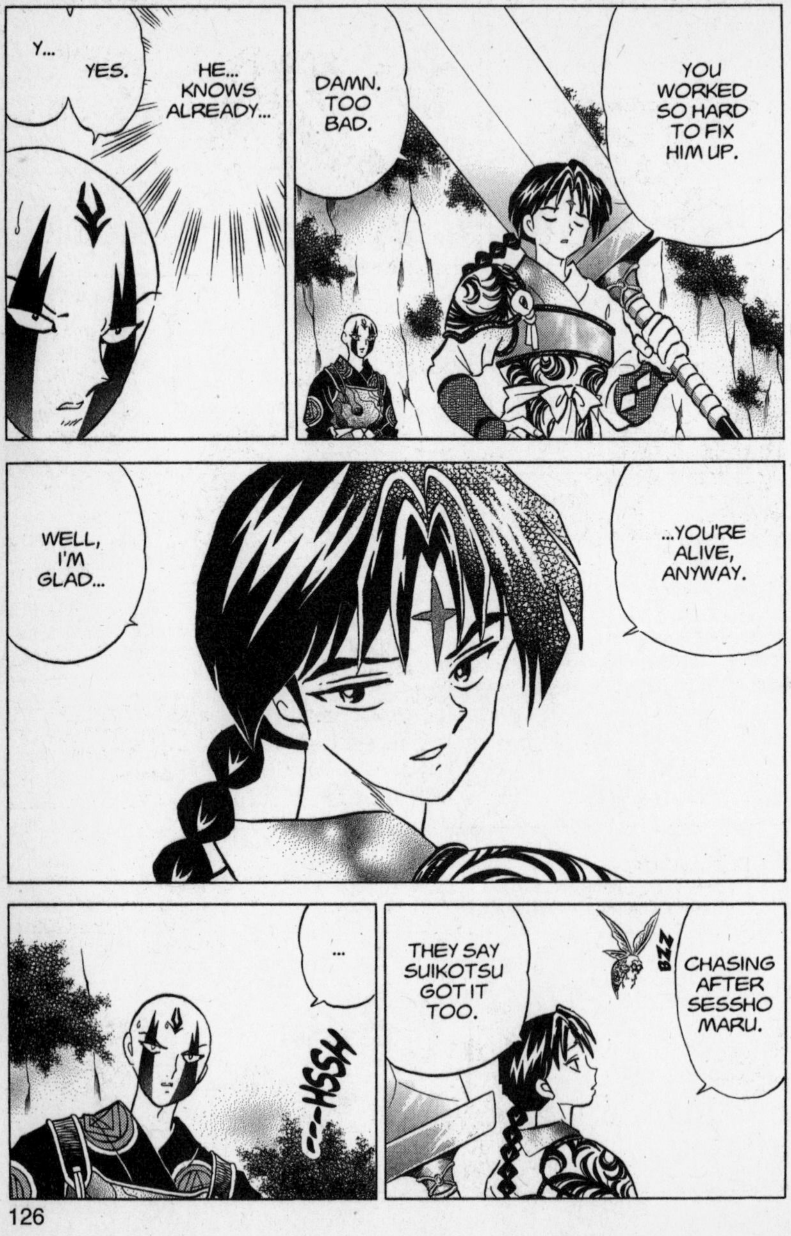
Y...
YES.
HE... KNOWS ALREADY...
DAMN. TOO BAD.
YOU WORKED SO HARD TO FIX HIM UP.
WELL, I'M GLAD...
...YOU'RE ALIVE, ANYWAY.
...
--HSSH
THEY SAY SUIKOTSU GOT IT TOO.
BZZ
CHASING AFTER SESSHO MARU.

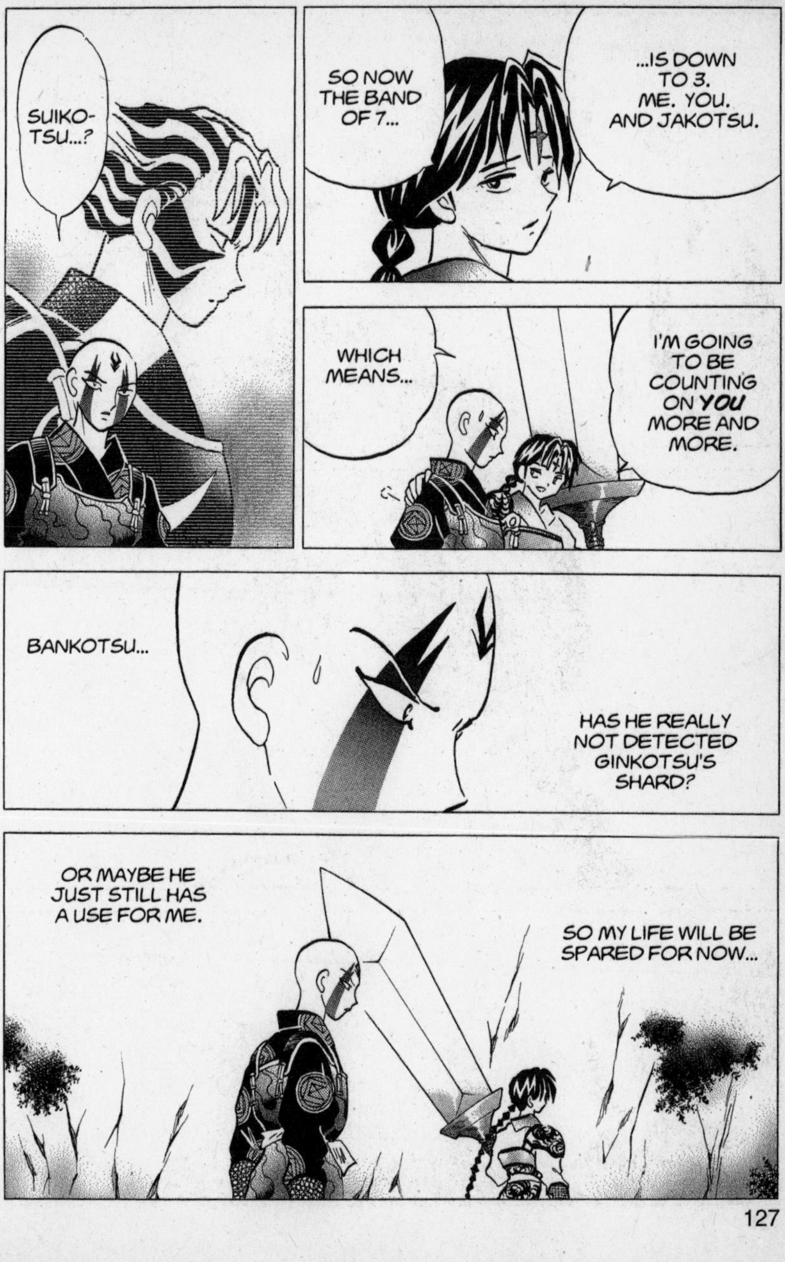
SUIKO-TSU...?
SO NOW THE BAND OF 7...
...IS DOWN TO 3. ME. YOU. AND JAKOTSU.
WHICH MEANS...
I'M GOING TO BE COUNTING ON *YOU* MORE AND MORE.
BANKOTSU...
HAS HE REALLY NOT DETECTED GINKOTSU'S SHARD?
OR MAYBE HE JUST STILL HAS A USE FOR ME.
SO MY LIFE WILL BE SPARED FOR NOW...

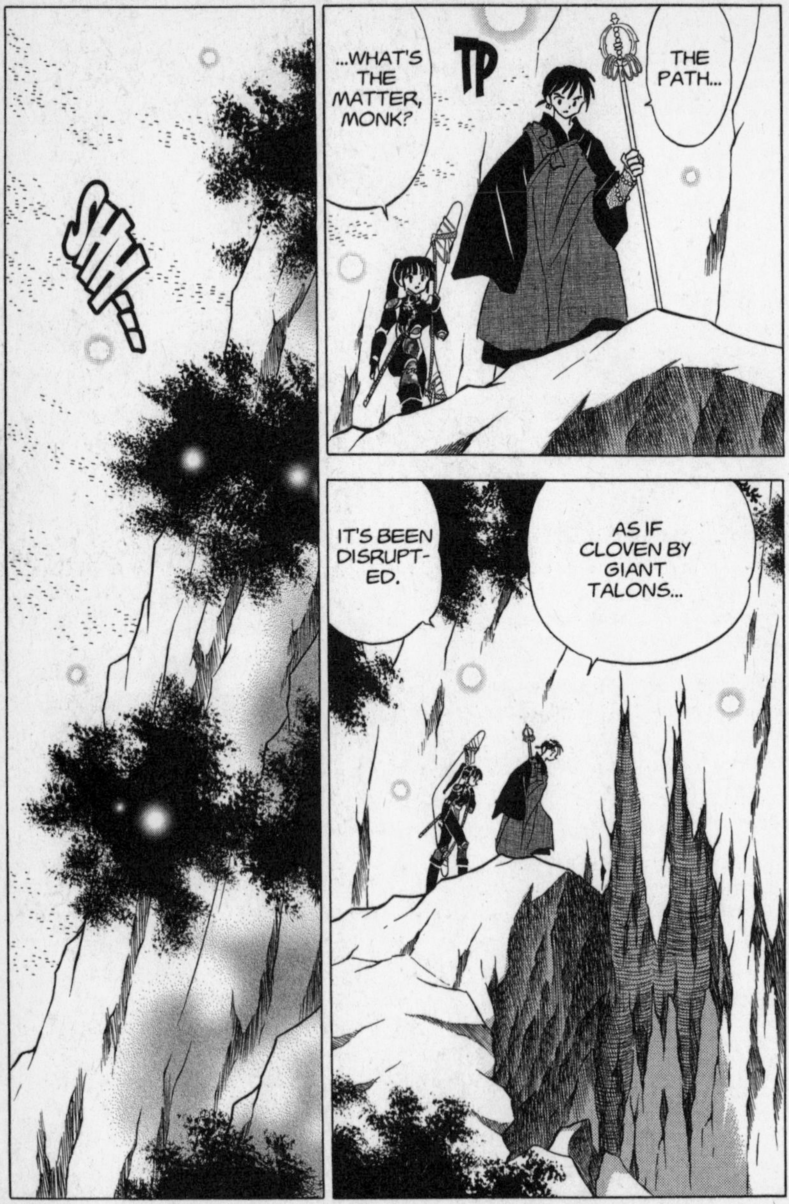
THE PATH...
TP
...WHAT'S THE MATTER, MONK?
AS IF CLOVEN BY GIANT TALONS...
IT'S BEEN DISRUPT-ED.
SHH

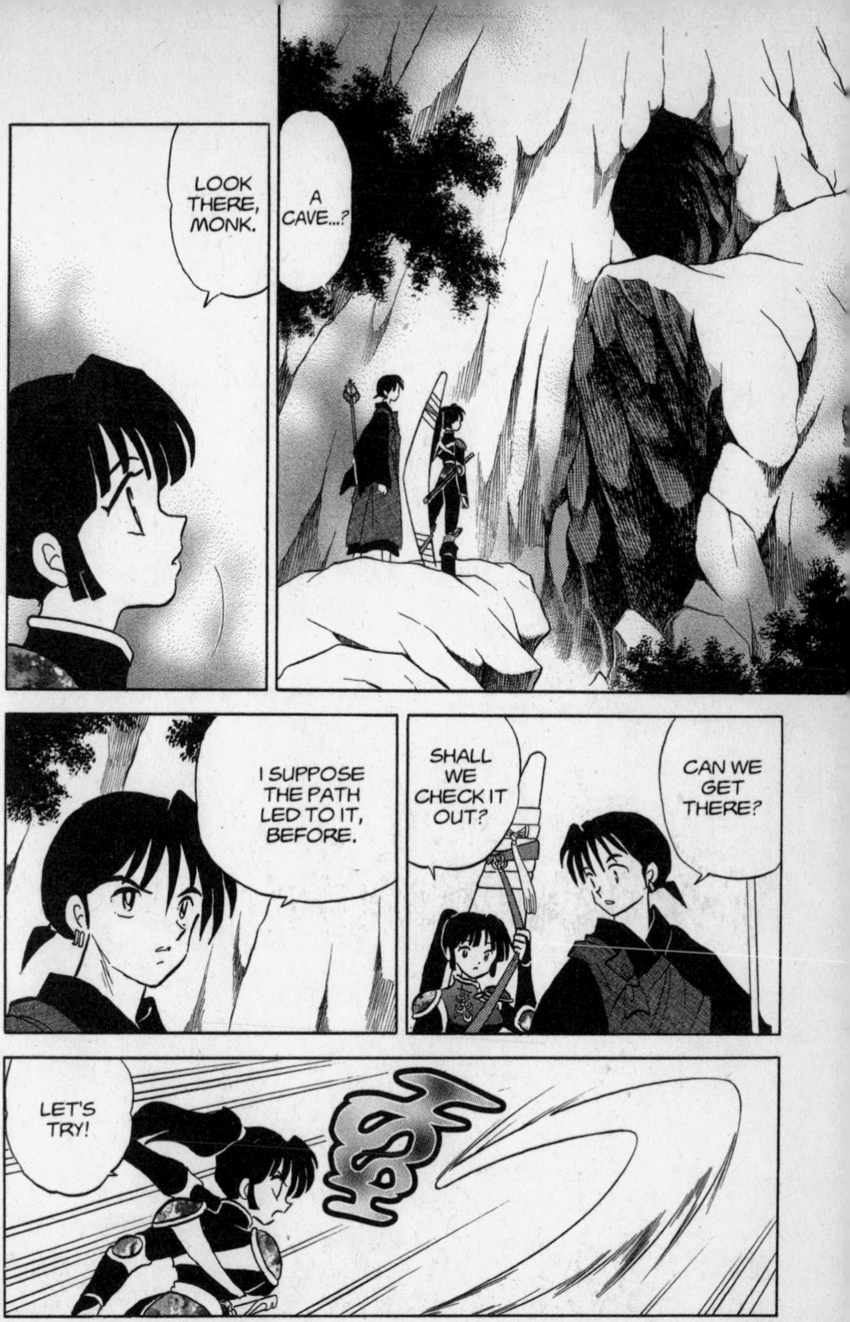
A CAVE...?
LOOK THERE, MONK.
CAN WE GET THERE?
SHALL WE CHECK IT OUT?
I SUPPOSE THE PATH LED TO IT, BEFORE.
LET'S TRY!

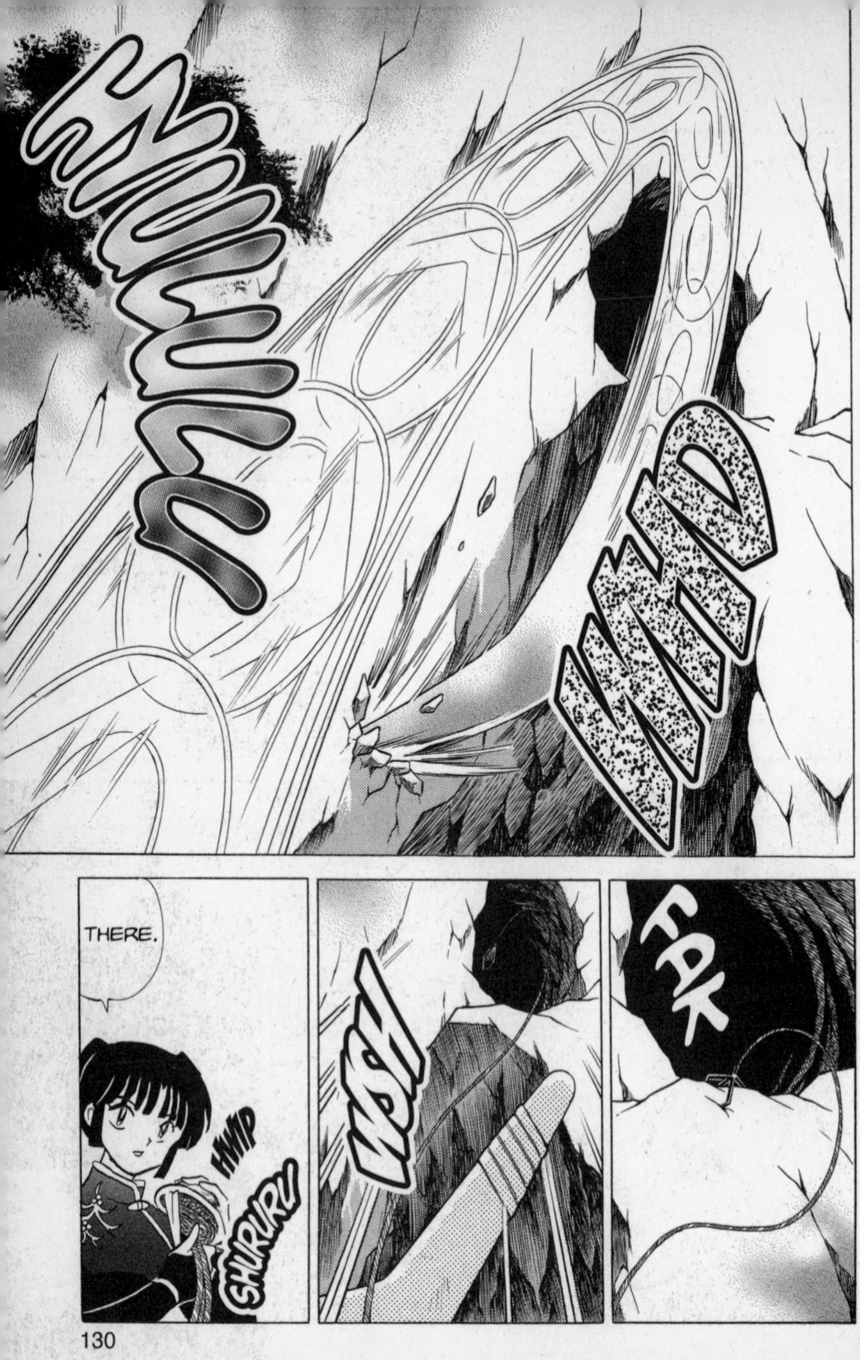
THUD
FAK
WOSH
THERE.
HWIP
SHURURU

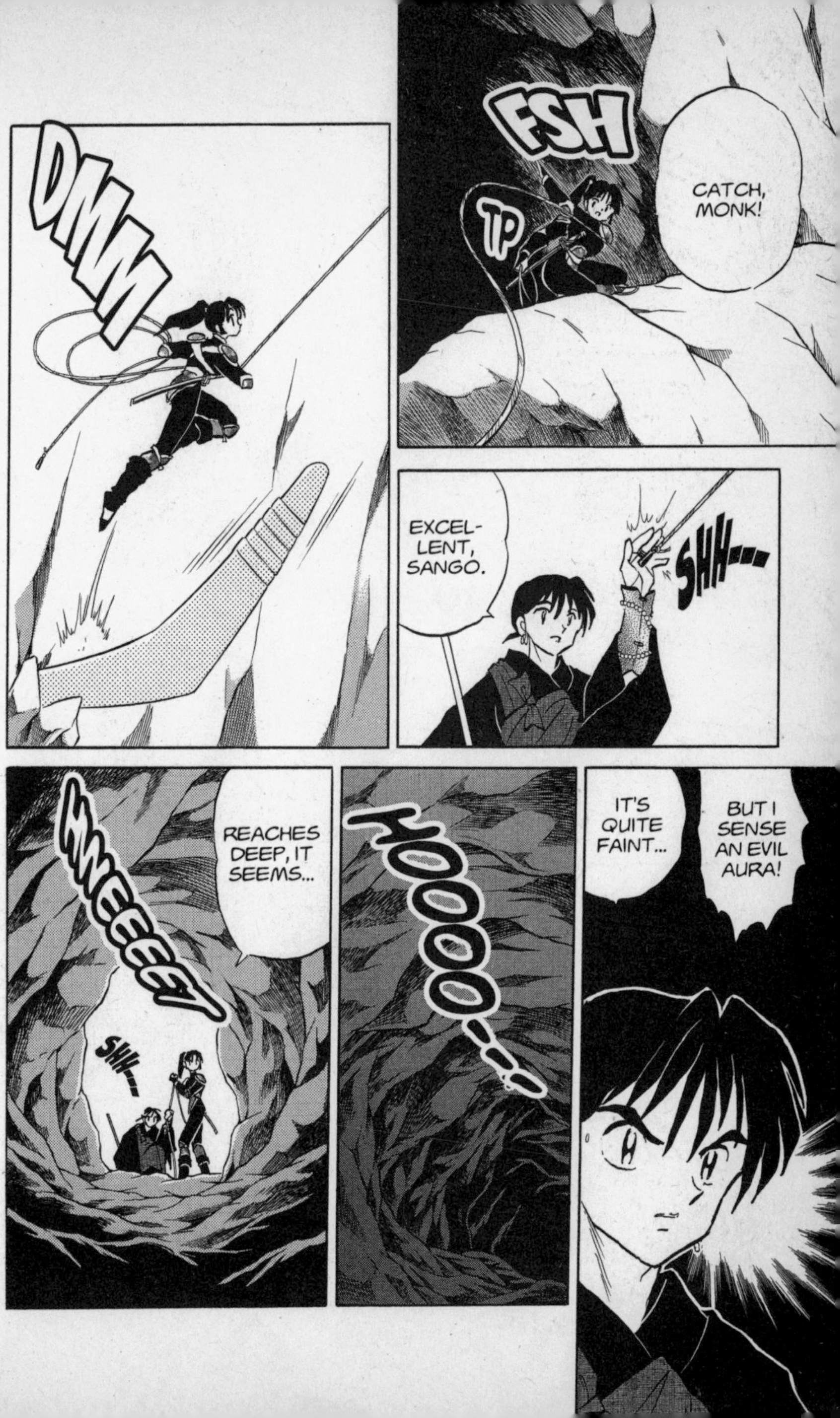
DMM
FSH
TP
CATCH, MONK!
EXCEL-LENT, SANGO.
SHH...
REACHES DEEP, IT SEEMS...
HWEEEEE!
SHH...
HOOOOO...!!
IT'S QUITE FAINT...
BUT I SENSE AN EVIL AURA!

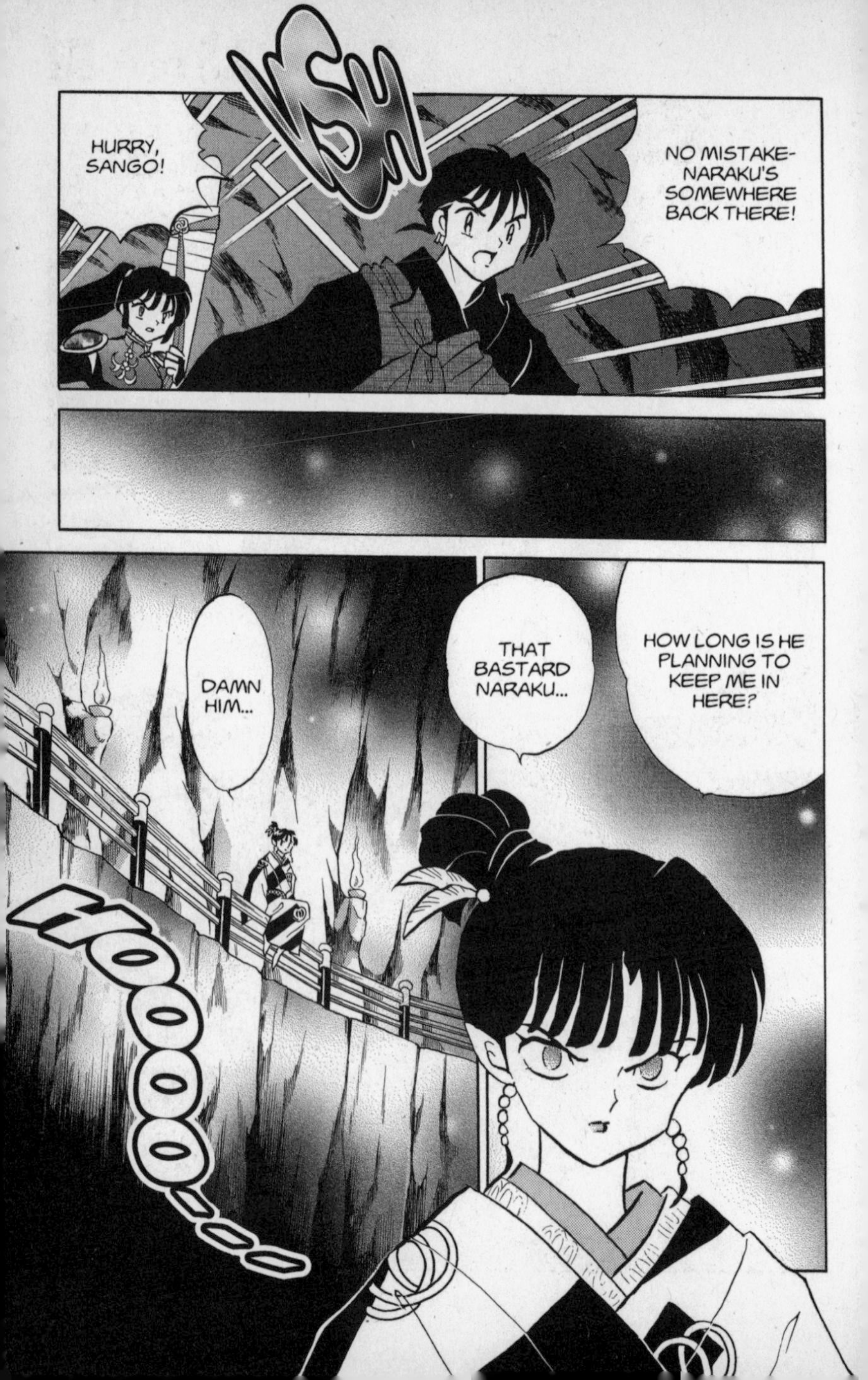
VSH
NO MISTAKE-NARAKU'S SOMEWHERE BACK THERE!
HURRY, SANGO!
HOW LONG IS HE PLANNING TO KEEP ME IN HERE?
THAT BASTARD NARAKU...
DAMN HIM...
HOOOOO---

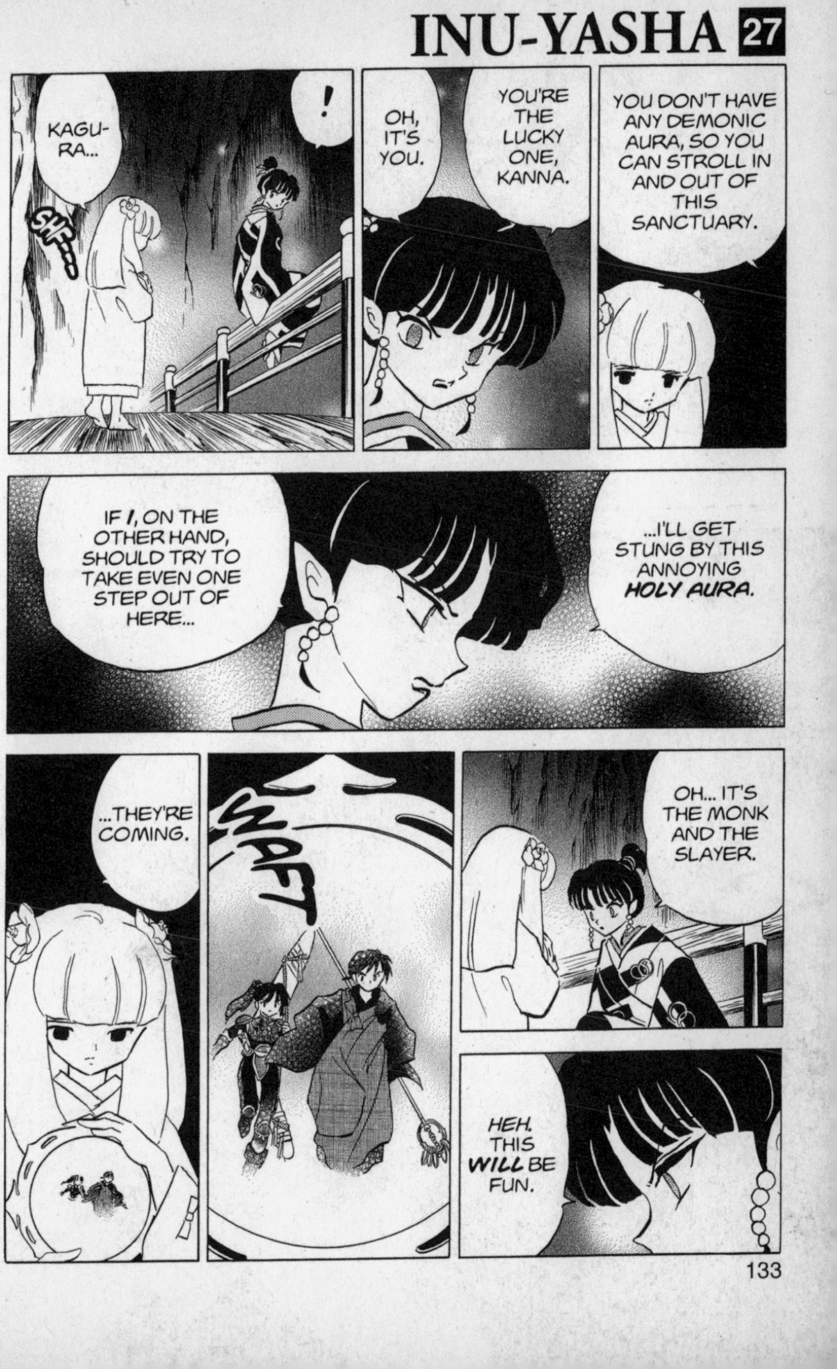
KAGU-RA...
SHF
!
OH, IT'S YOU.
YOU'RE THE LUCKY ONE, KANNA.
YOU DON'T HAVE ANY DEMONIC AURA, SO YOU CAN STROLL IN AND OUT OF THIS SANCTUARY.
IF *I*, ON THE OTHER HAND, SHOULD TRY TO TAKE EVEN ONE STEP OUT OF HERE...
...I'LL GET STUNG BY THIS ANNOYING ***HOLY AURA.***
...THEY'RE COMING.
WAFT
OH... IT'S THE MONK AND THE SLAYER.
HEH. THIS ***WILL*** BE FUN.

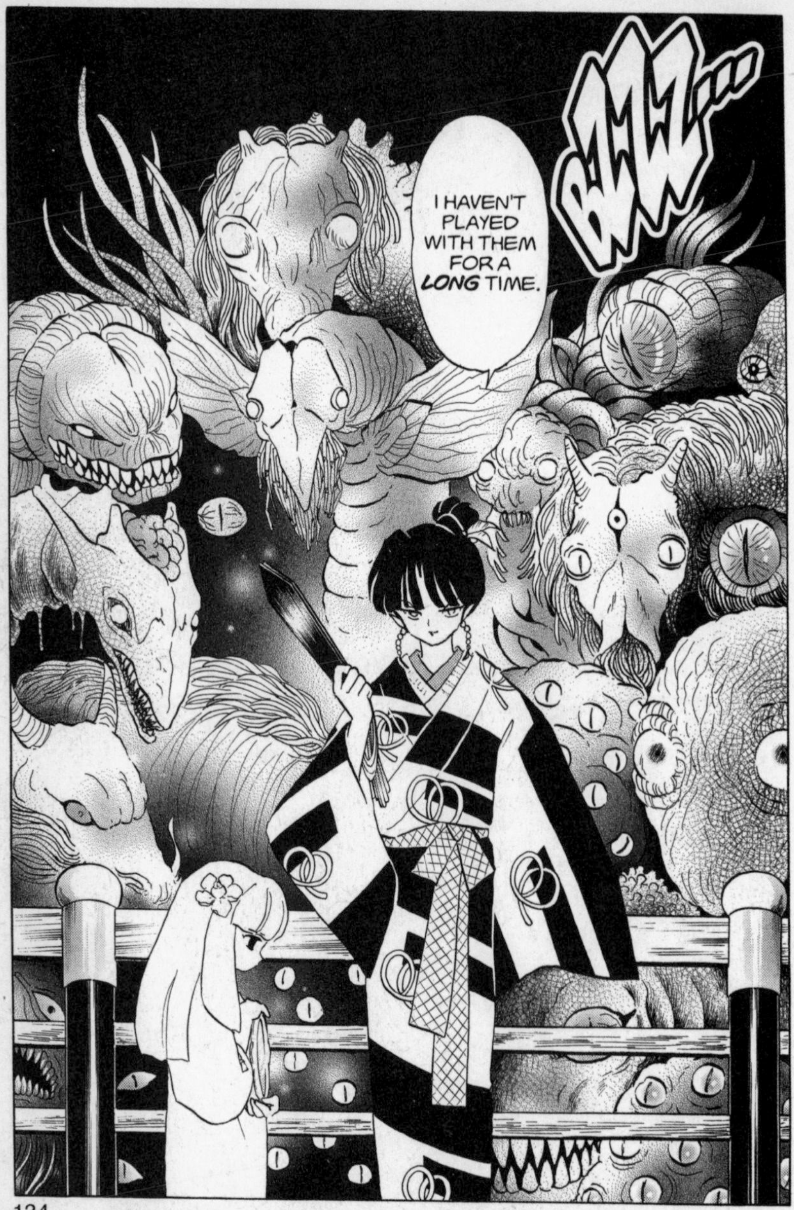
BZZZ...
I HAVEN'T PLAYED WITH THEM FOR A *LONG* TIME.

SCROLL 8
THE CORRIDOR

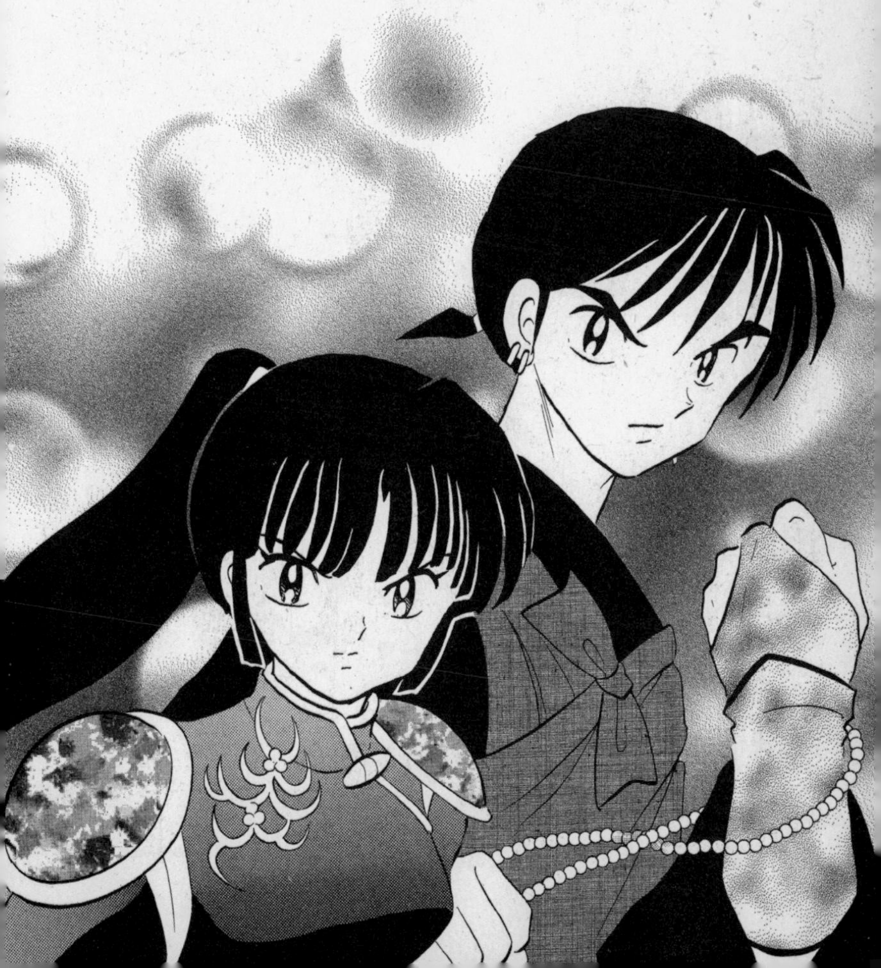

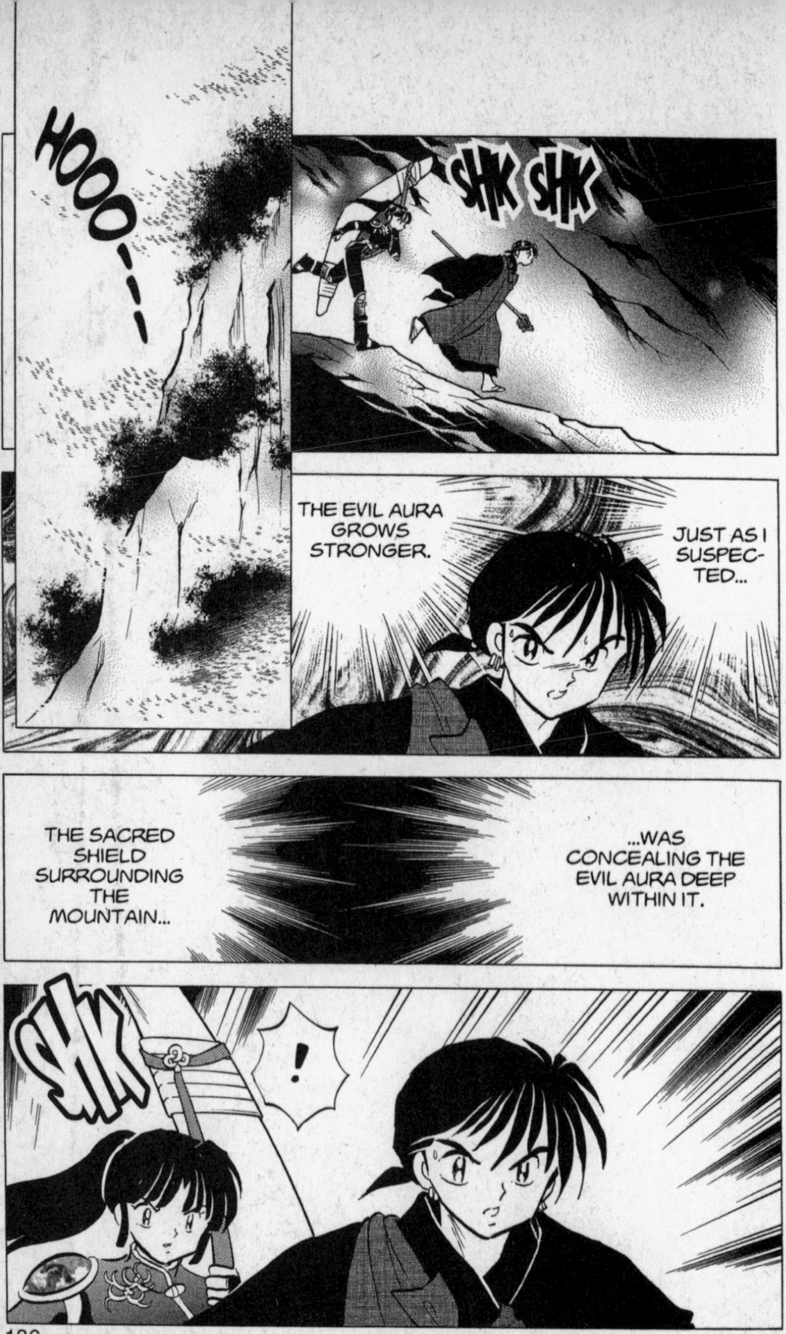
HOOO...
SHK SHK
JUST AS I SUSPECTED...
THE EVIL AURA GROWS STRONGER.
...WAS CONCEALING THE EVIL AURA DEEP WITHIN IT.
THE SACRED SHIELD SURROUNDING THE MOUNTAIN...
!
SHK

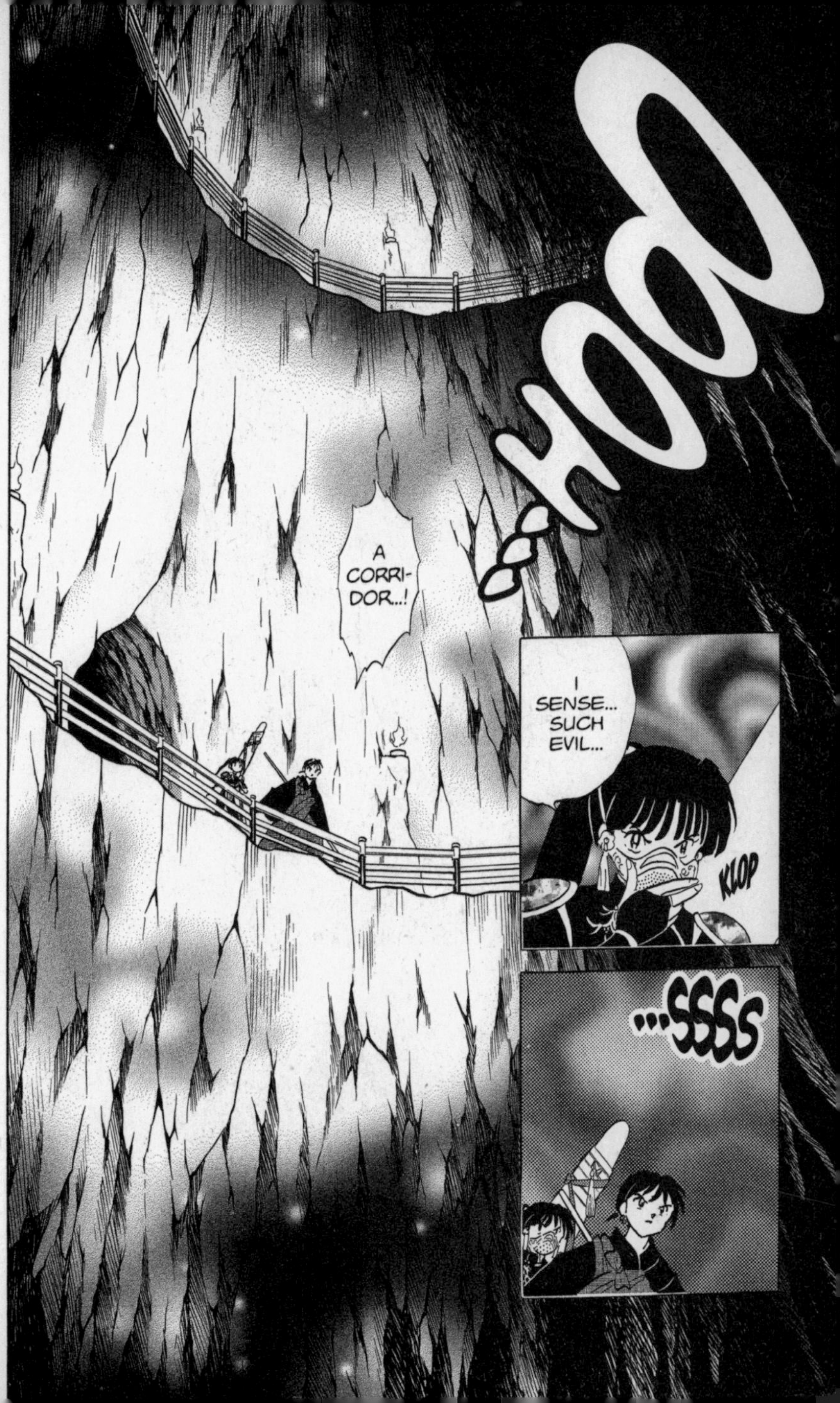
DOOH
I SENSE... SUCH EVIL...
KLOP
...SSSS
A CORRI-DOR...!

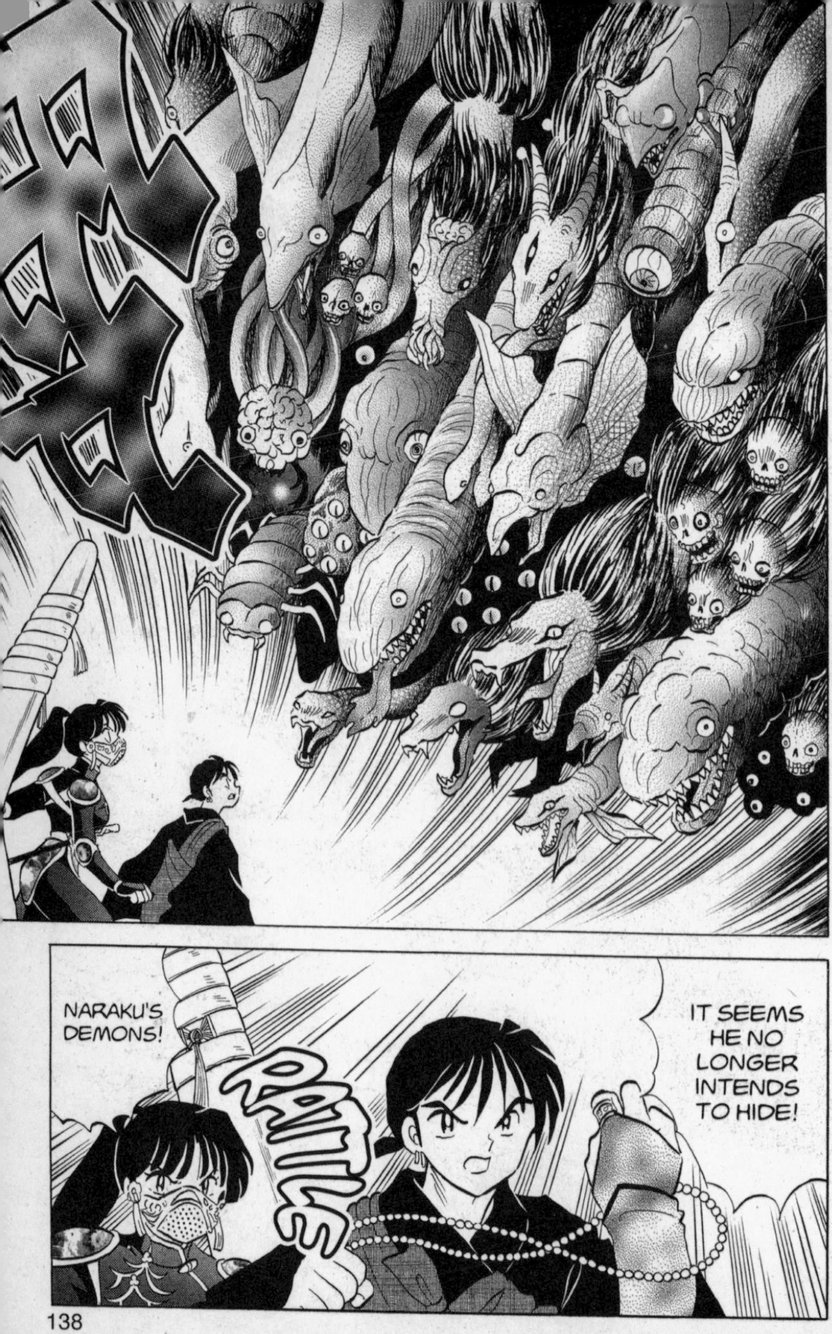
IT SEEMS HE NO LONGER INTENDS TO HIDE!
RATTLE
NARAKU'S DEMONS!

SAIMYO-SHO?!

DON'T USE THE WIND TUNNEL, MONK!

IF YOU SUCK THEM IN, THEIR VENOM WILL KILL YOU!

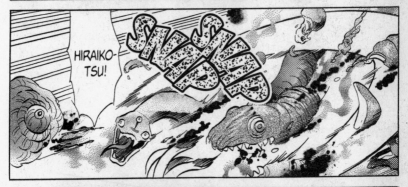

HIRAIKO-TSU!

BEGONE!

WSSH

BZZT

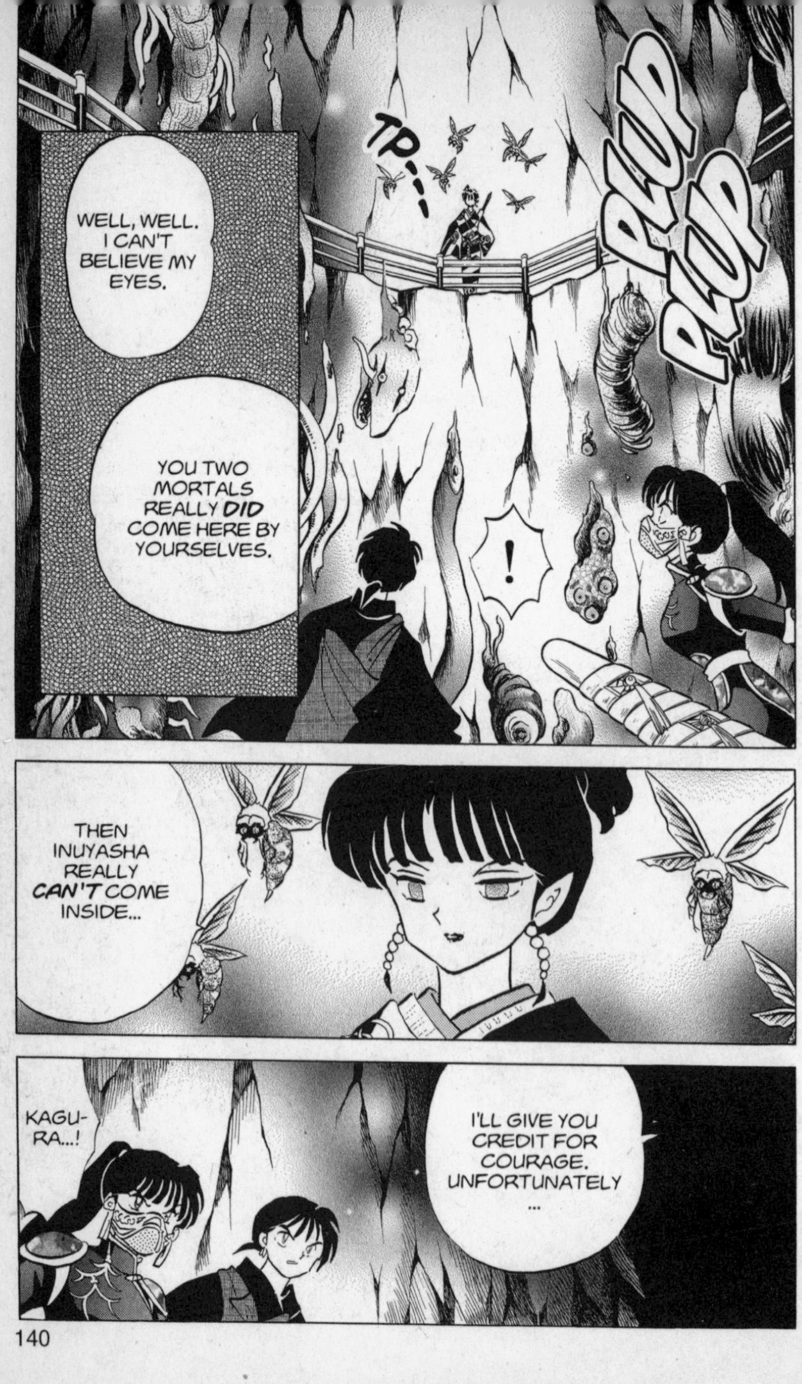
PLUP
PLUP
TP...
!
WELL, WELL. I CAN'T BELIEVE MY EYES.
YOU TWO MORTALS REALLY DID COME HERE BY YOURSELVES.
THEN INUYASHA REALLY CAN'T COME INSIDE...
I'LL GIVE YOU CREDIT FOR COURAGE. UNFORTUNATELY ...
KAGU-RA...!

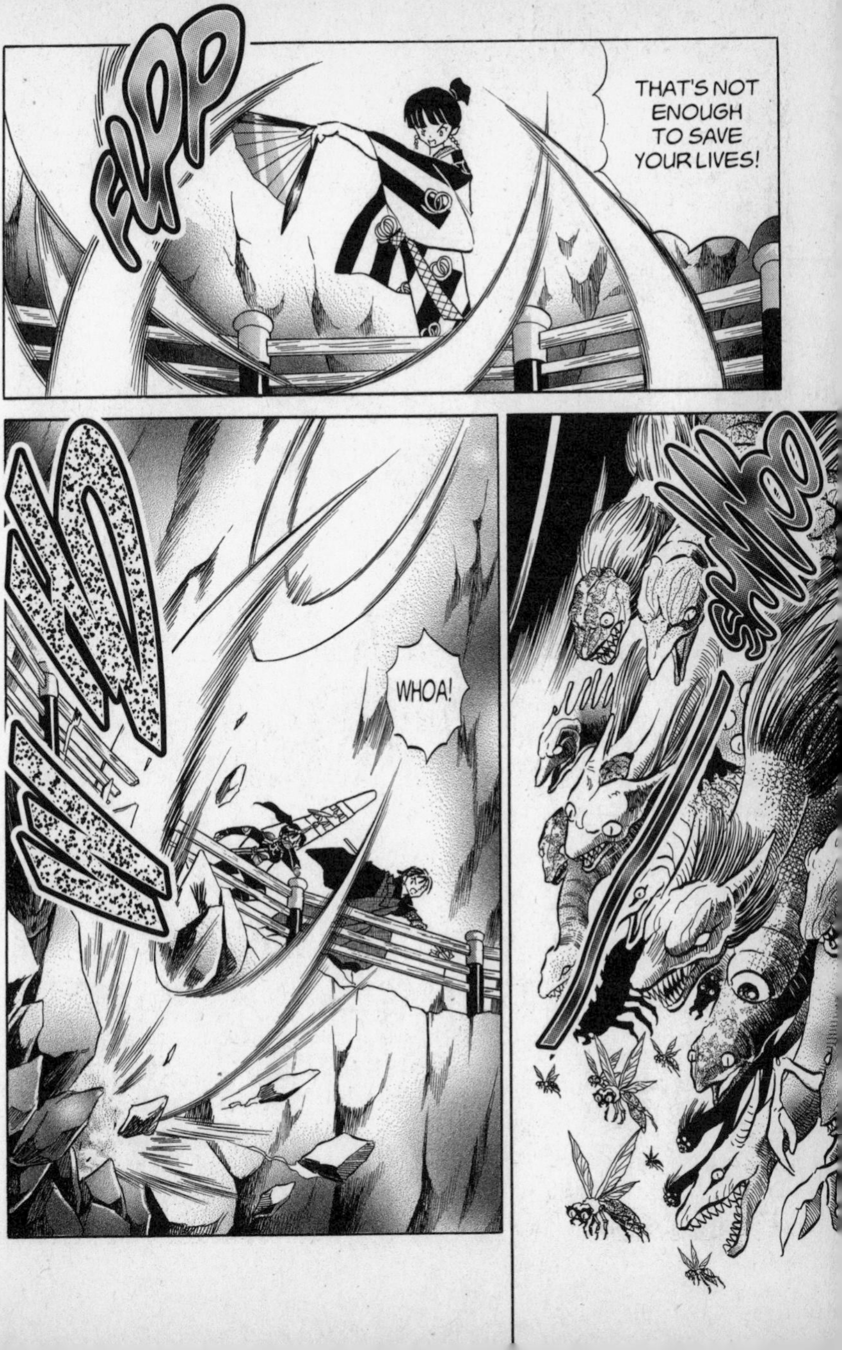
FLIPP
THAT'S NOT ENOUGH TO SAVE YOUR LIVES!
SWOO
WHOA!

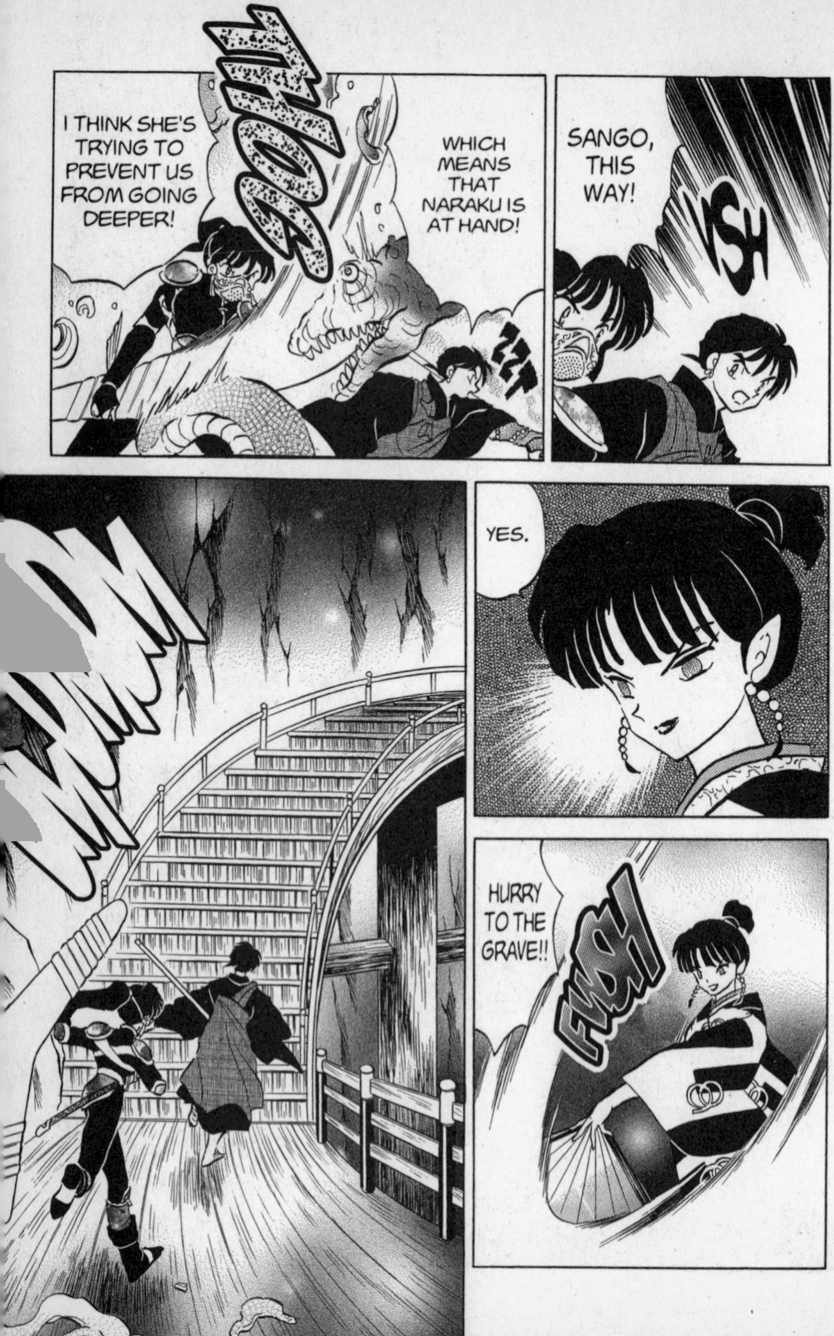
SANGO, THIS WAY!
VSH
WHICH MEANS THAT NARAKU IS AT HAND!
I THINK SHE'S TRYING TO PREVENT US FROM GOING DEEPER!
THOOG
ZZT
YES.
HURRY TO THE GRAVE!!
FWOSH

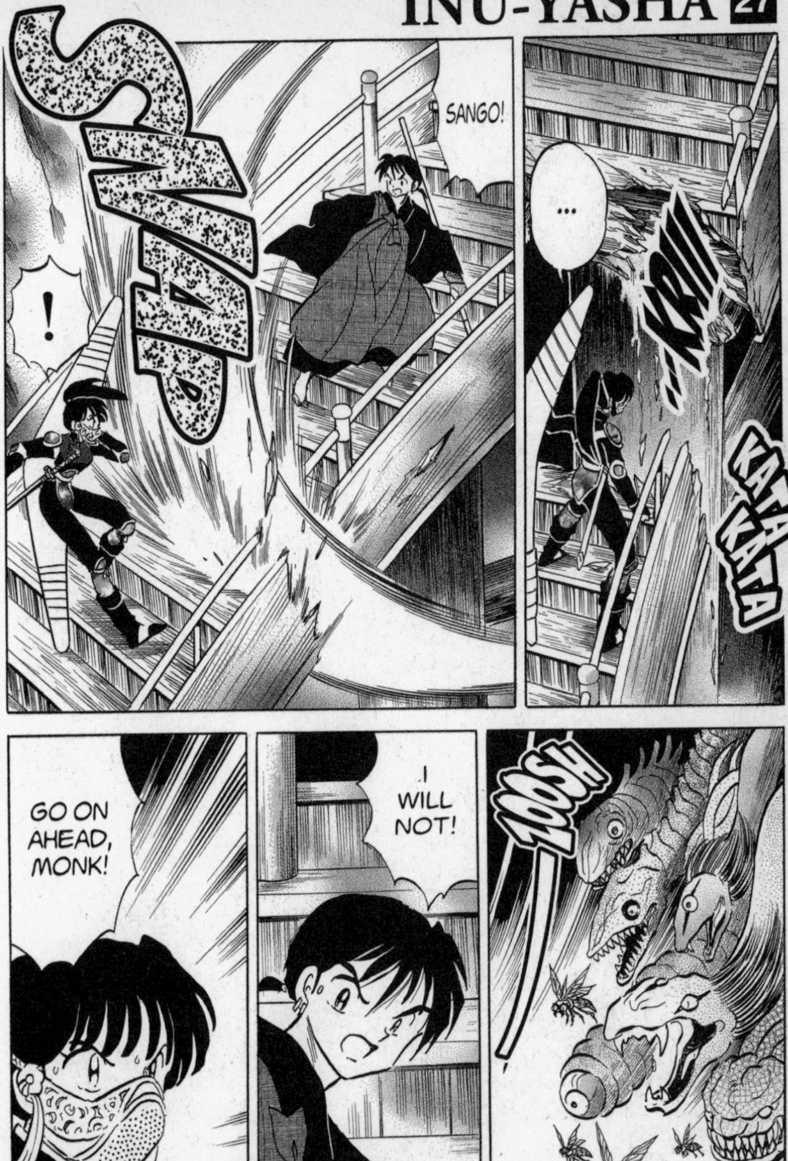
...
...KRIII
KATA KATA
SANGO!
SNAP
!
WOOSH
I WILL NOT!
GO ON AHEAD, MONK!

THE ONLY THING WE CAN CARE ABOUT IS FINDING NARAKU!

HSSH

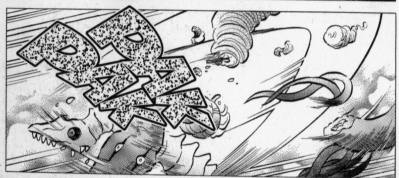

PAKK

HWRRR

...

YOU DON'T HONESTLY EXPECT TO DEFEAT ME?

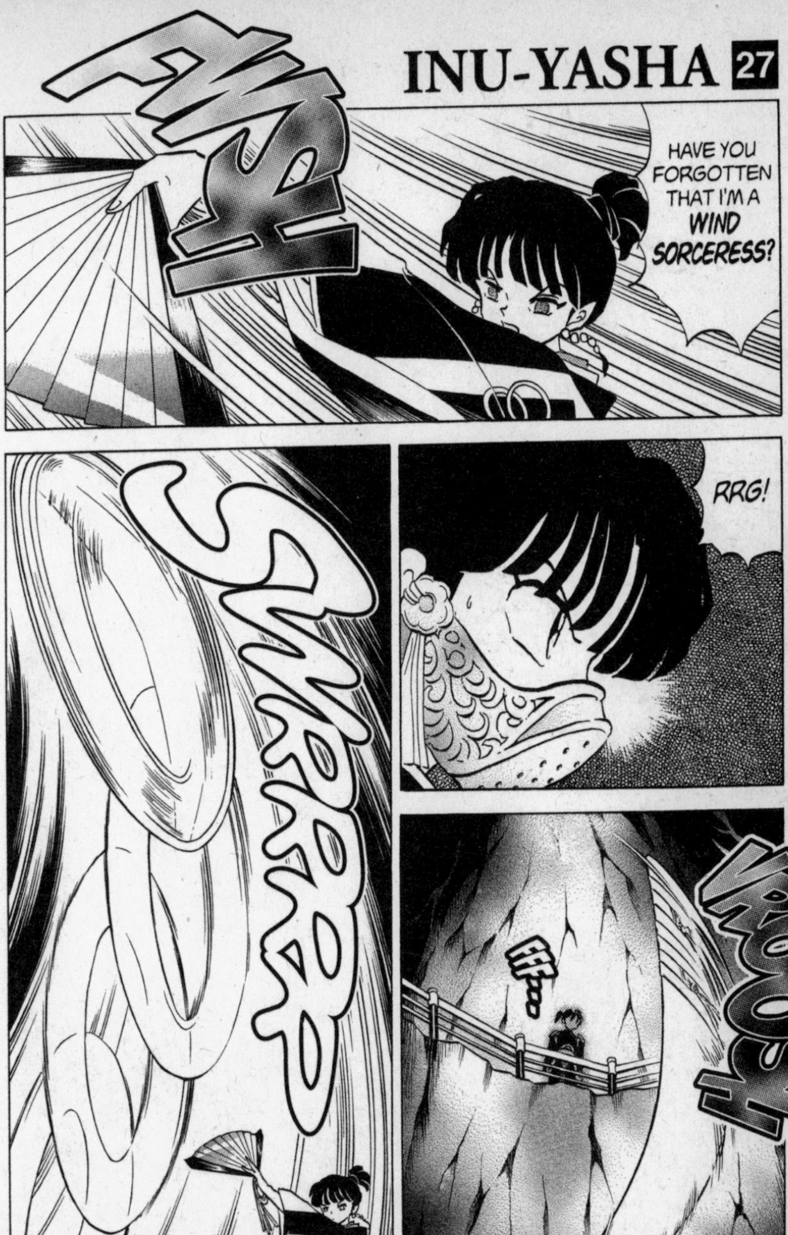
HAVE YOU FORGOTTEN THAT I'M A WIND SORCERESS?
RRG!

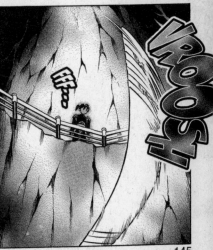

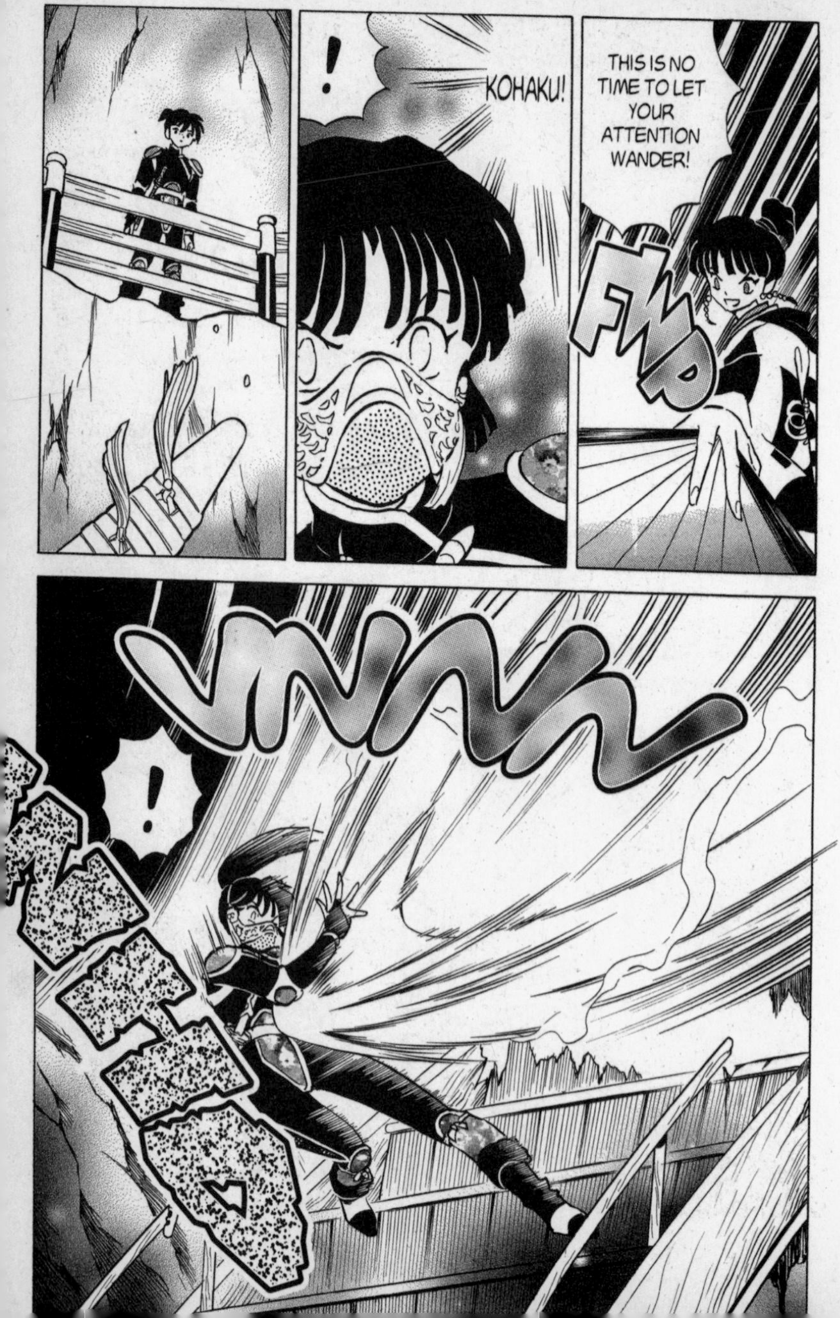
THIS IS NO TIME TO LET YOUR ATTENTION WANDER!
FWP
!
KOHAKU!
!

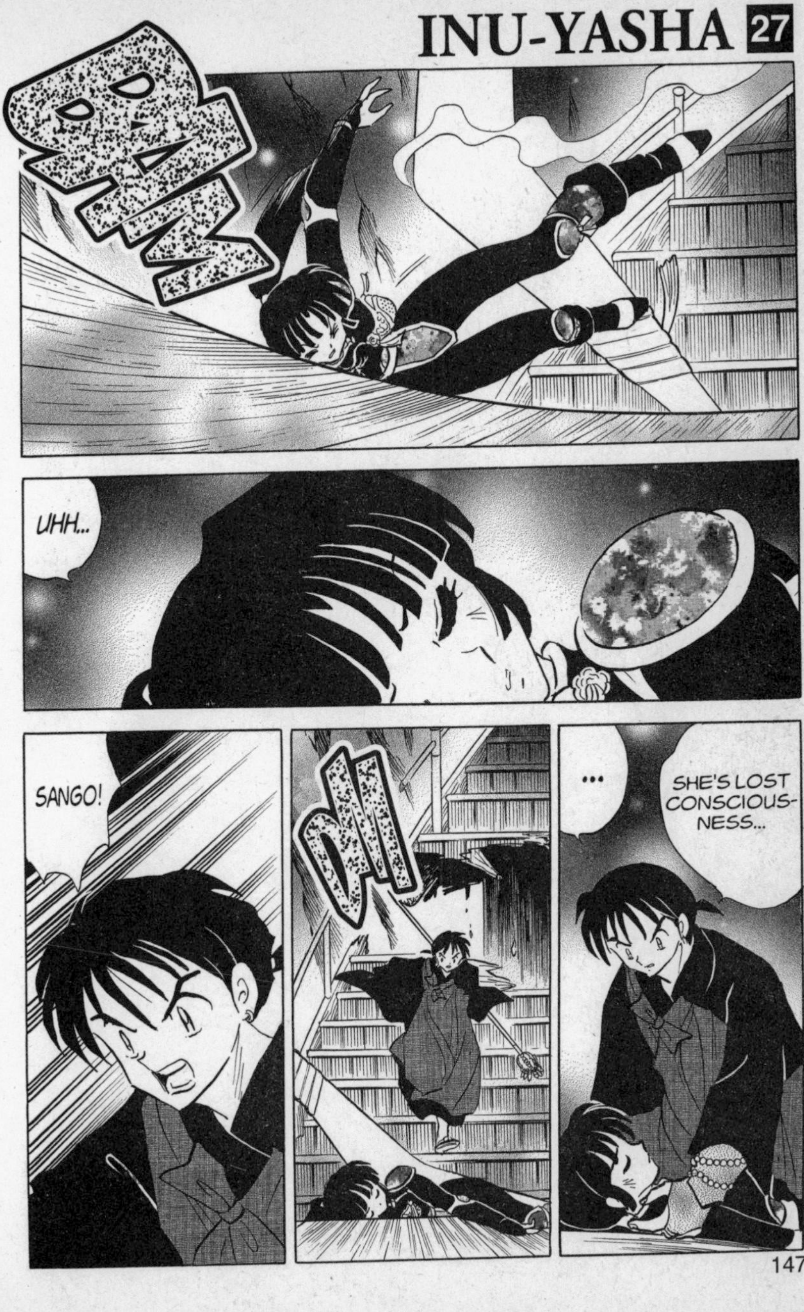
DAMN
UHH...
...
SHE'S LOST CONSCIOUS-NESS...
DM
SANGO!

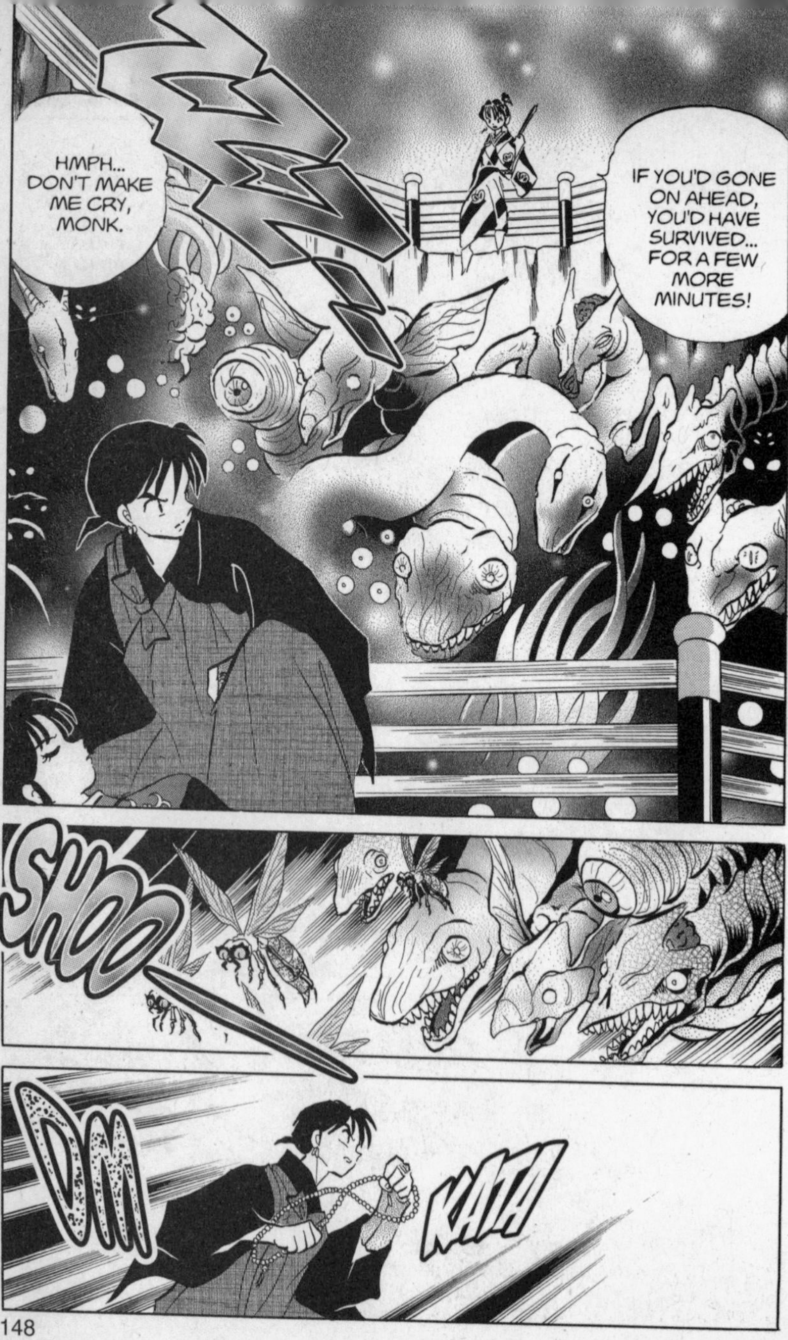
IF YOU'D GONE ON AHEAD, YOU'D HAVE SURVIVED... FOR A FEW MORE MINUTES!
HMPH... DON'T MAKE ME CRY, MONK.
SHOO
KATA
DM

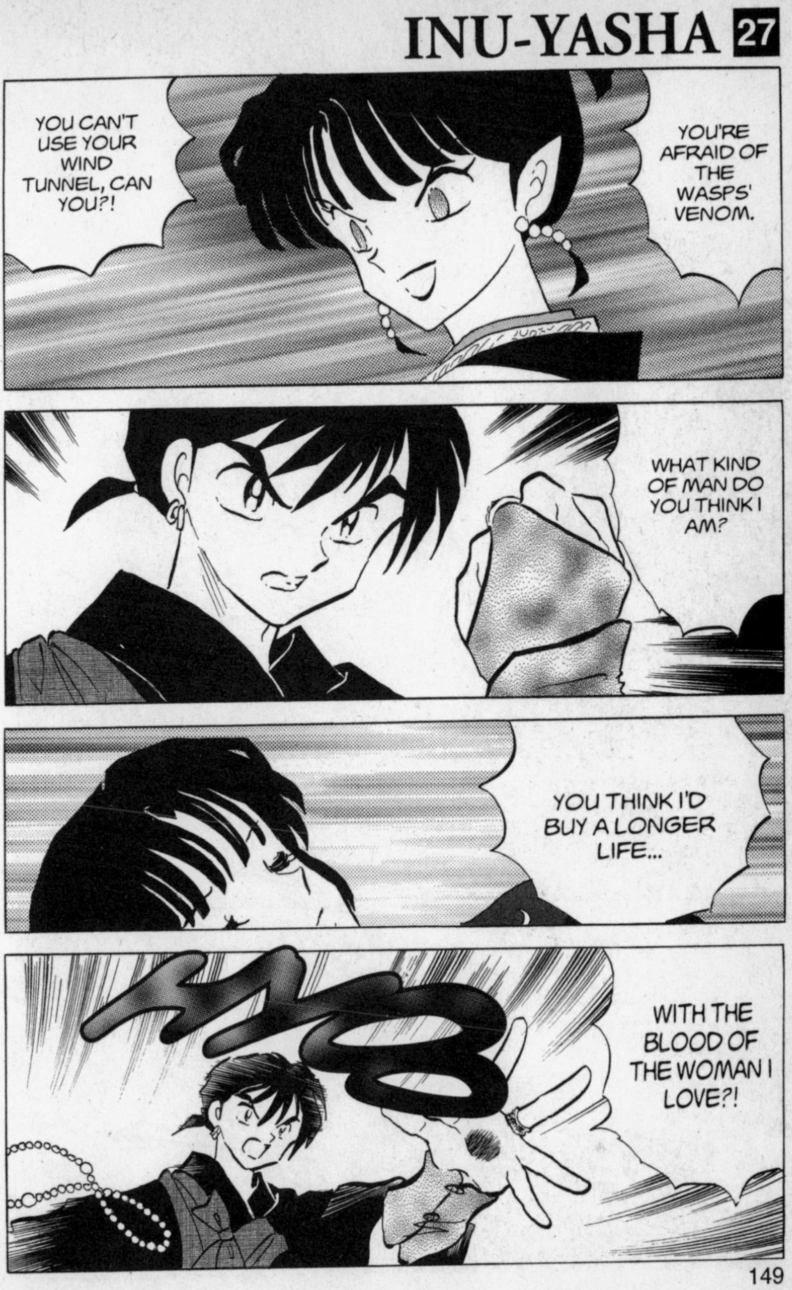
YOU CAN'T USE YOUR WIND TUNNEL, CAN YOU?!
YOU'RE AFRAID OF THE WASPS' VENOM.
WHAT KIND OF MAN DO YOU THINK I AM?
YOU THINK I'D BUY A LONGER LIFE...
WITH THE BLOOD OF THE WOMAN I LOVE?!

WIND
TUNNEL!

VOOOO...!

BCH BCH BCH

WHAT?!

HE
REALLY
DID IT...?!

BZZ BZZ

BCH BCH

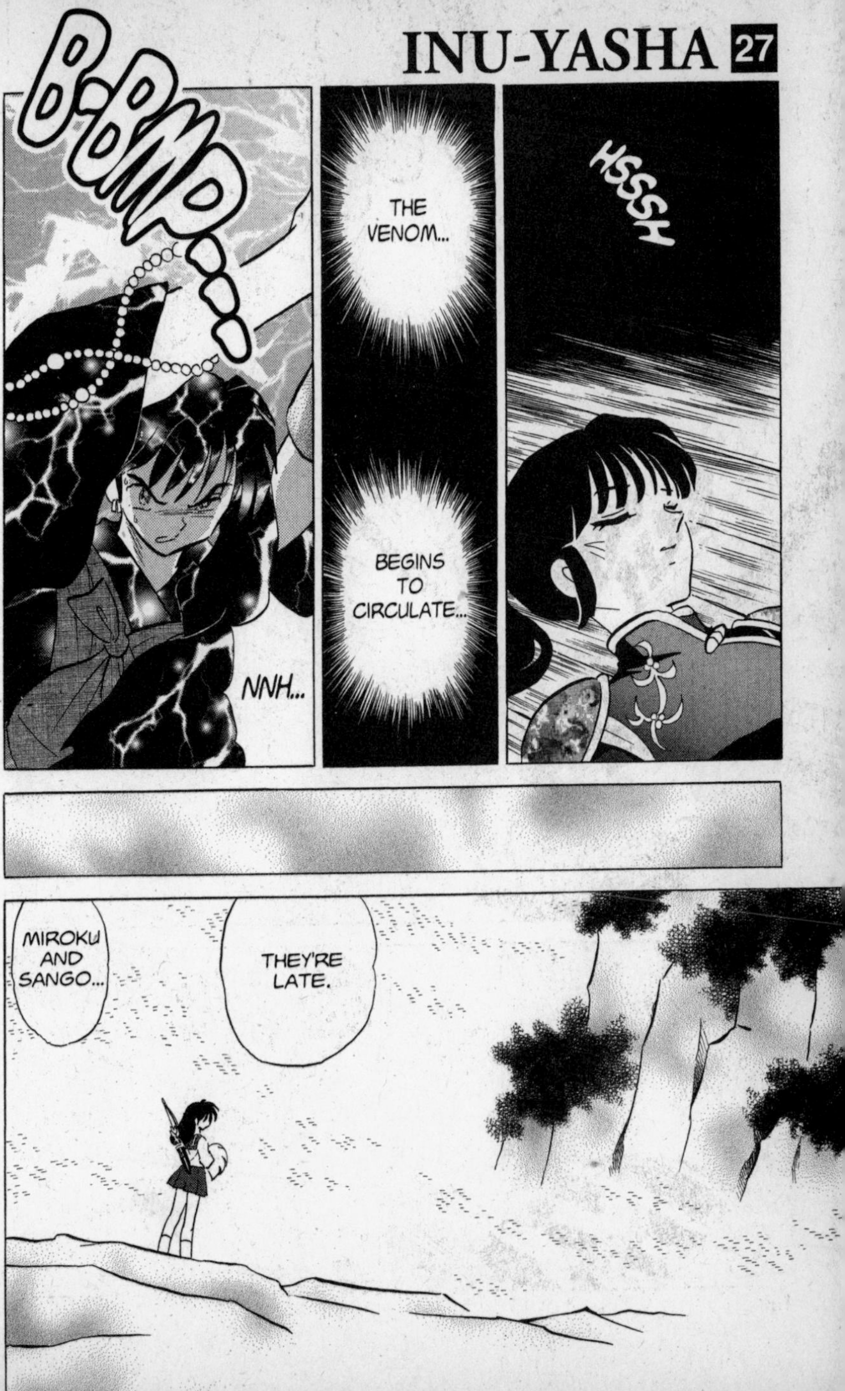
B-BOMP...
NNH...
THE VENOM...
BEGINS TO CIRCULATE...
HSSSH
MIROKU AND SANGO...
THEY'RE LATE.

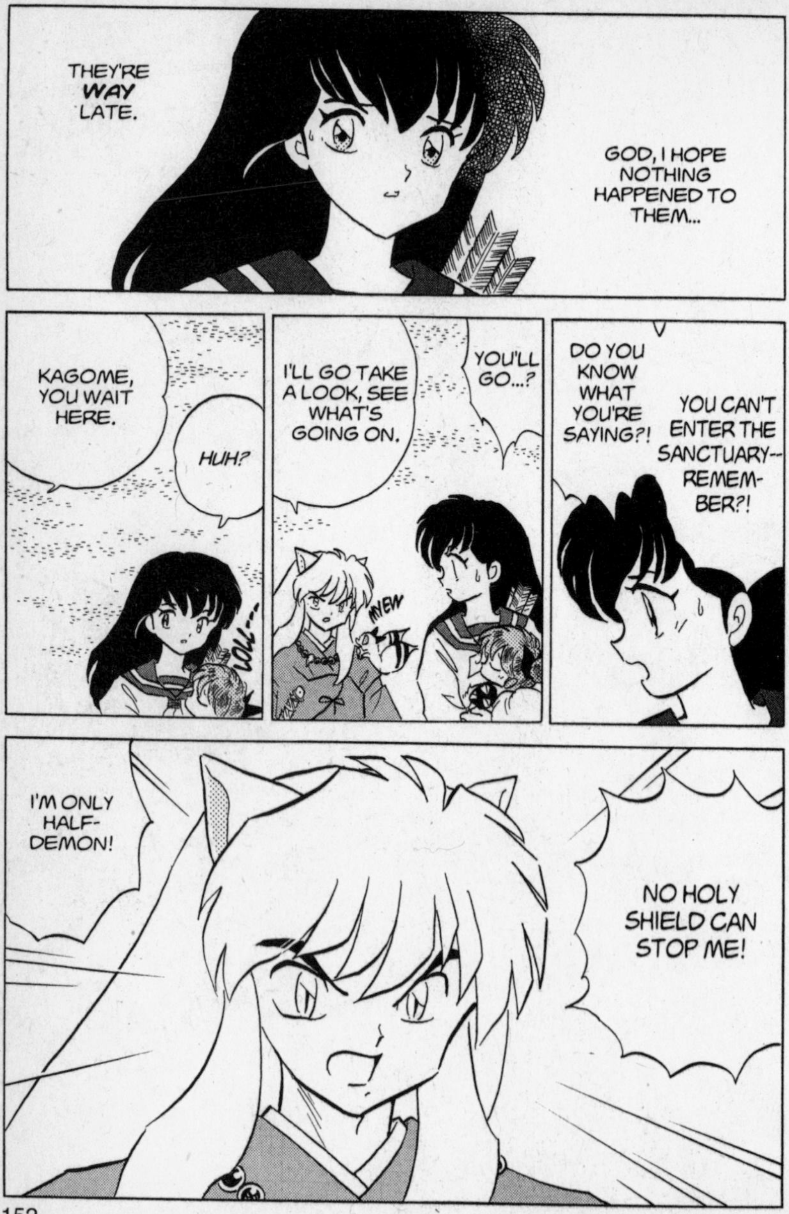

THEY'RE WAY LATE.
GOD, I HOPE NOTHING HAPPENED TO THEM...
KAGOME, YOU WAIT HERE.
HUH?
I'LL GO TAKE A LOOK, SEE WHAT'S GOING ON.
YOU'LL GO...?
DO YOU KNOW WHAT YOU'RE SAYING?!
YOU CAN'T ENTER THE SANCTUARY-- REMEMBER?!
I'M ONLY HALF-DEMON!
NO HOLY SHIELD CAN STOP ME!

SCROLL 9
THE LIMIT

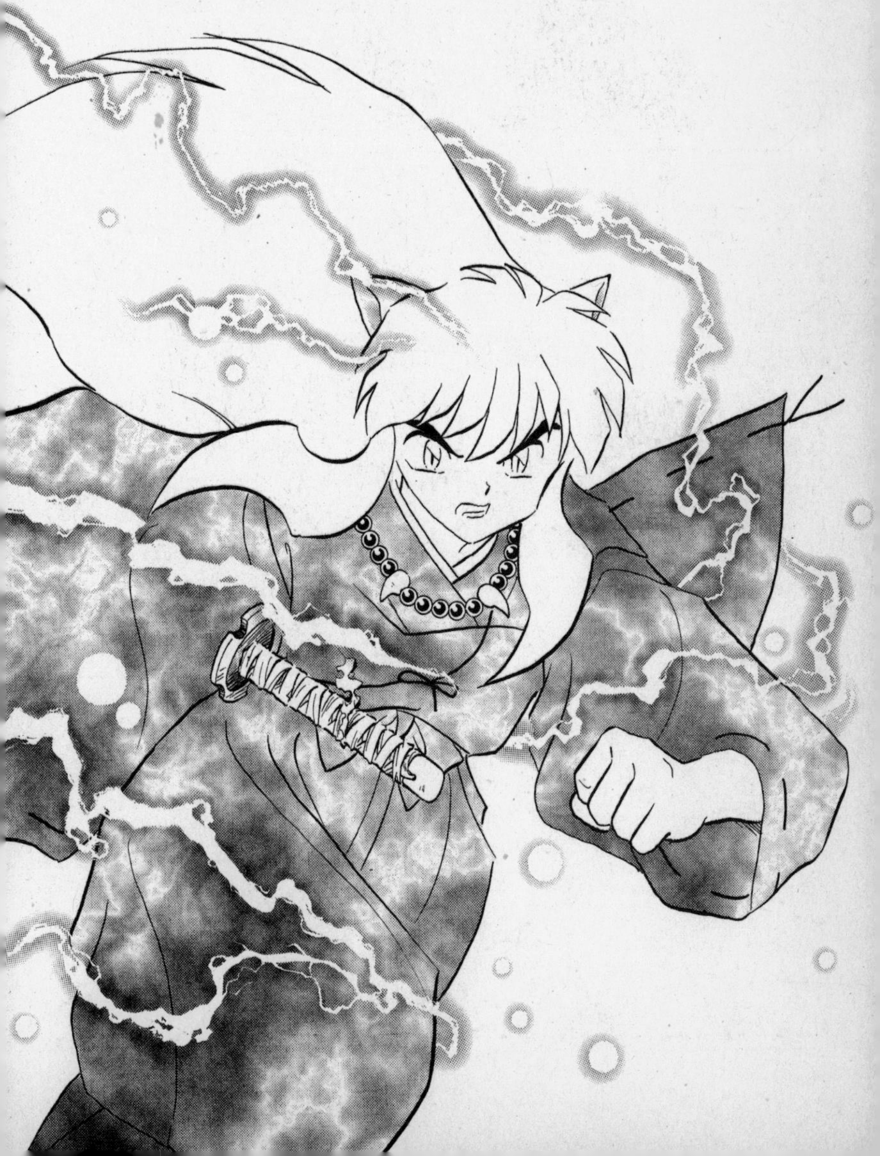

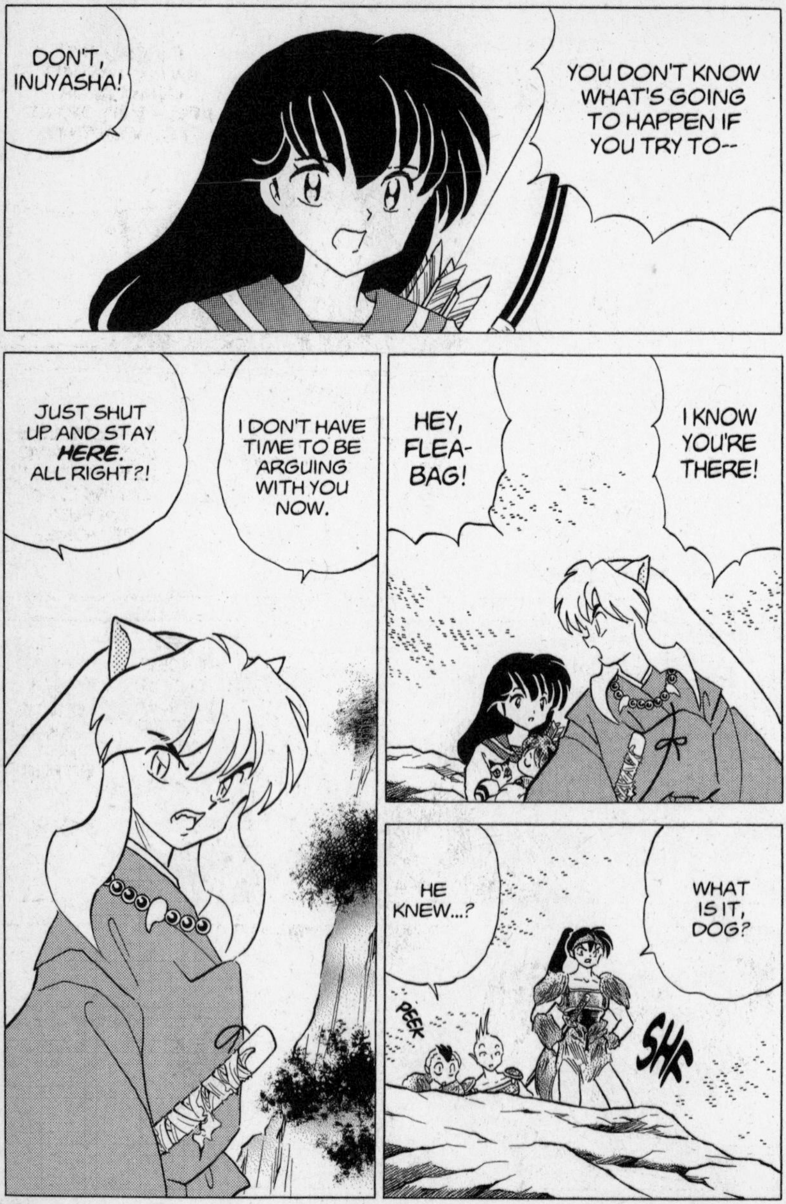
YOU DON'T KNOW WHAT'S GOING TO HAPPEN IF YOU TRY TO--
DON'T, INUYASHA!
I KNOW YOU'RE THERE!
HEY, FLEA-BAG!
WHAT IS IT, DOG?
SHF
HE KNEW...?
PEEK
I DON'T HAVE TIME TO BE ARGUING WITH YOU NOW.
JUST SHUT UP AND STAY HERE. ALL RIGHT?!

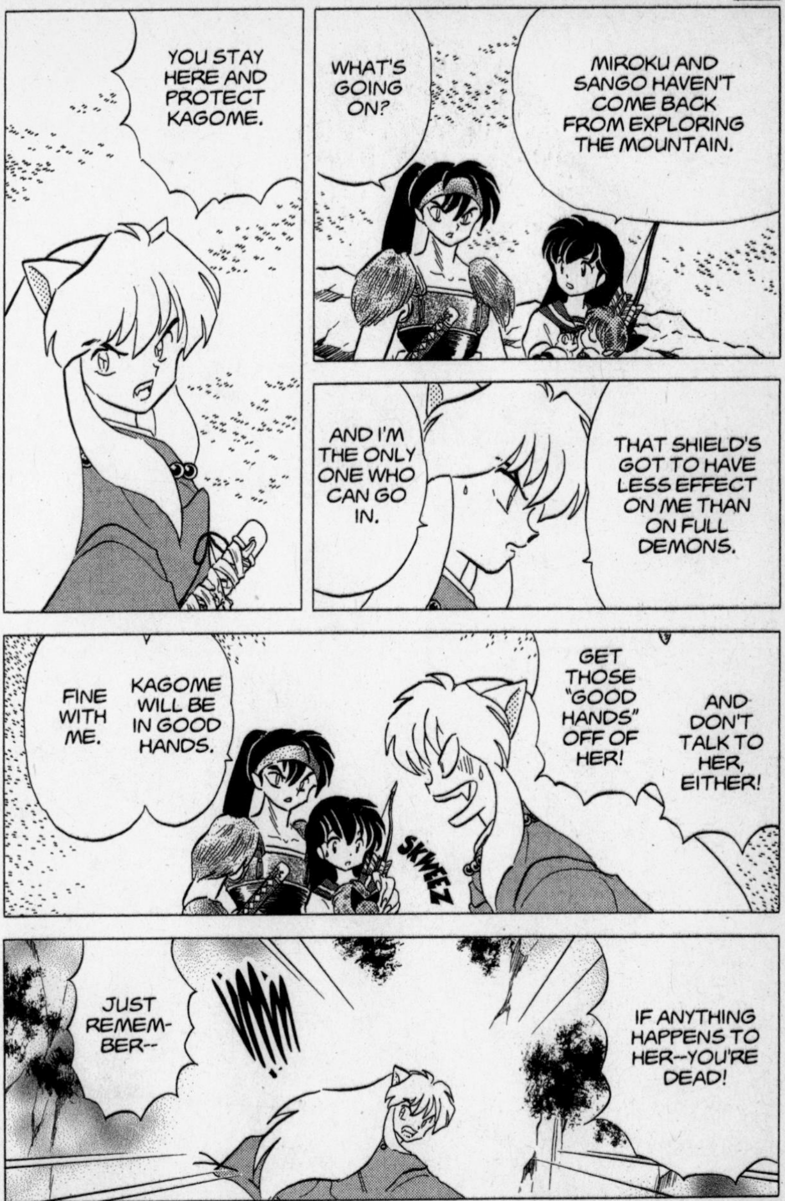
MIROKU AND SANGO HAVEN'T COME BACK FROM EXPLORING THE MOUNTAIN.
WHAT'S GOING ON?
YOU STAY HERE AND PROTECT KAGOME.
THAT SHIELD'S GOT TO HAVE LESS EFFECT ON ME THAN ON FULL DEMONS.
AND I'M THE ONLY ONE WHO CAN GO IN.
KAGOME WILL BE IN GOOD HANDS.
FINE WITH ME.
AND DON'T TALK TO HER, EITHER!
GET THOSE "GOOD HANDS" OFF OF HER!
SKWEEZ
IF ANYTHING HAPPENS TO HER--YOU'RE DEAD!
JUST REMEM-BER--

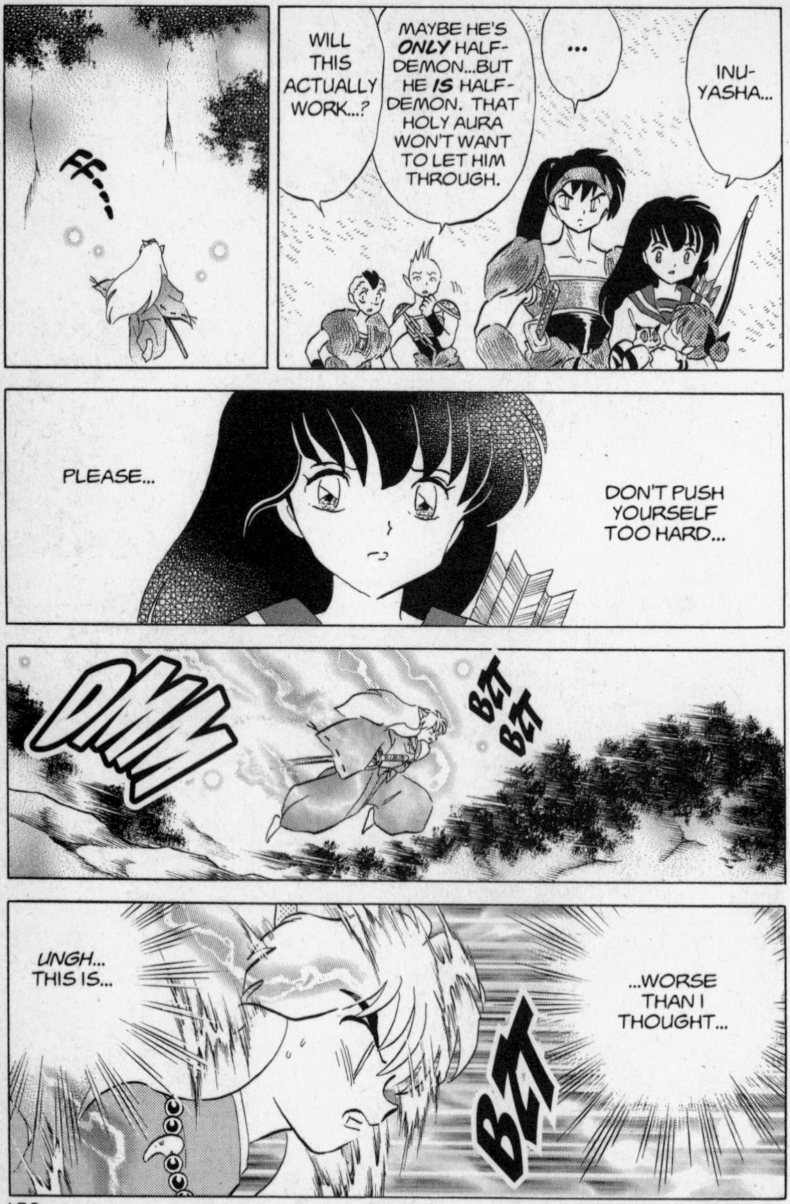
FF...
WILL THIS ACTUALLY WORK...?
MAYBE HE'S ONLY HALF-DEMON...BUT HE IS HALF-DEMON. THAT HOLY AURA WON'T WANT TO LET HIM THROUGH.
...
INU-YASHA...
PLEASE...
DON'T PUSH YOURSELF TOO HARD...
DMN
BZT BZT
UNGH... THIS IS...
...WORSE THAN I THOUGHT...
BZT

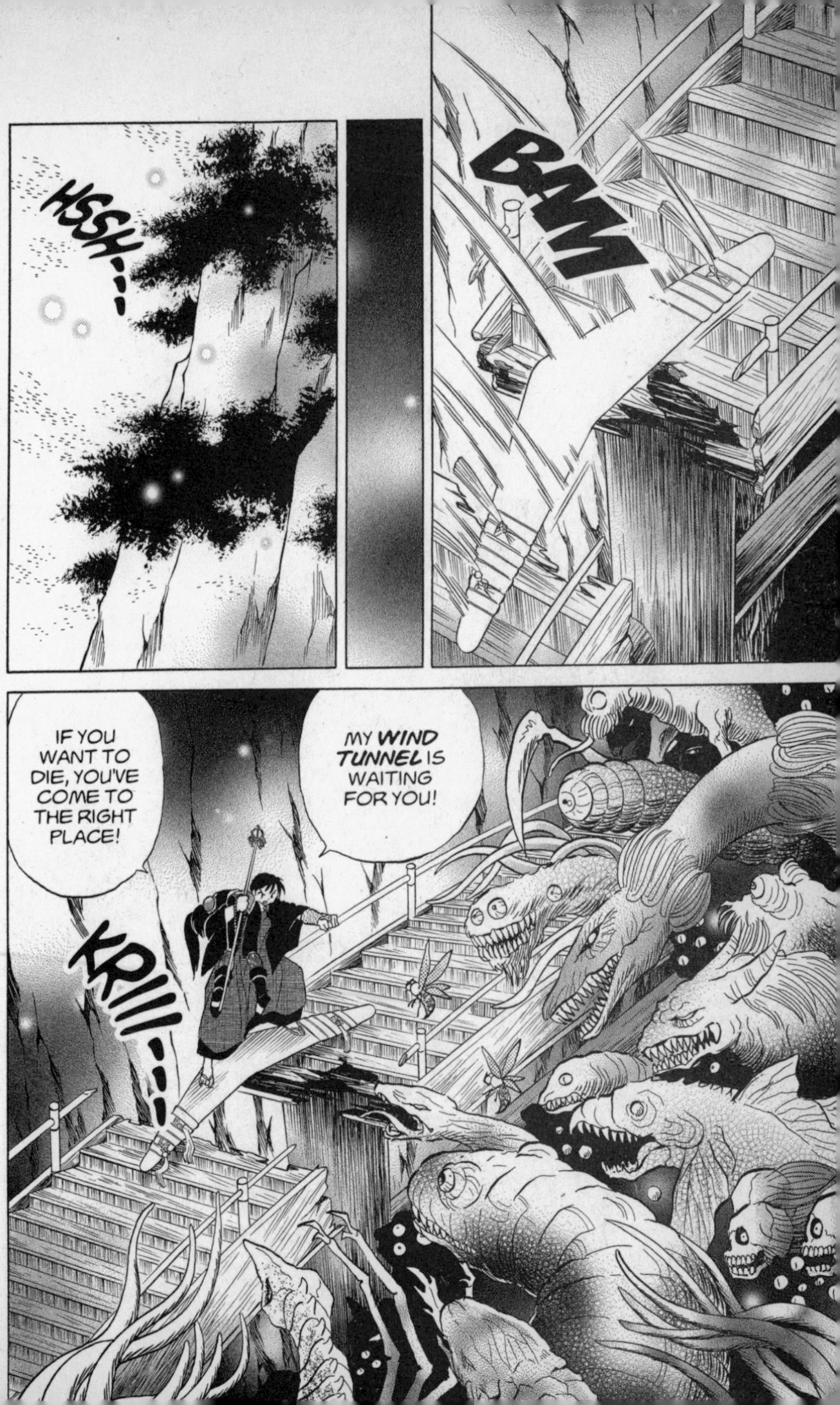
BAM
HSSH...
MY WIND TUNNEL IS WAITING FOR YOU!
IF YOU WANT TO DIE, YOU'VE COME TO THE RIGHT PLACE!
KRIII...

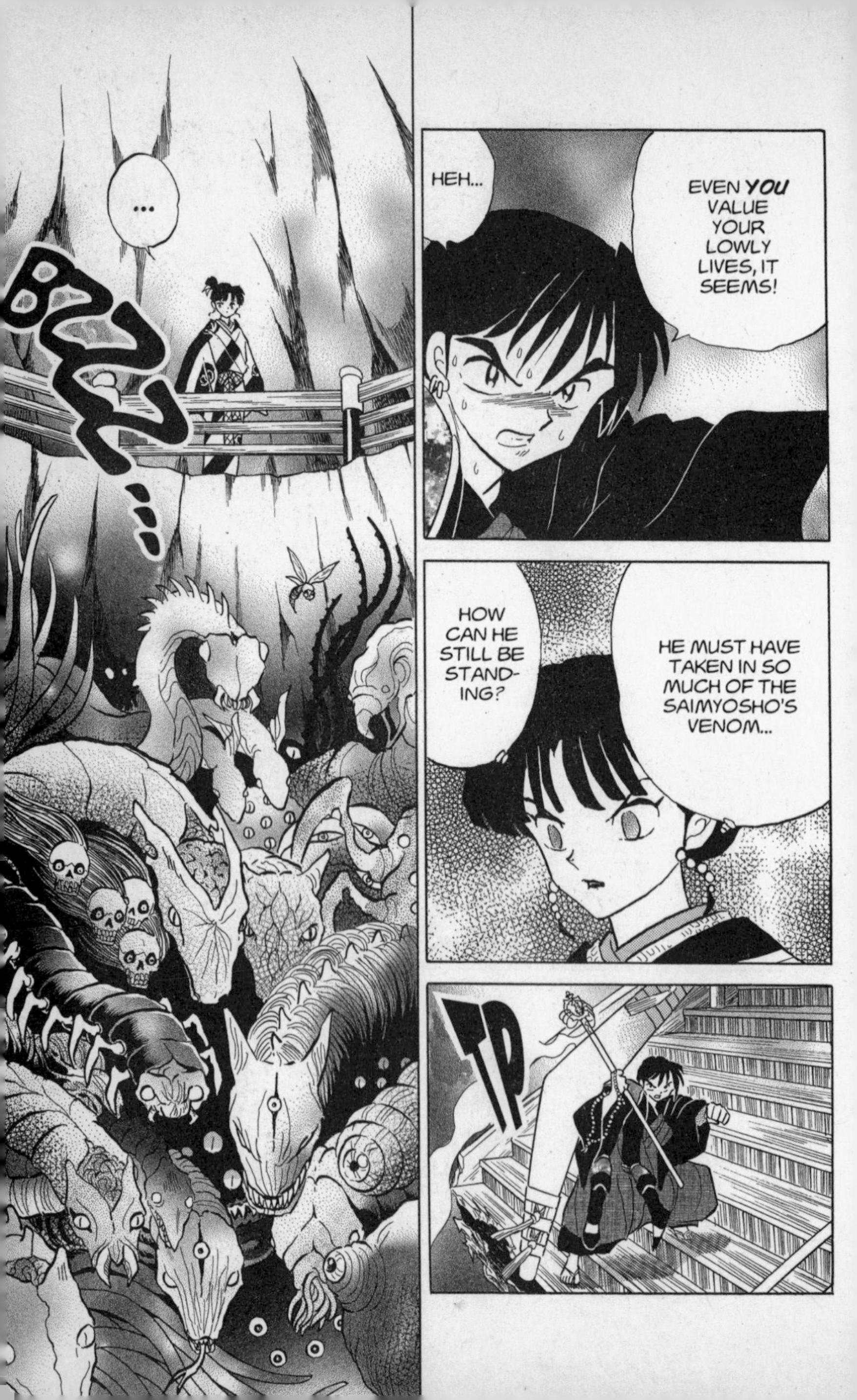
HEH...
EVEN YOU VALUE YOUR LOWLY LIVES, IT SEEMS!
HE MUST HAVE TAKEN IN SO MUCH OF THE SAIMYOSHO'S VENOM...
HOW CAN HE STILL BE STAND-ING?
TP
...
BZZ...

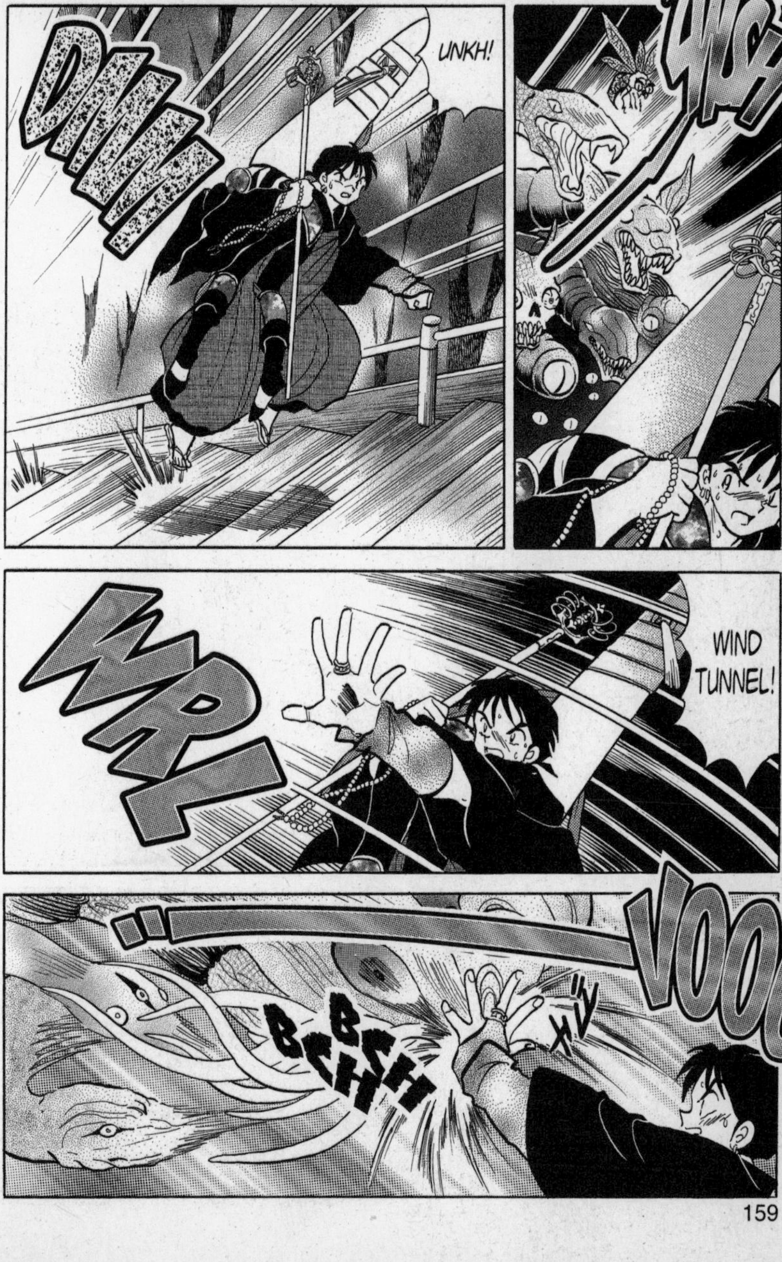
ZWUSH
UNKH!
WIND TUNNEL!
WRL
VOOOO

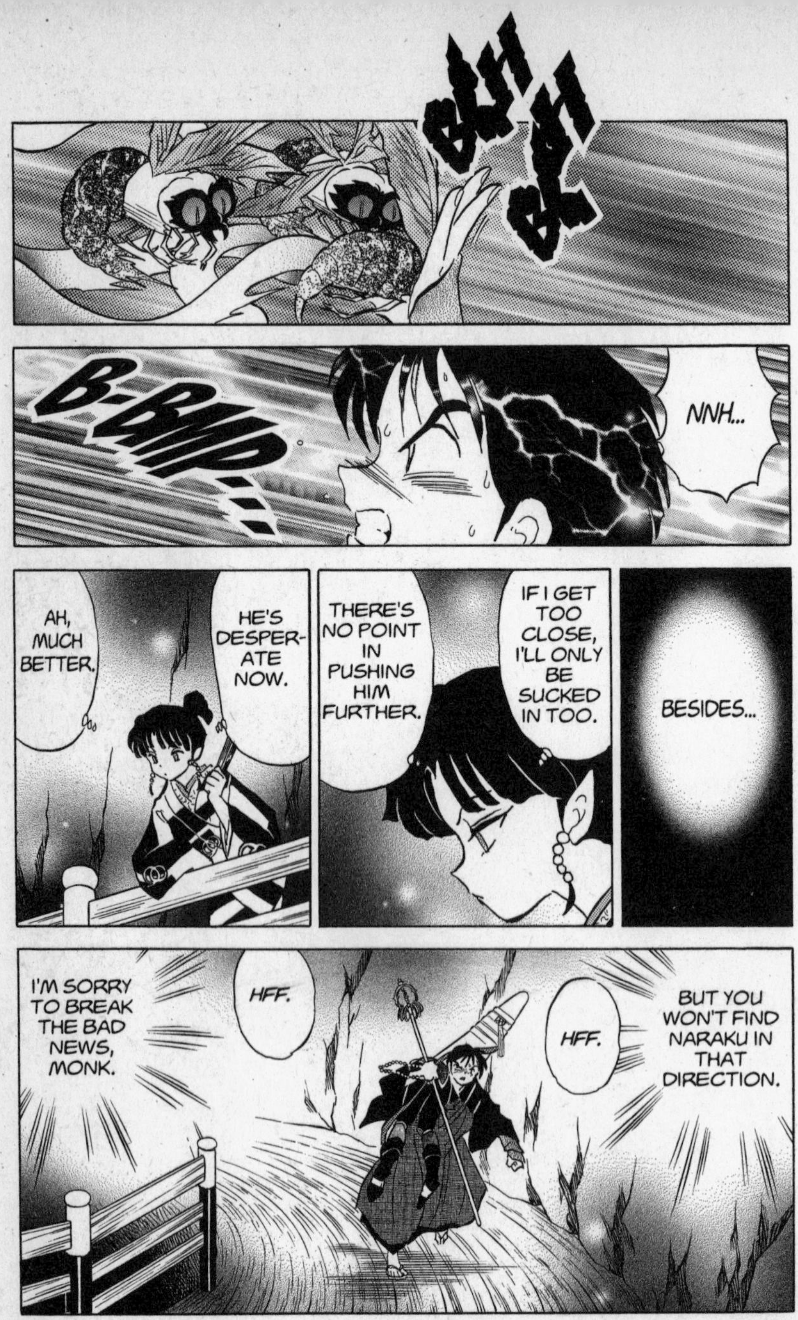
NNH...
B-BMP...
BESIDES...
IF I GET TOO CLOSE, I'LL ONLY BE SUCKED IN TOO.
THERE'S NO POINT IN PUSHING HIM FURTHER.
HE'S DESPER-ATE NOW.
AH, MUCH BETTER.
BUT YOU WON'T FIND NARAKU IN THAT DIRECTION.
HFF.
HFF.
I'M SORRY TO BREAK THE BAD NEWS, MONK.

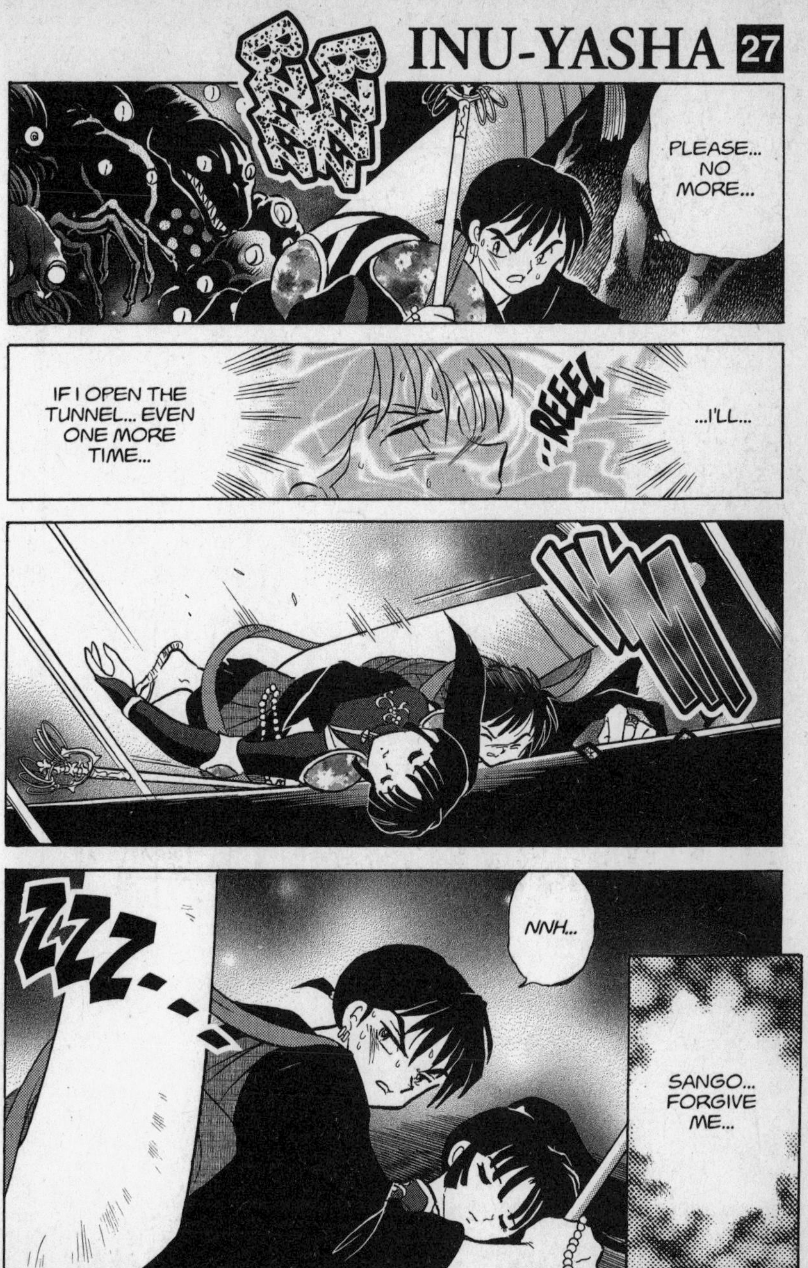
PLEASE... NO MORE...
IF I OPEN THE TUNNEL... EVEN ONE MORE TIME...
...I'LL...
-REEE!
NNH...
SANGO... FORGIVE ME...
ZZZ...

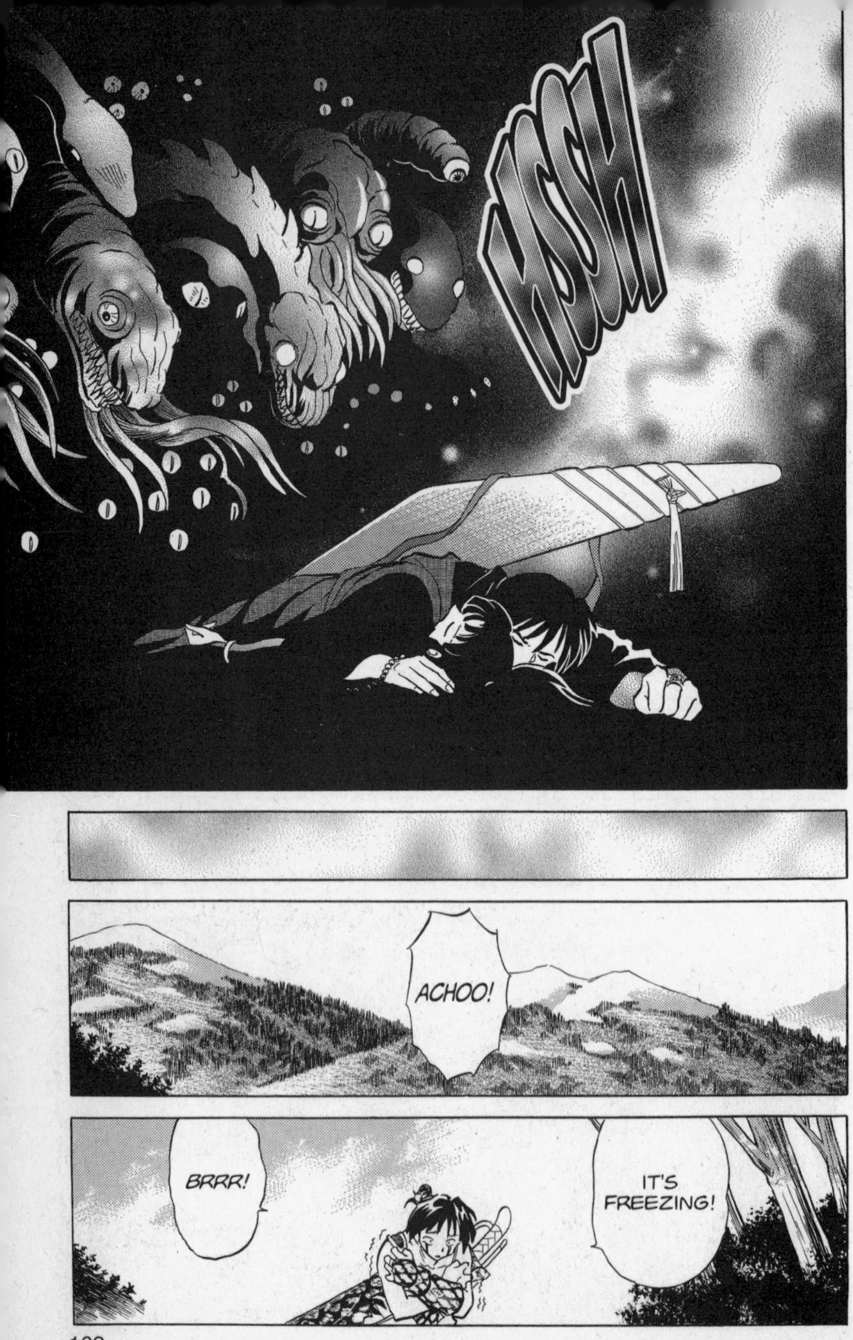
HSSH
ACHOO!
IT'S FREEZING!
BRRR!

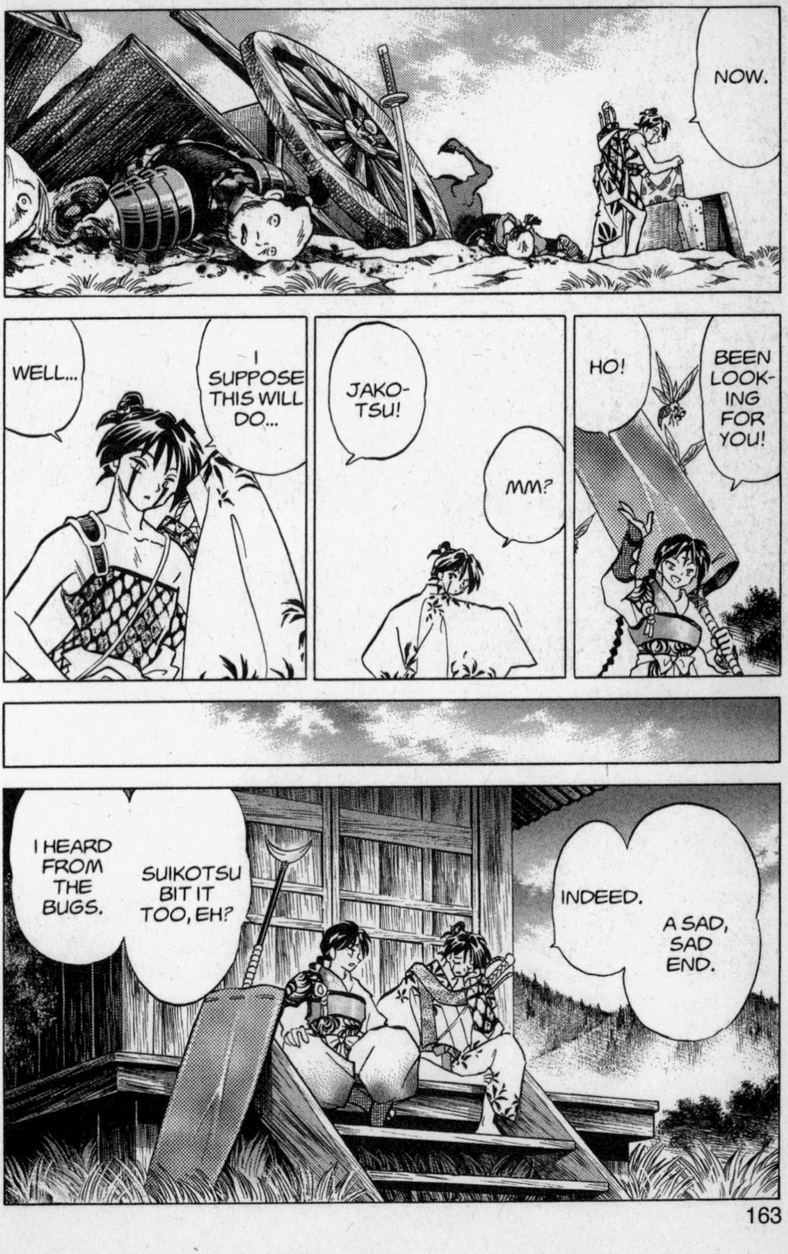
NOW.
WELL...
I SUPPOSE THIS WILL DO...
JAKO-TSU!
MM?
HO!
BEEN LOOK-ING FOR YOU!
I HEARD FROM THE BUGS.
SUIKOTSU BIT IT TOO, EH?
INDEED.
A SAD, SAD END.

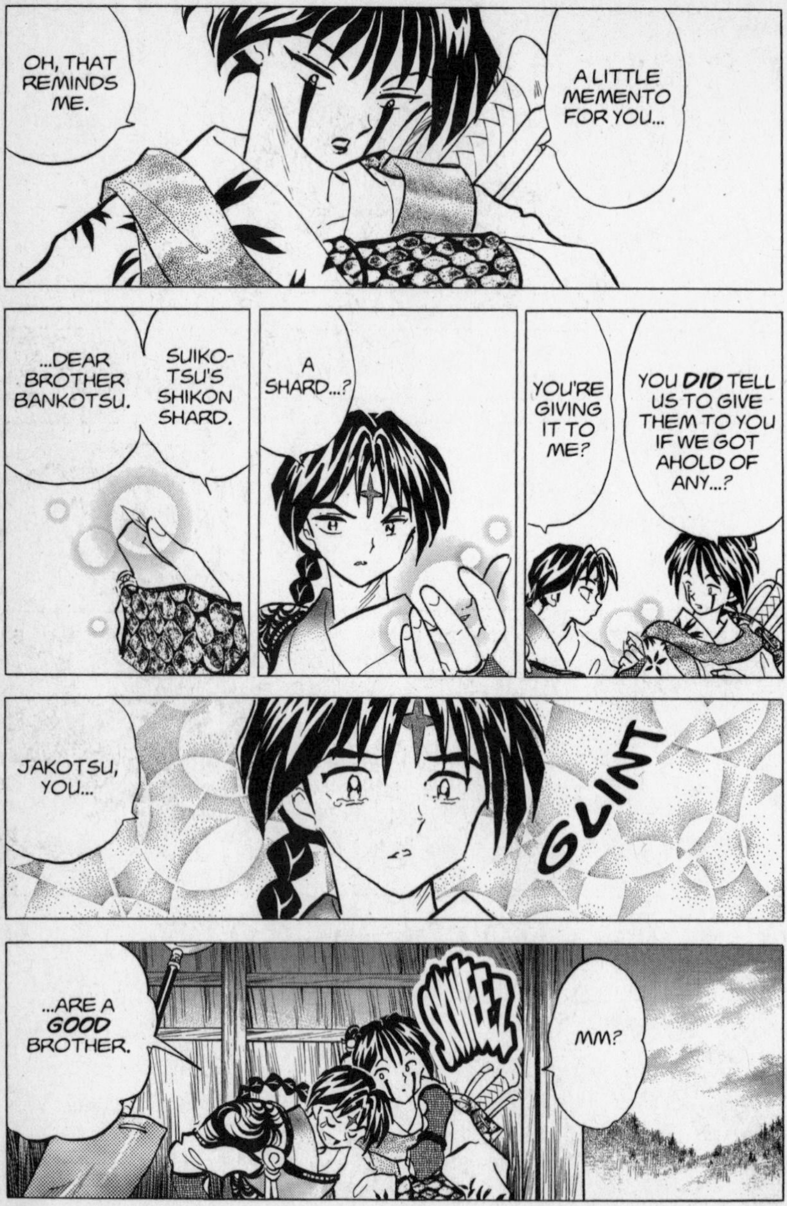
OH, THAT REMINDS ME.
A LITTLE MEMENTO FOR YOU...
...DEAR BROTHER BANKOTSU.
SUIKO-TSU'S SHIKON SHARD.
A SHARD...?
YOU'RE GIVING IT TO ME?
YOU **DID** TELL US TO GIVE THEM TO YOU IF WE GOT AHOLD OF ANY...?
JAKOTSU, YOU...
GLINT
...ARE A **GOOD** BROTHER.
SNEEZ
MM?

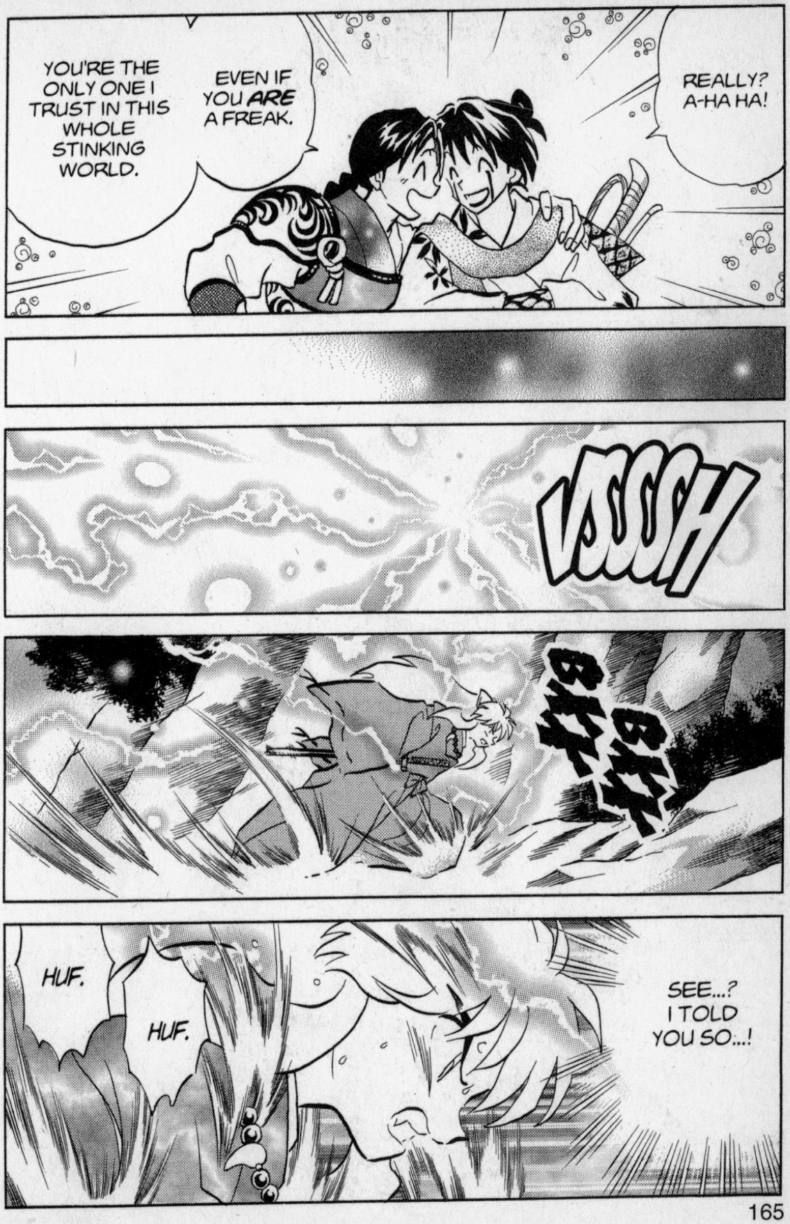
YOU'RE THE ONLY ONE I TRUST IN THIS WHOLE STINKING WORLD.
EVEN IF YOU *ARE* A FREAK.
REALLY? A-HA HA!
VSSSH
BKKK BKKK
HUF.
HUF.
SEE...? I TOLD YOU SO...!

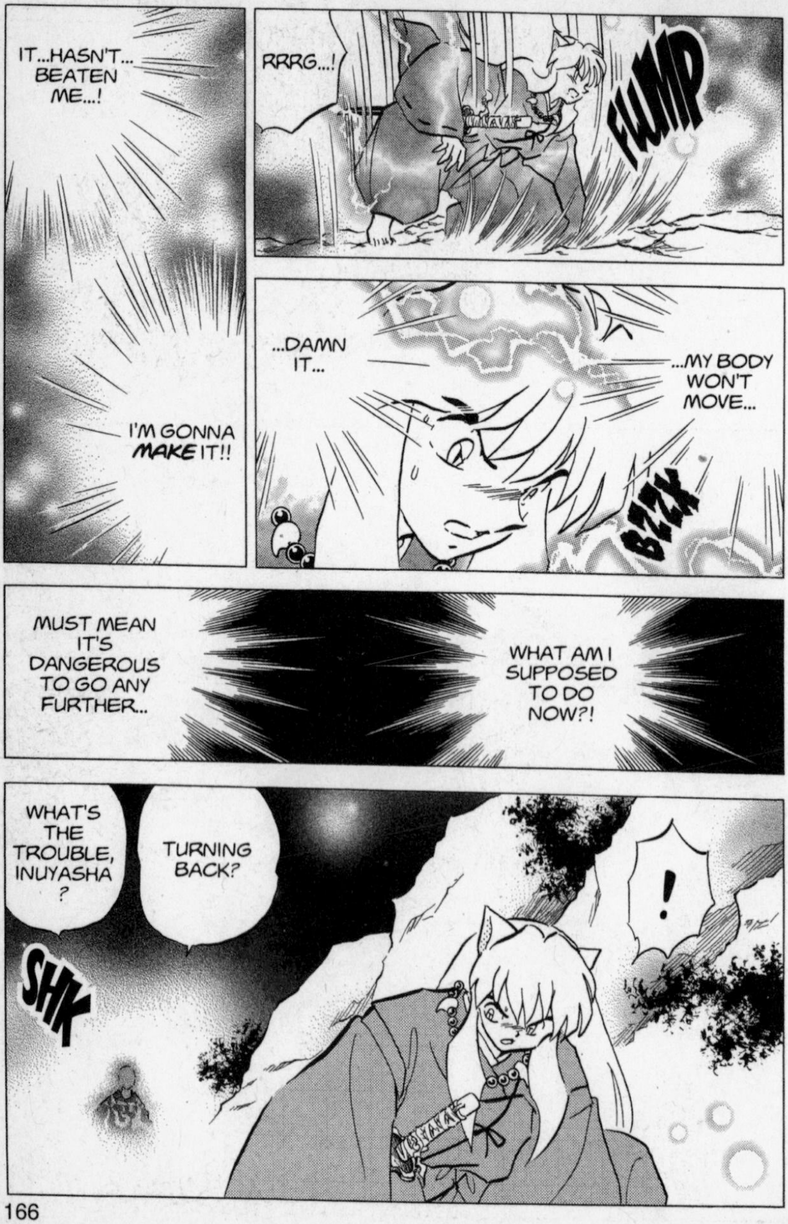
IT...HASN'T... BEATEN ME...!
I'M GONNA MAKE IT!!
RRRG...!
FUMP
...DAMN IT...
...MY BODY WON'T MOVE...
BZZK
MUST MEAN IT'S DANGEROUS TO GO ANY FURTHER...
WHAT AM I SUPPOSED TO DO NOW?!
WHAT'S THE TROUBLE, INUYASHA?
TURNING BACK?
SHK
!

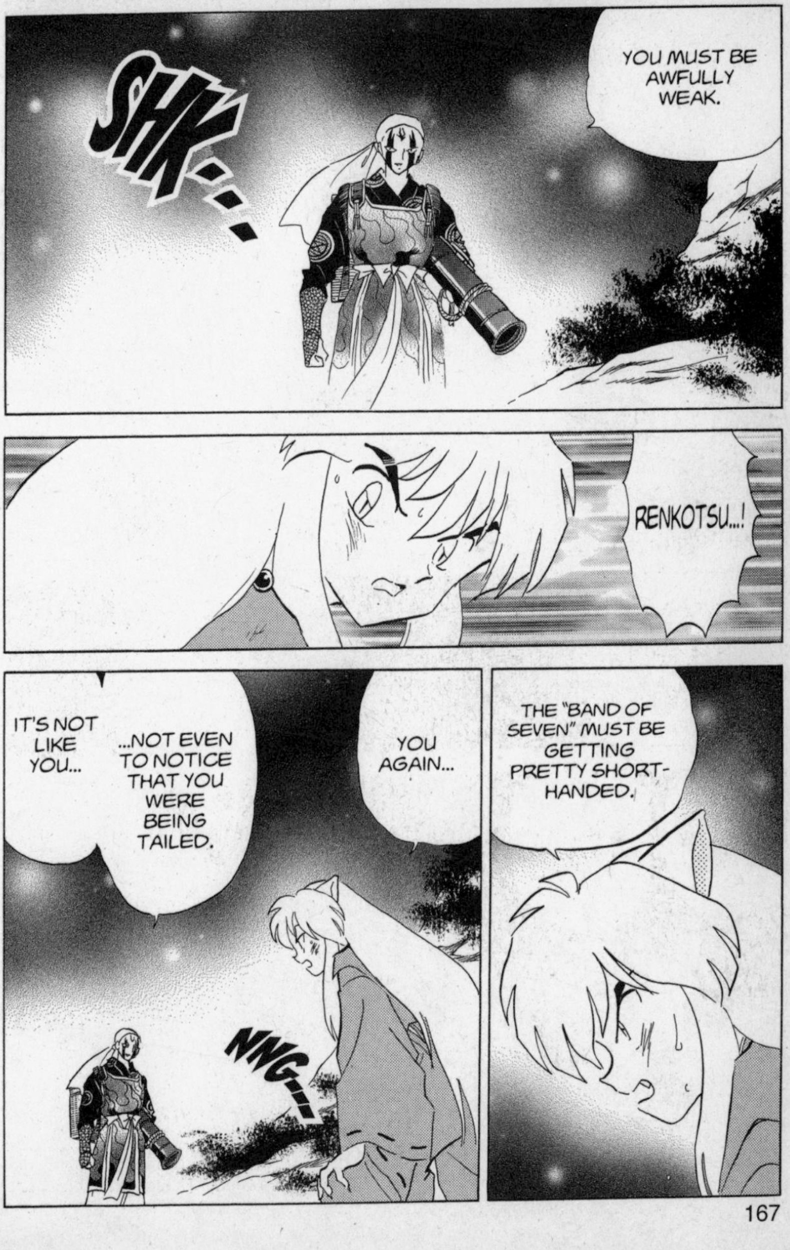
YOU MUST BE AWFULLY WEAK.
SHK...
RENKOTSU...!
THE "BAND OF SEVEN" MUST BE GETTING PRETTY SHORT-HANDED.
YOU AGAIN...
IT'S NOT LIKE YOU...
...NOT EVEN TO NOTICE THAT YOU WERE BEING TAILED.
NNG...

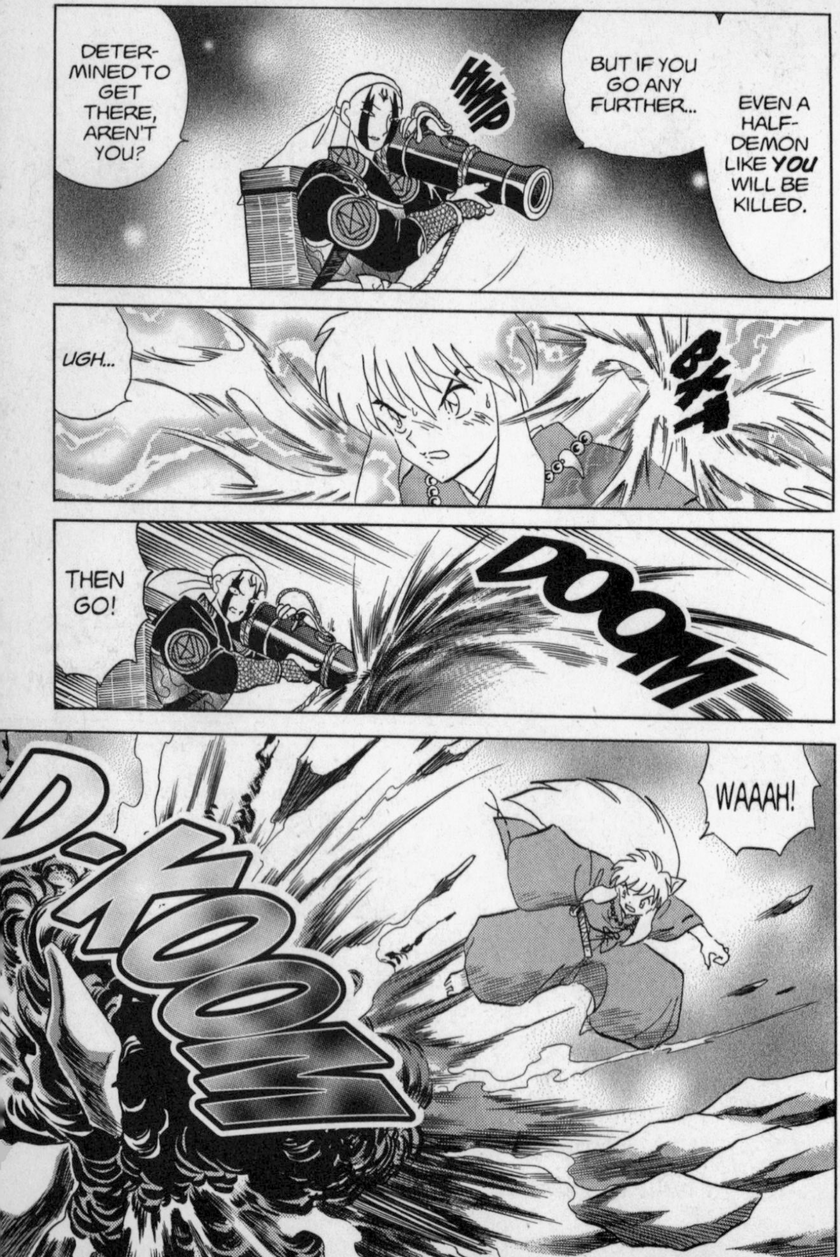
DETERMINED TO GET THERE, AREN'T YOU?
HMMP
BUT IF YOU GO ANY FURTHER...
EVEN A HALF-DEMON LIKE **YOU** WILL BE KILLED.
UGH...
BKT
THEN GO!
DOOM
D-KOOM
WAAAH!

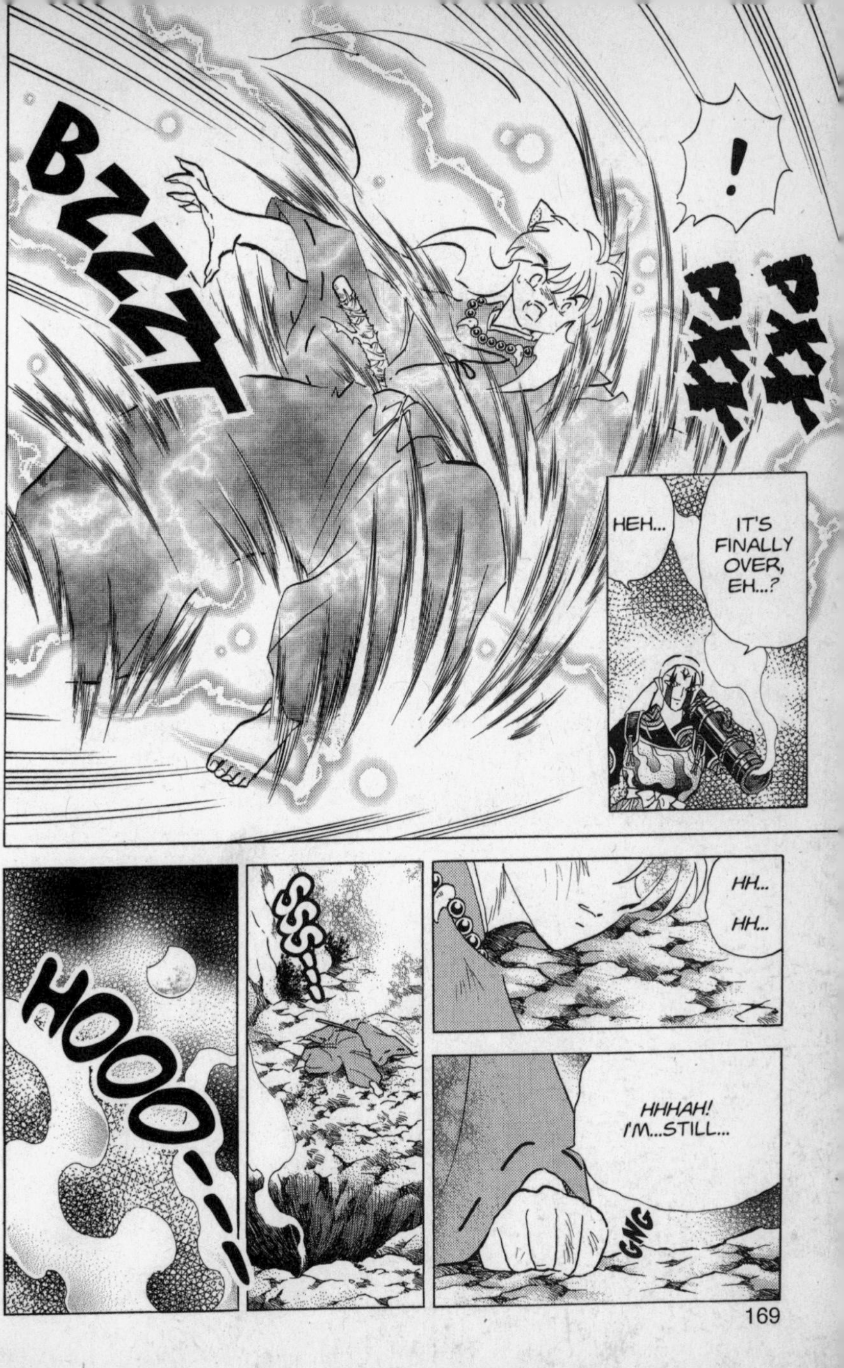
!
DKK DKK
BZZZT
IT'S FINALLY OVER, EH...?
HEH...
HH... HH...
HHHAH! I'M...STILL...
GNG
SSS
HOOO---

HUH...?!

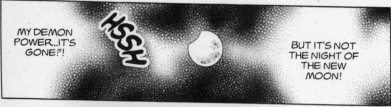

MY DEMON POWER...IT'S GONE?!

BUT IT'S NOT THE NIGHT OF THE NEW MOON!

DAMN IT TO HELL...

THE BARRIER DID THIS!

SCROLL 10
HAKUSHIN THE HOLY

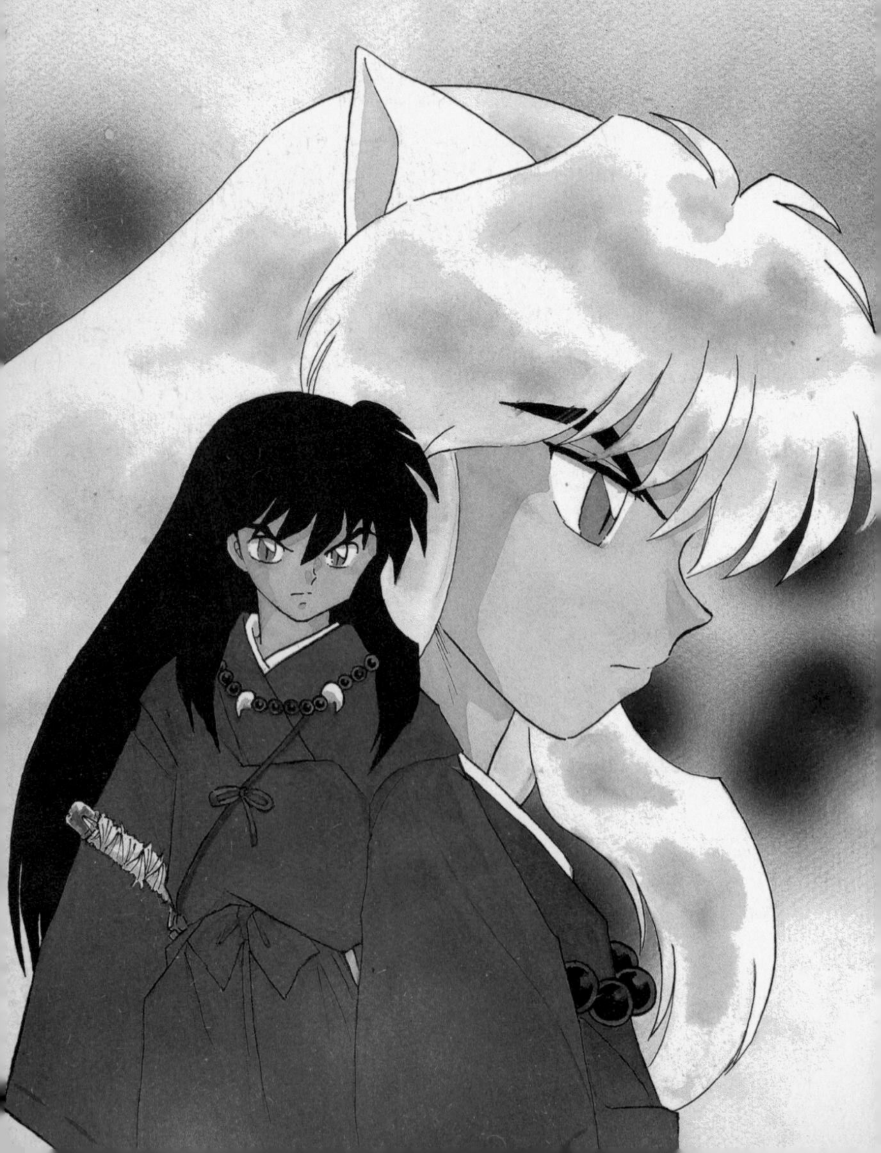

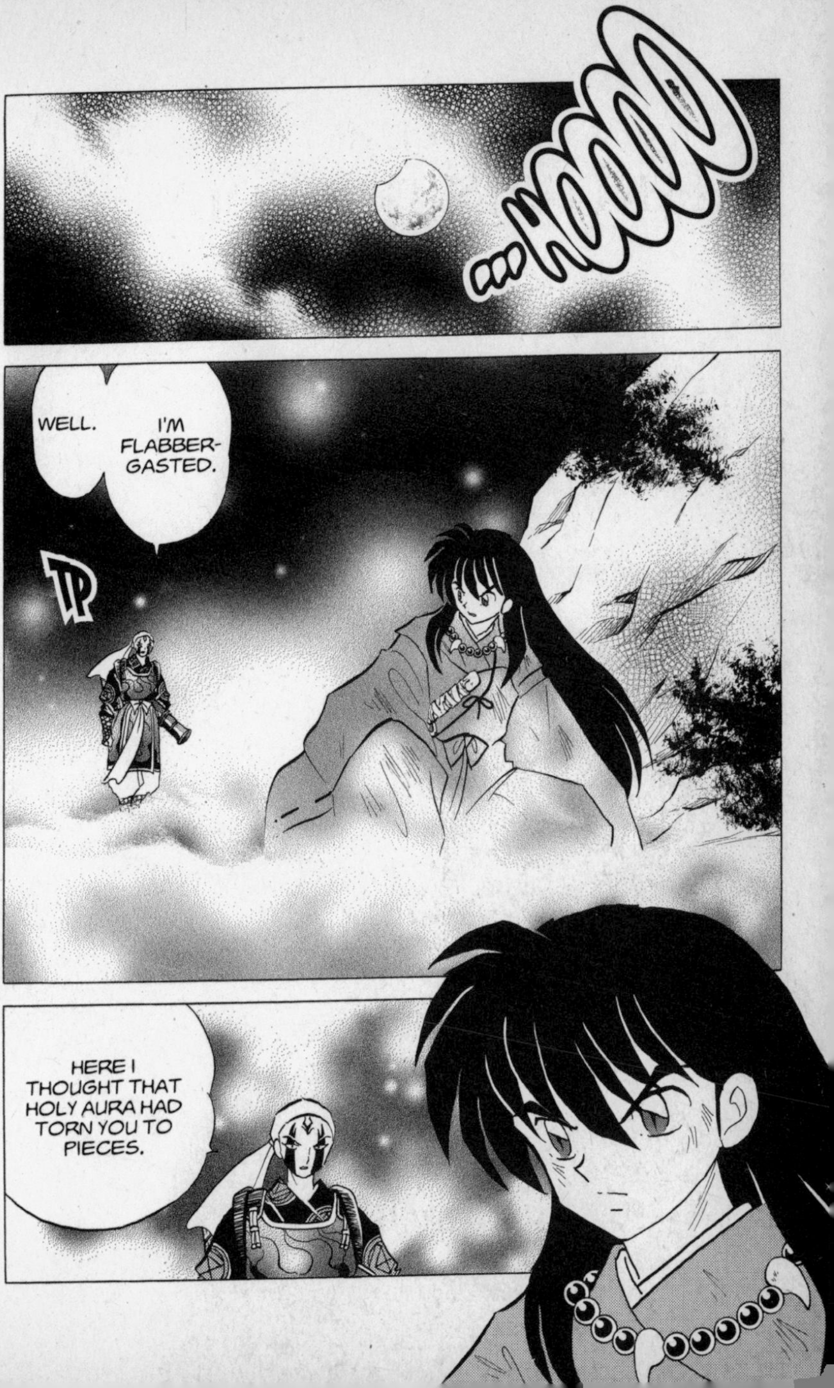

...HOOOO
WELL.
I'M FLABBERGASTED.
TP
HERE I THOUGHT THAT HOLY AURA HAD TORN YOU TO PIECES.

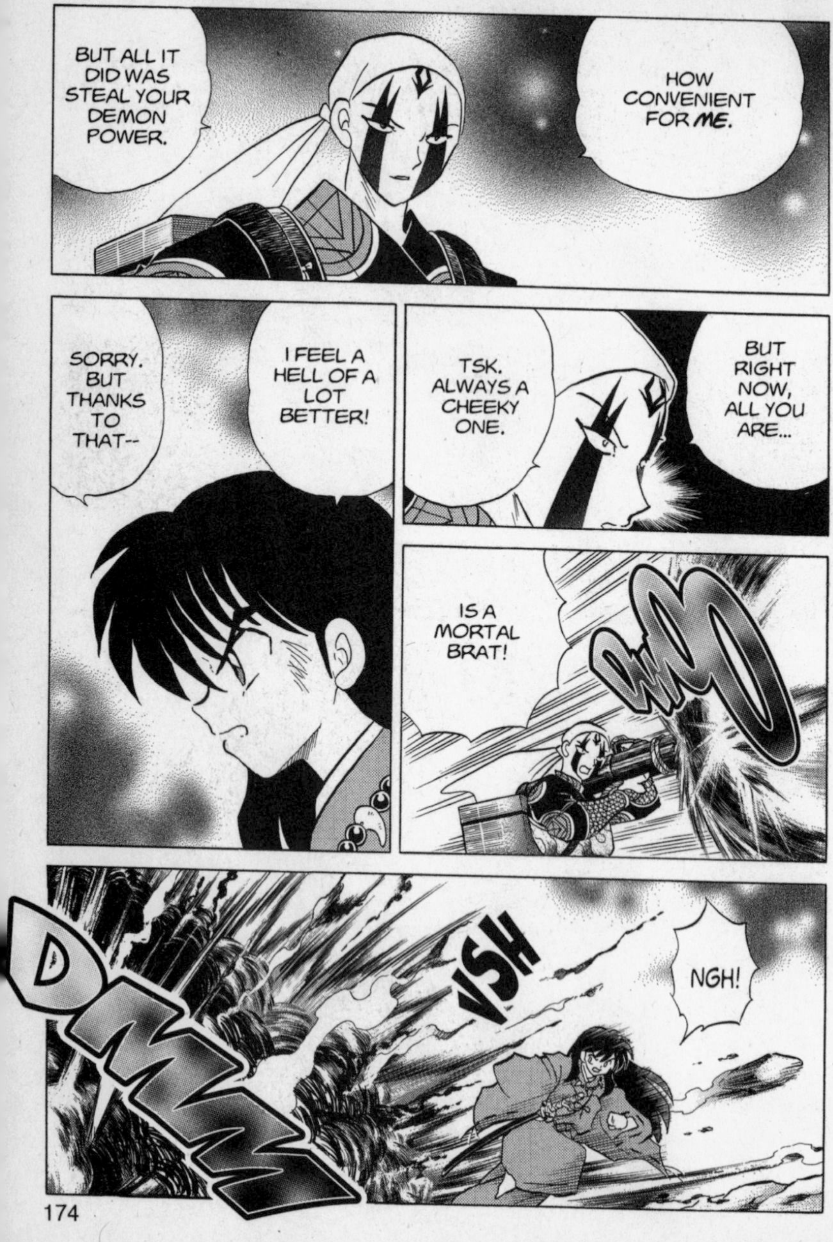
BUT ALL IT DID WAS STEAL YOUR DEMON POWER.
HOW CONVENIENT FOR *ME*.
SORRY. BUT THANKS TO THAT--
I FEEL A HELL OF A LOT BETTER!
TSK. ALWAYS A CHEEKY ONE.
BUT RIGHT NOW, ALL YOU ARE...
IS A MORTAL BRAT!
NGH!

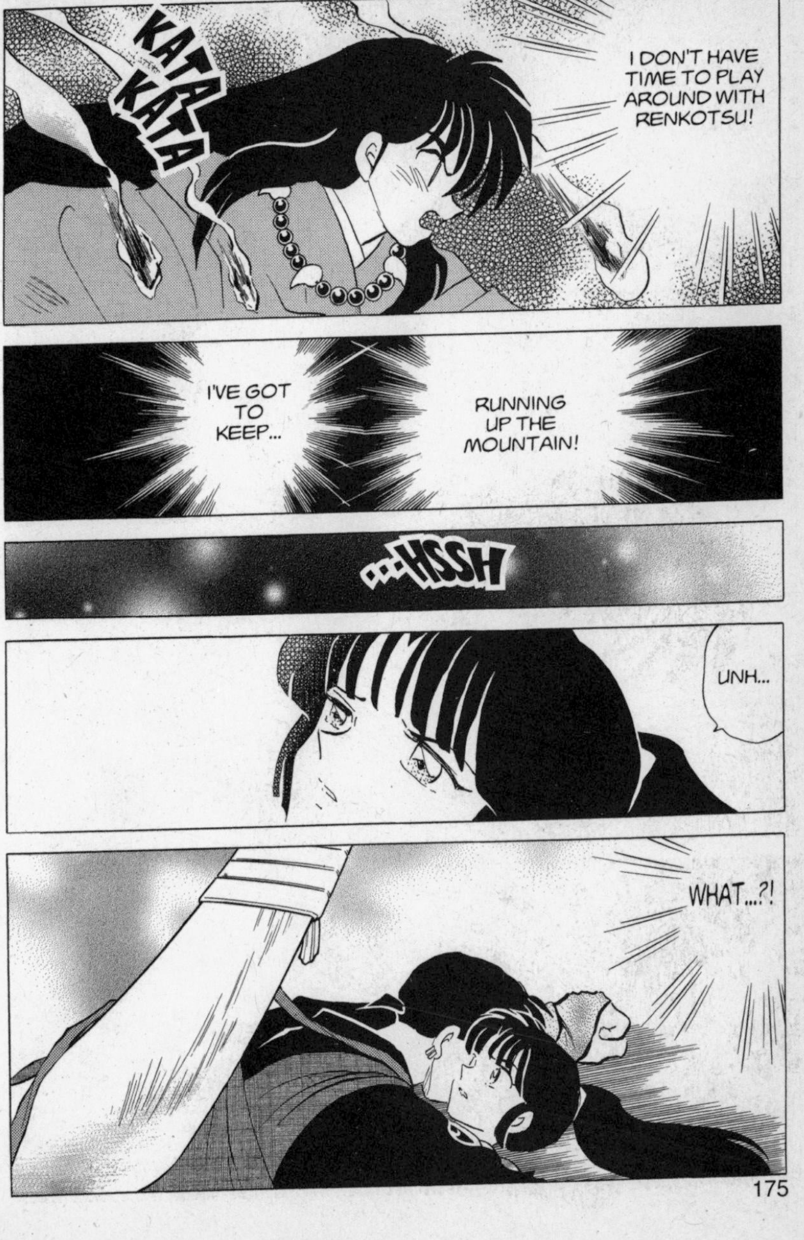
I DON'T HAVE TIME TO PLAY AROUND WITH RENKOTSU!
KATA KATA
RUNNING UP THE MOUNTAIN!
I'VE GOT TO KEEP...
...HSSH
UNH...
WHAT...?!

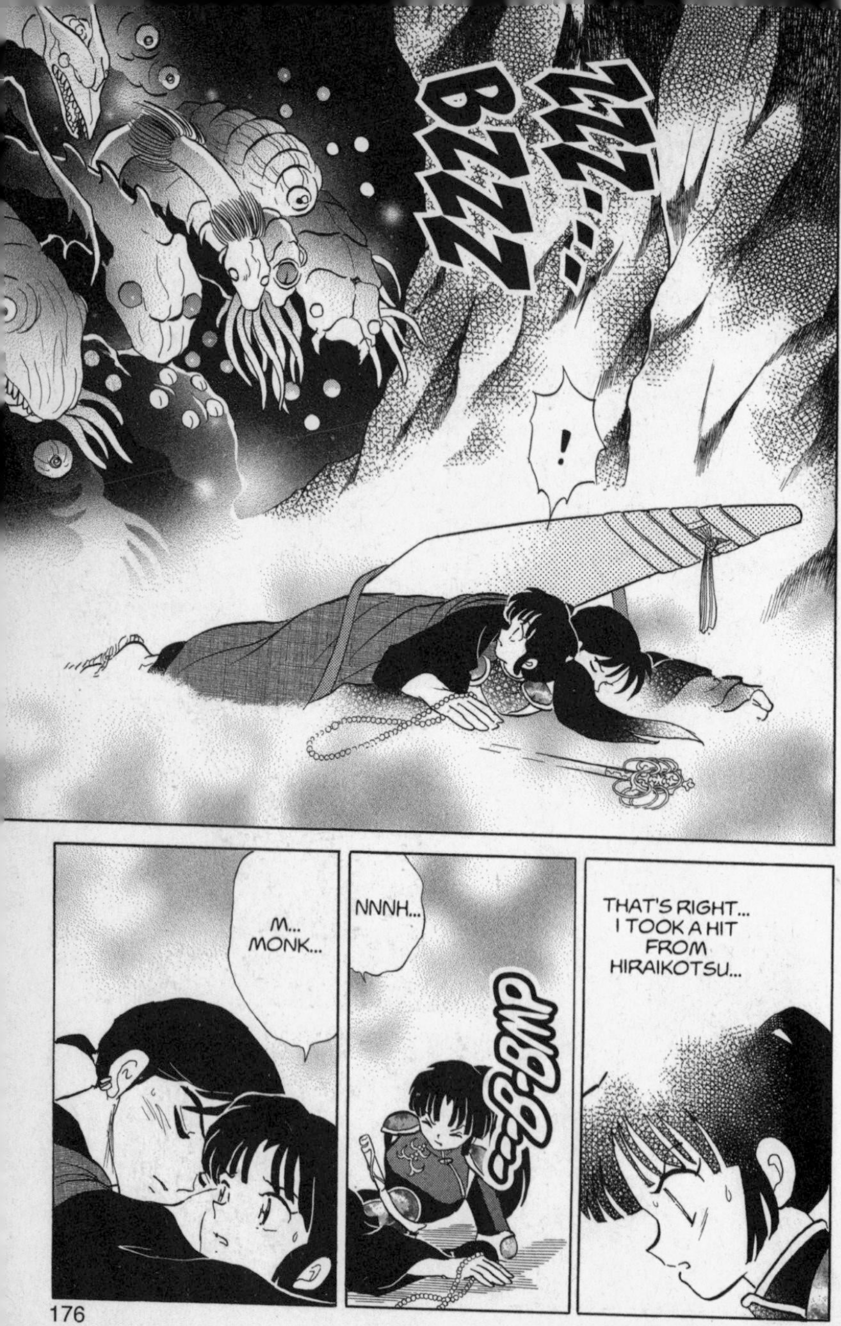
ZZZ...
BZZZ
!
THAT'S RIGHT... I TOOK A HIT FROM HIRAIKOTSU...
NNNH...
..B-B-BMP
M... MONK...

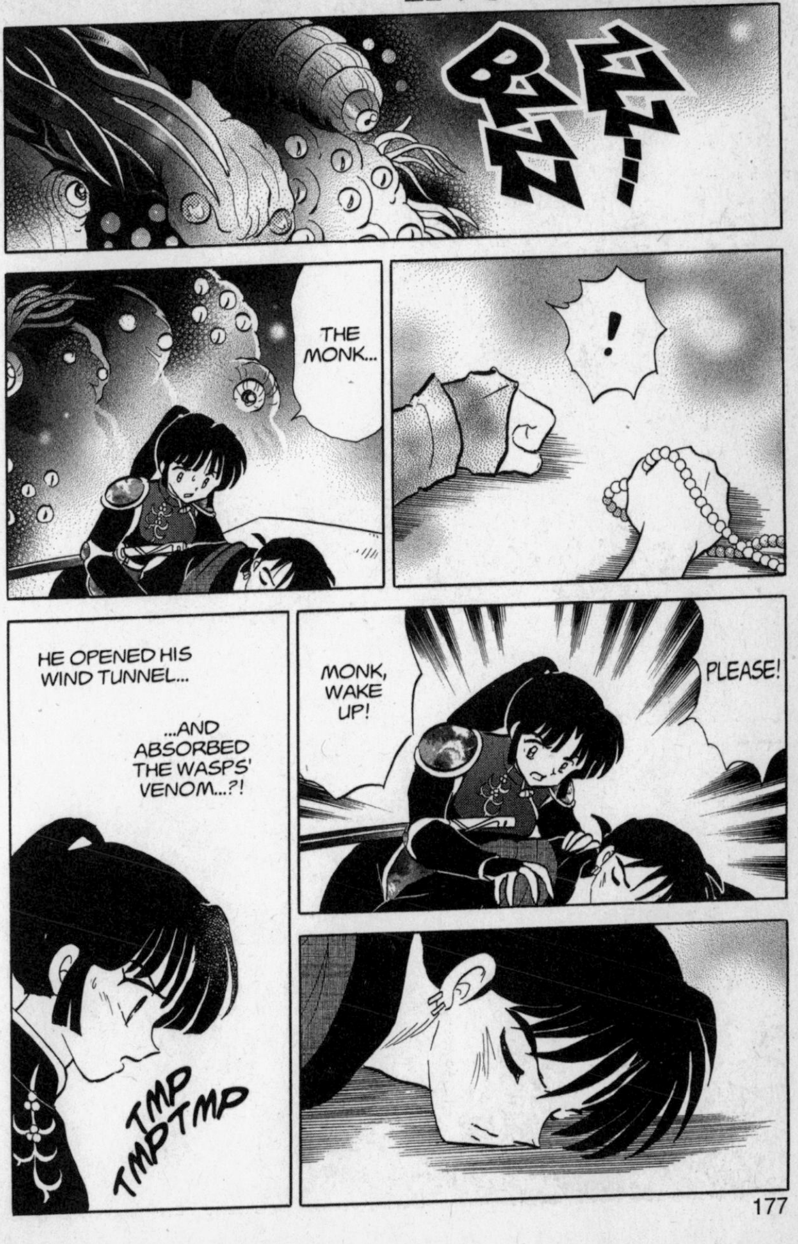
BZZZZZ...
!
THE MONK...
MONK, WAKE UP!
PLEASE!
HE OPENED HIS WIND TUNNEL...
...AND ABSORBED THE WASPS' VENOM...?!
TMP TMPTMP

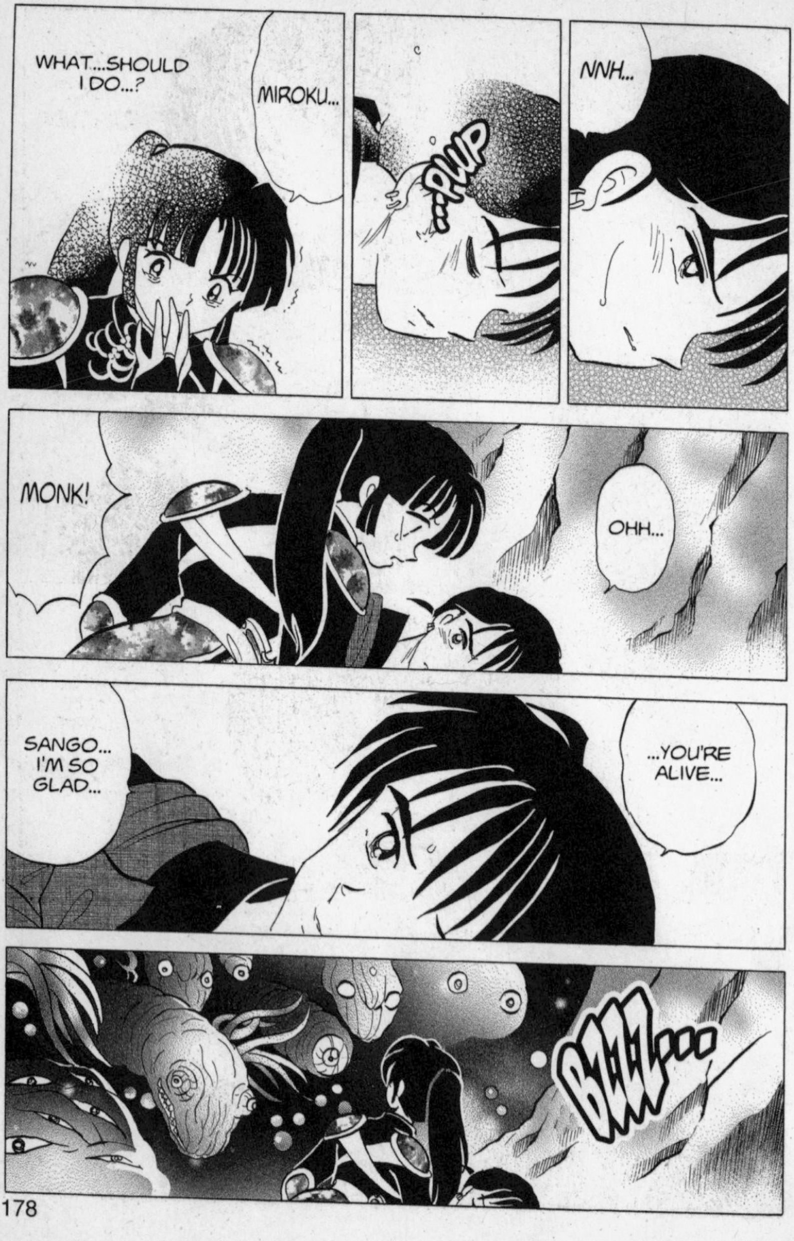

WHAT...SHOULD I DO...?
MIROKU...
PLIP
NNH...
MONK!
OHH...
SANGO... I'M SO GLAD...
...YOU'RE ALIVE...
BZZZ...

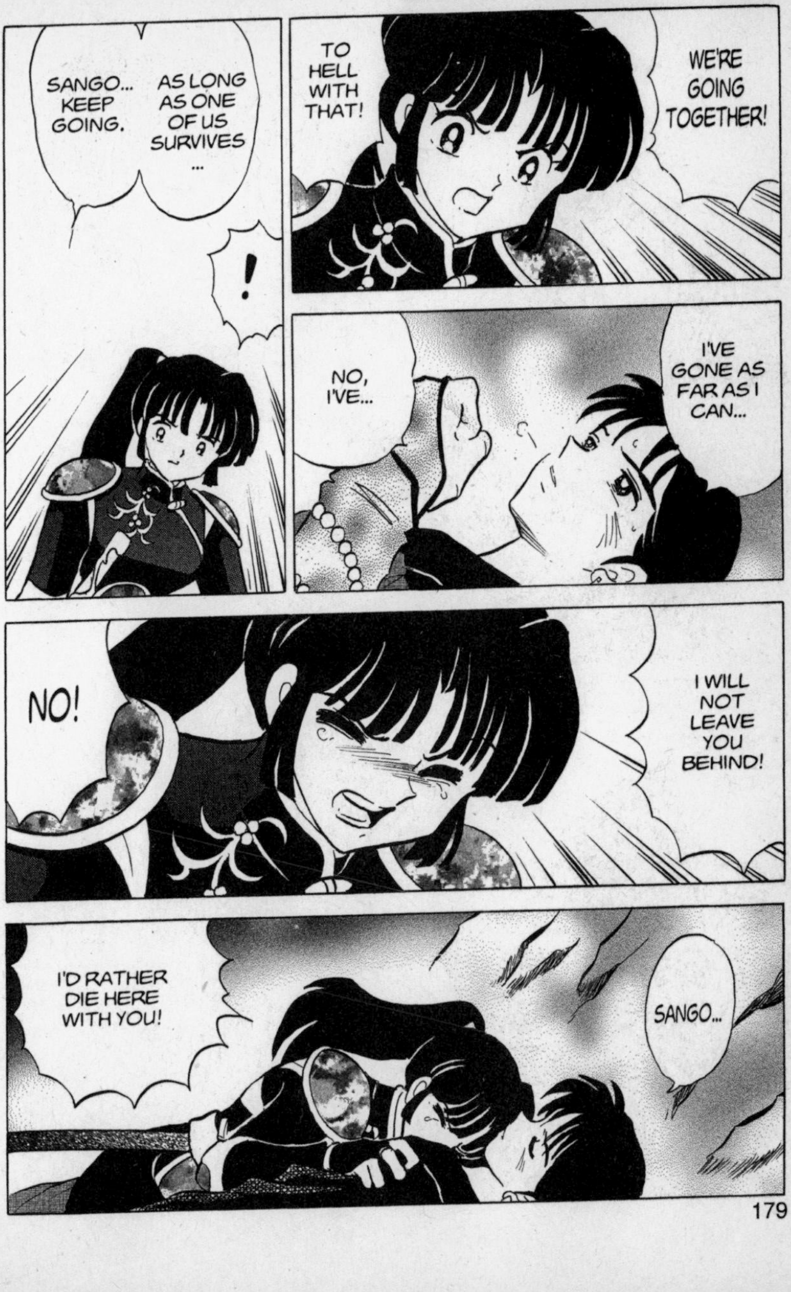
SANGO... KEEP GOING.
AS LONG AS ONE OF US SURVIVES ...
TO HELL WITH THAT!
WE'RE GOING TOGETHER!
!
NO, I'VE...
I'VE GONE AS FAR AS I CAN...
NO!
I WILL NOT LEAVE YOU BEHIND!
I'D RATHER DIE HERE WITH YOU!
SANGO...

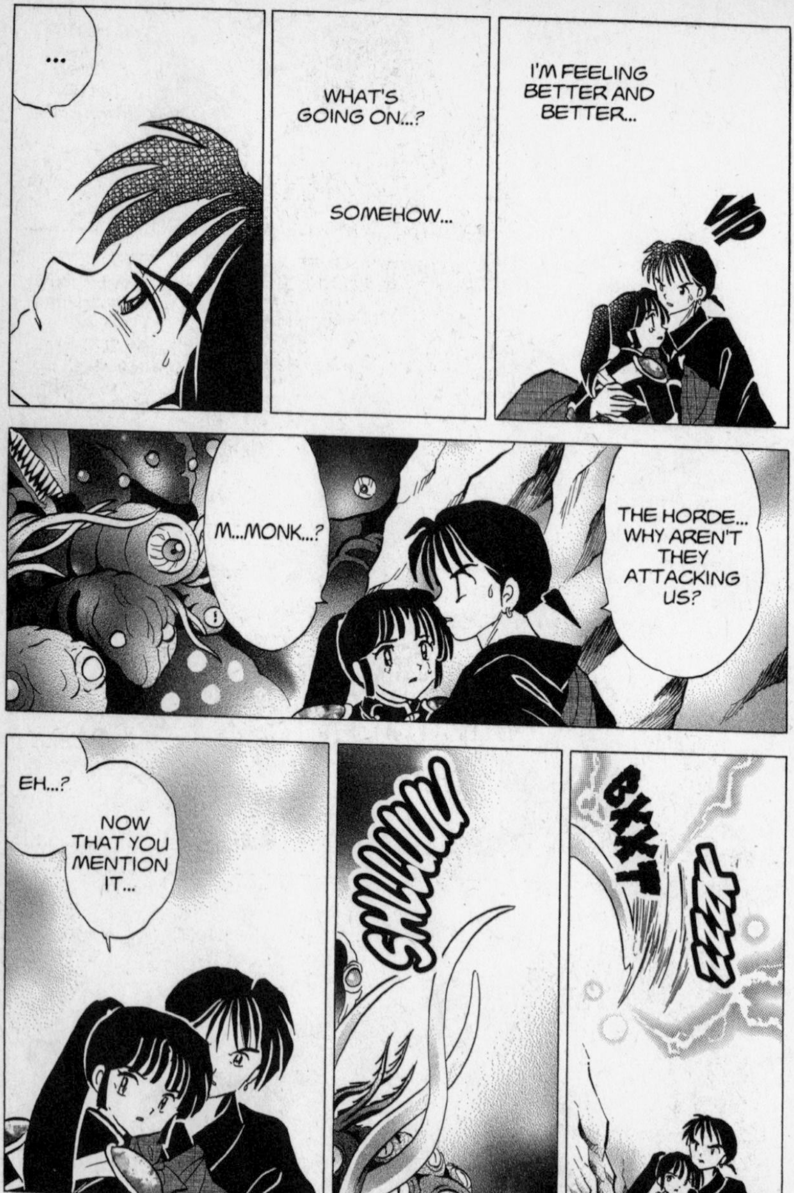
I'M FEELING BETTER AND BETTER...
VIP
WHAT'S GOING ON...?
SOMEHOW...
...
THE HORDE... WHY AREN'T THEY ATTACKING US?
M...MONK...?
BKKT
ZZZZ
EH...?
NOW THAT YOU MENTION IT...

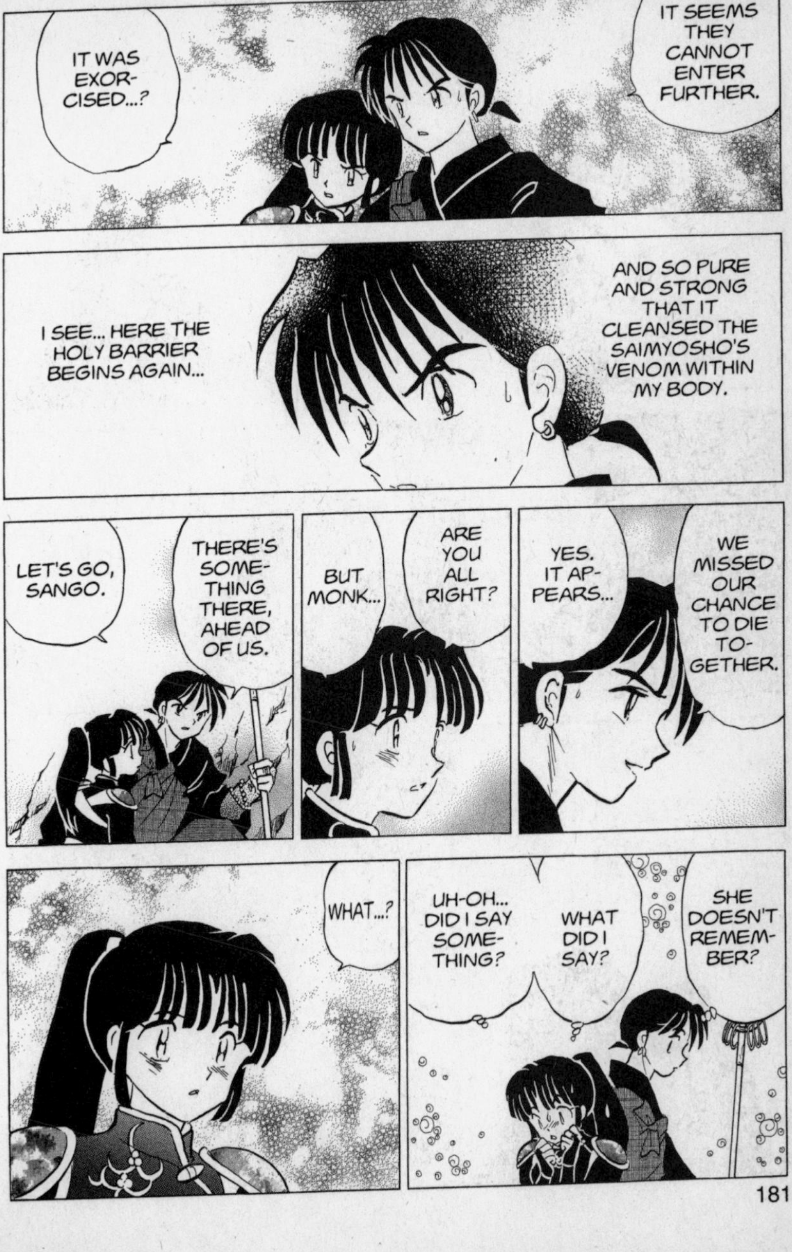
IT WAS EXORCISED...?
IT SEEMS THEY CANNOT ENTER FURTHER.
I SEE... HERE THE HOLY BARRIER BEGINS AGAIN...
AND SO PURE AND STRONG THAT IT CLEANSED THE SAIMYOSHO'S VENOM WITHIN MY BODY.
LET'S GO, SANGO.
THERE'S SOMETHING THERE, AHEAD OF US.
BUT MONK...
ARE YOU ALL RIGHT?
YES. IT APPEARS...
WE MISSED OUR CHANCE TO DIE TOGETHER.
WHAT...?
UH-OH... DID I SAY SOMETHING?
WHAT DID I SAY?
SHE DOESN'T REMEMBER?

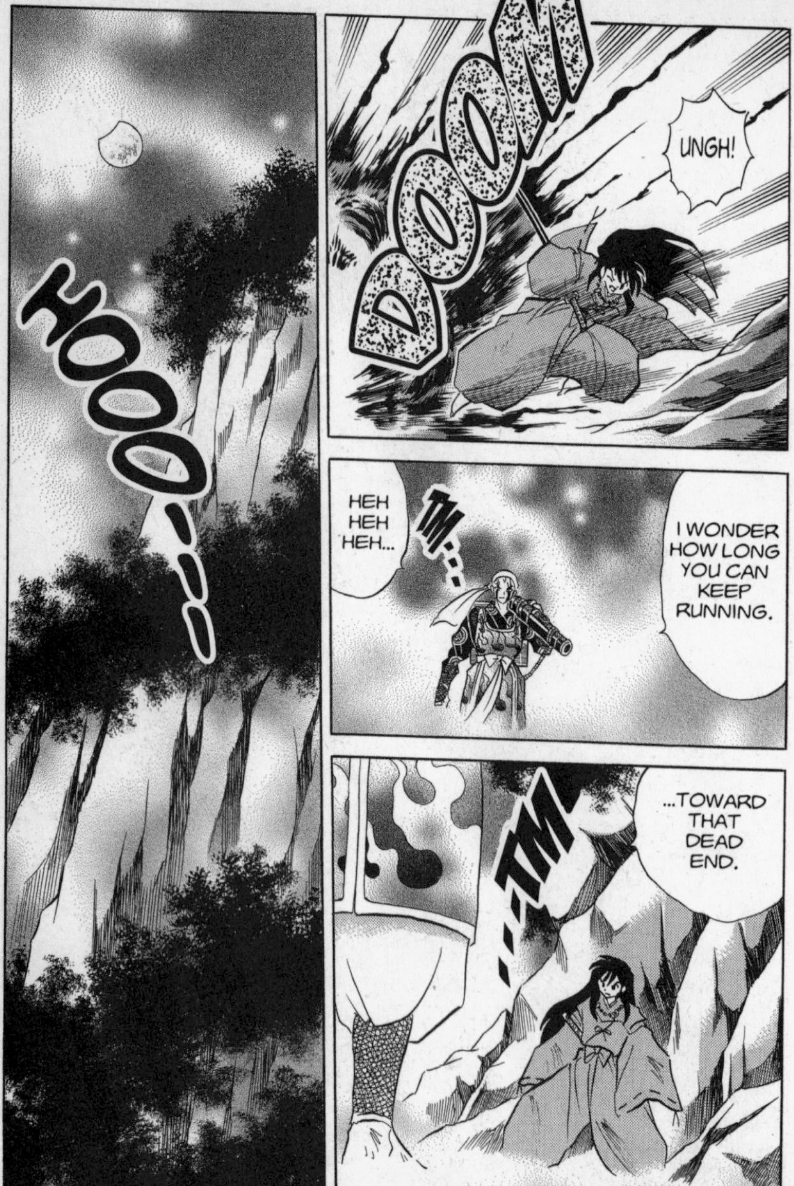

DOOOM
UNGH!
I WONDER HOW LONG YOU CAN KEEP RUNNING.
TM...
HEH HEH HEH...
...TOWARD THAT DEAD END.
...TM
HOOOO-...

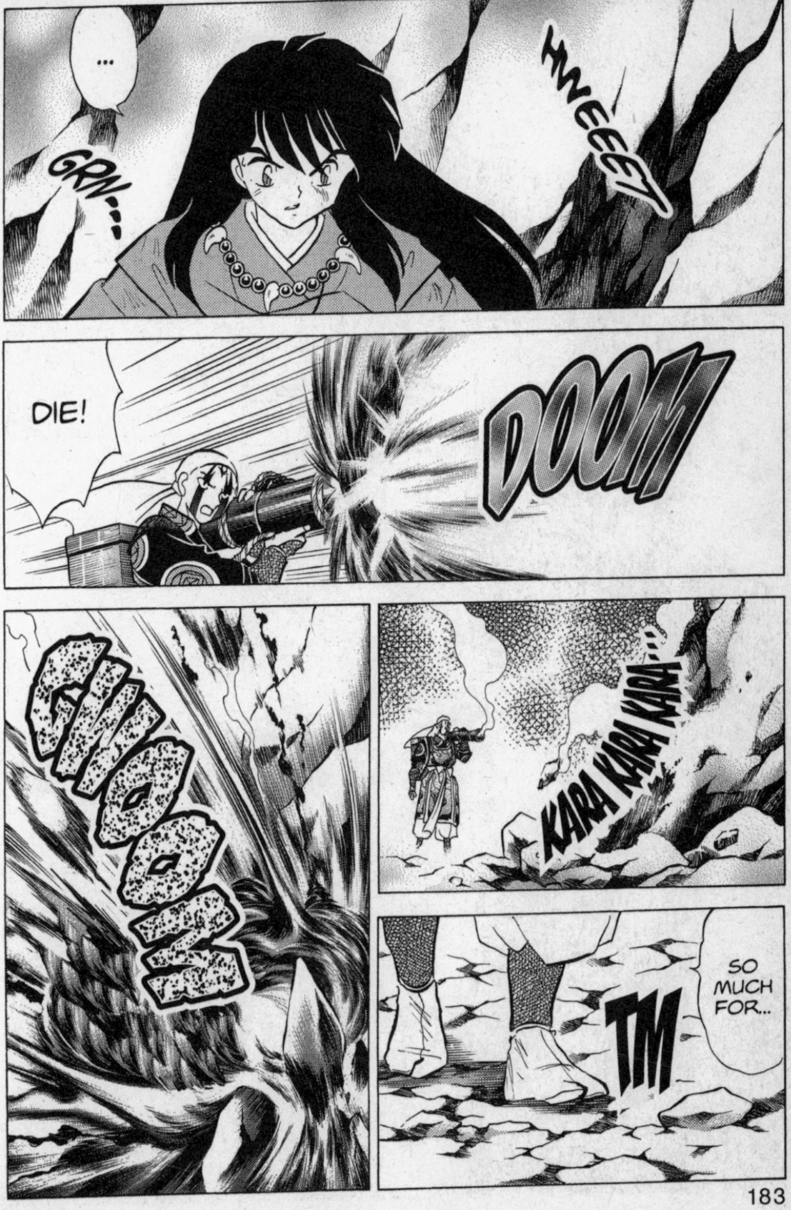
HWEEEE
...
GRN...
DOOM
DIE!
KARA KARA KARA KARA...
SO MUCH FOR...
TM
CHOOM

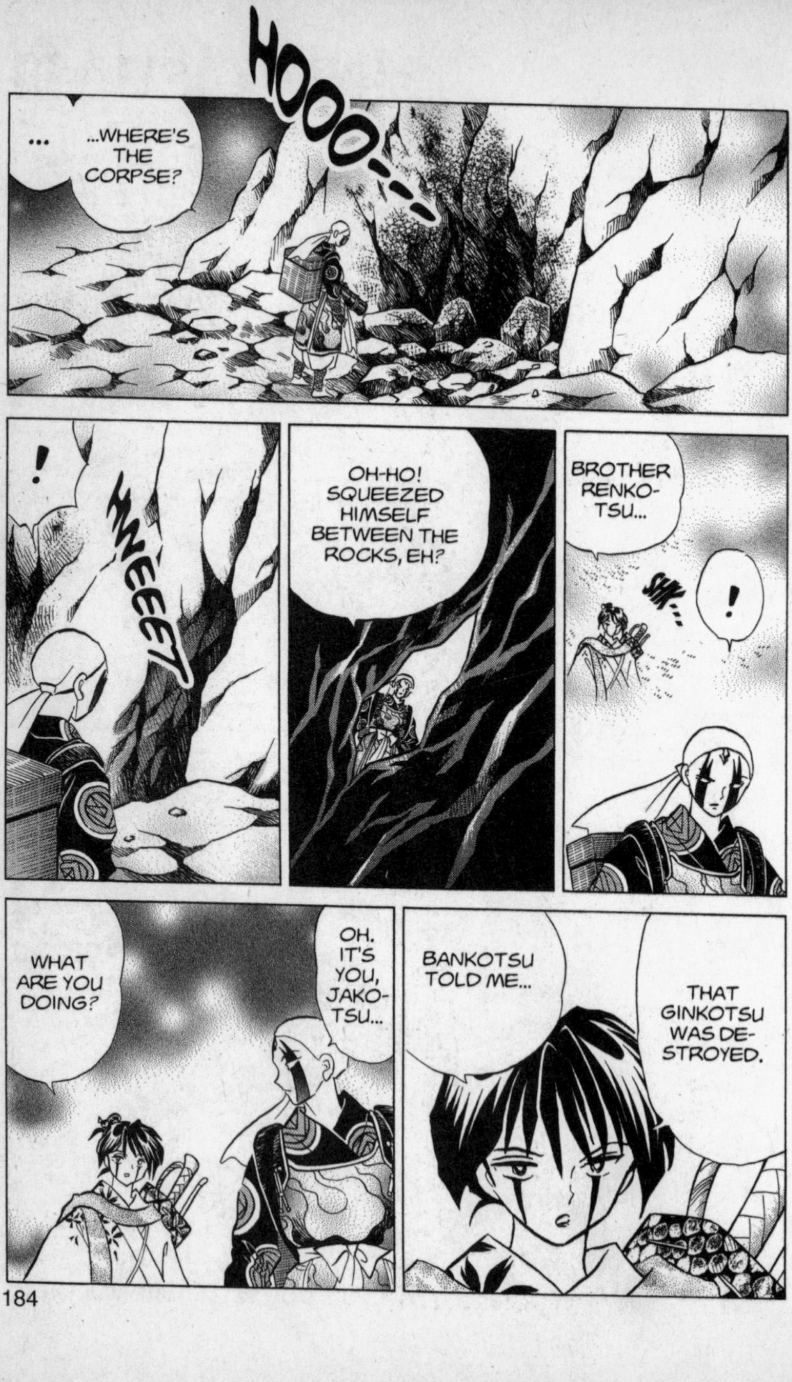
HOOO-...
...
...WHERE'S THE CORPSE?
!
HWEEET
OH-HO! SQUEEZED HIMSELF BETWEEN THE ROCKS, EH?
BROTHER RENKO-TSU...
SHK...
!
WHAT ARE YOU DOING?
OH. IT'S YOU, JAKO-TSU...
BANKOTSU TOLD ME...
THAT GINKOTSU WAS DE-STROYED.

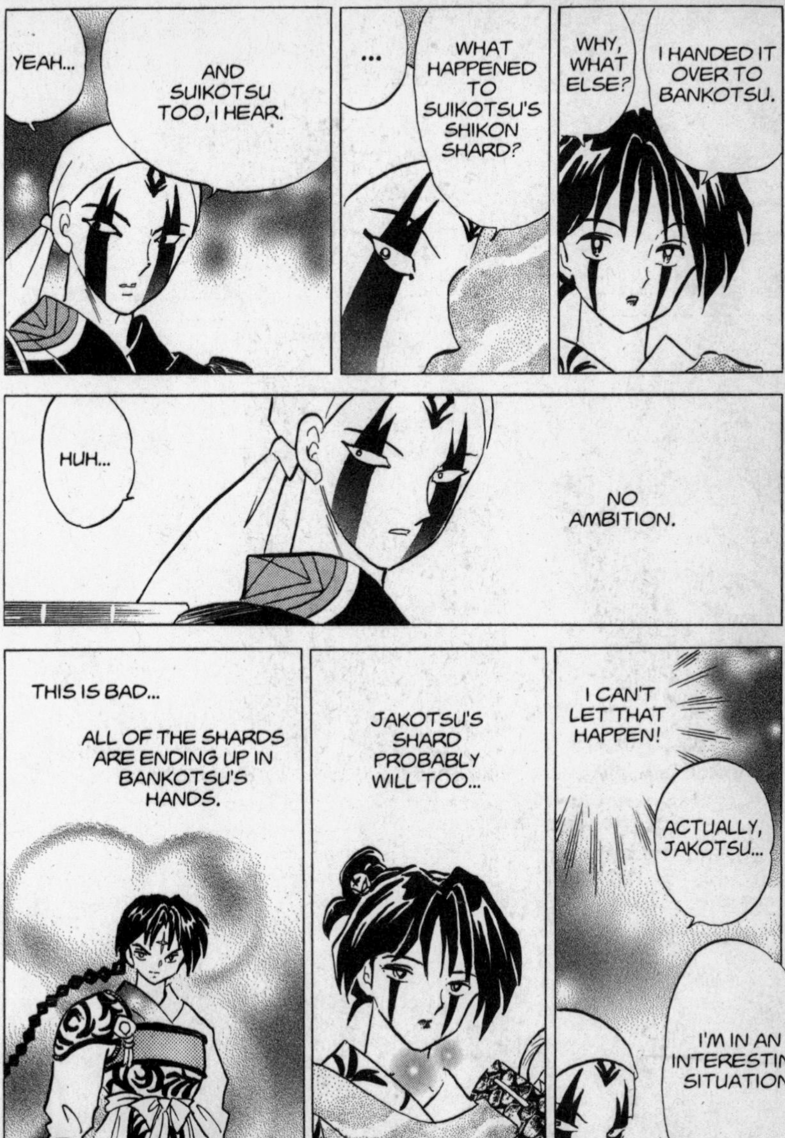
YEAH...
AND SUIKOTSU TOO, I HEAR.
...
WHAT HAPPENED TO SUIKOTSU'S SHIKON SHARD?
WHY, WHAT ELSE?
I HANDED IT OVER TO BANKOTSU.
HUH...
NO AMBITION.
THIS IS BAD...
ALL OF THE SHARDS ARE ENDING UP IN BANKOTSU'S HANDS.
JAKOTSU'S SHARD PROBABLY WILL TOO...
I CAN'T LET THAT HAPPEN!
ACTUALLY, JAKOTSU...
I'M IN AN INTERESTING SITUATION.

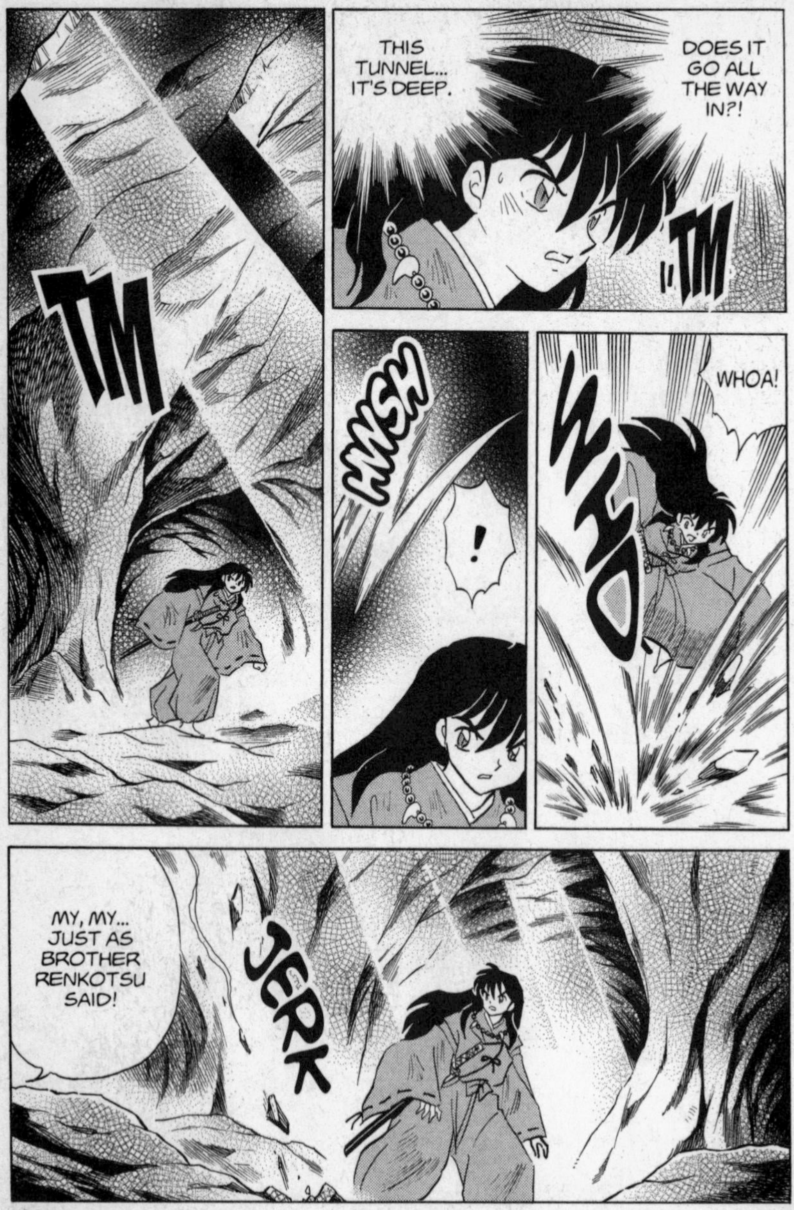
TM
THIS TUNNEL... IT'S DEEP.
DOES IT GO ALL THE WAY IN?!
TM
HWISH
!
WHO
WHOA!
MY, MY... JUST AS BROTHER RENKOTSU SAID!
JERK

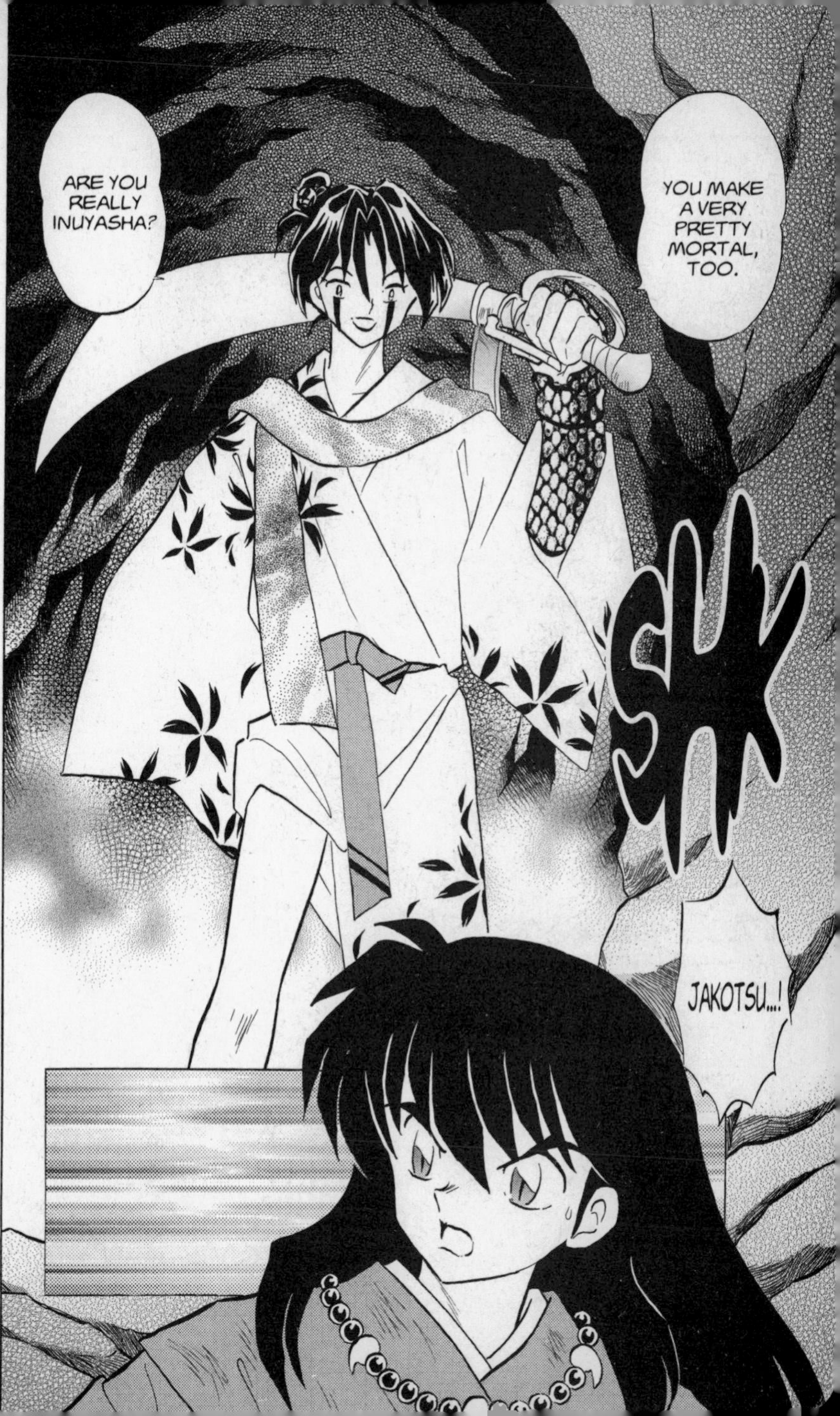
YOU MAKE A VERY PRETTY MORTAL, TOO.
ARE YOU REALLY INUYASHA?
SHK
JAKOTSU...!

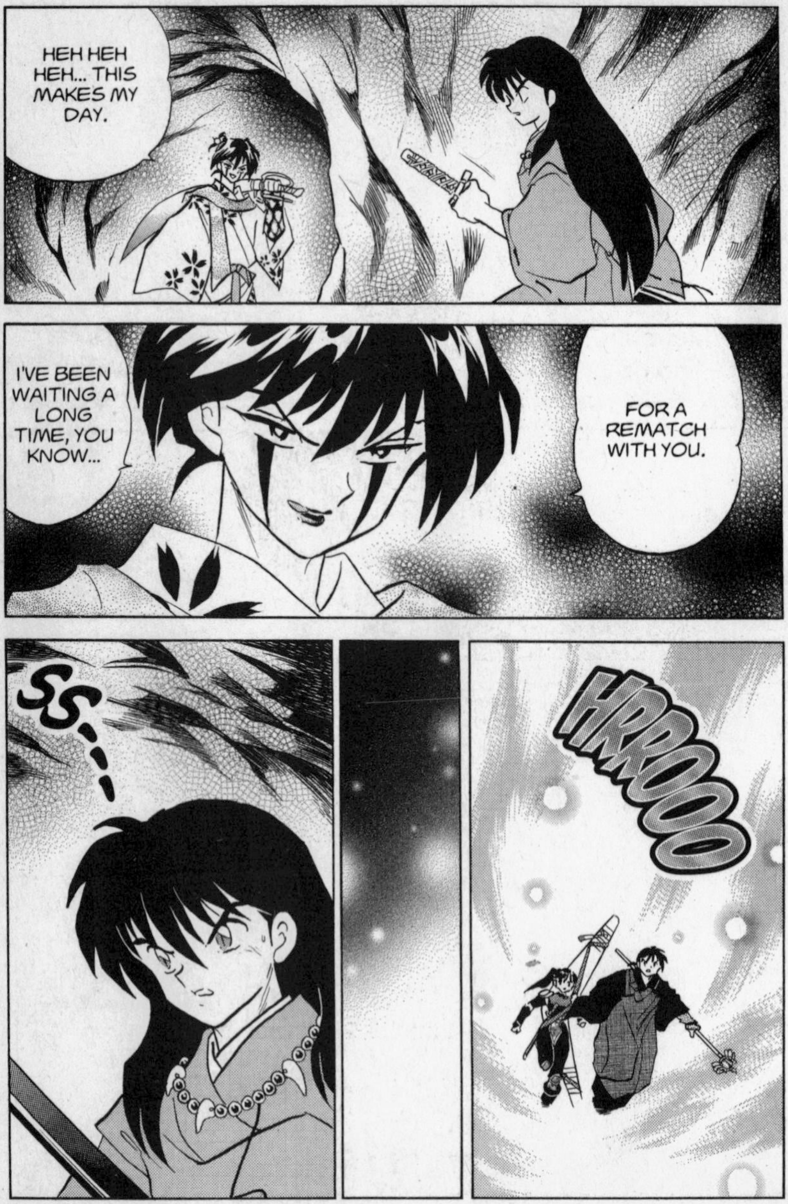
HEH HEH HEH... THIS MAKES MY DAY.
I'VE BEEN WAITING A LONG TIME, YOU KNOW...
FOR A REMATCH WITH YOU.
SS...
HRROOO

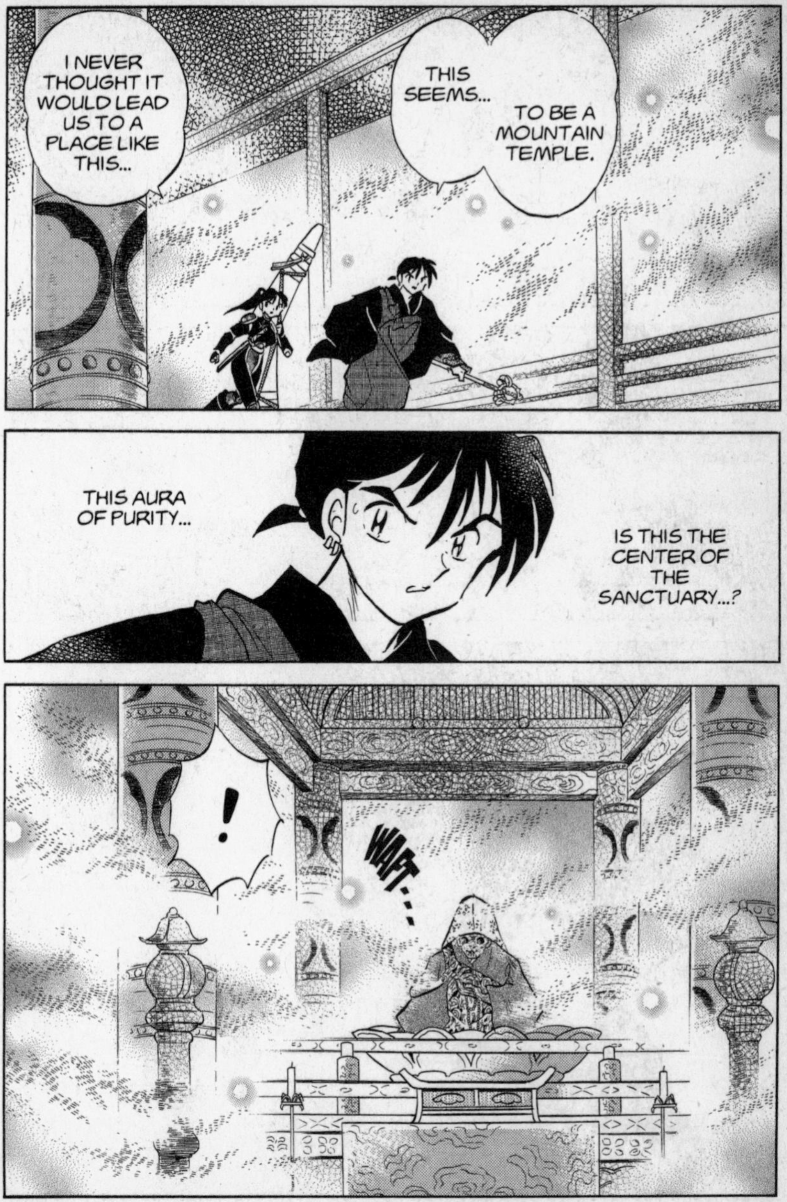
I NEVER THOUGHT IT WOULD LEAD US TO A PLACE LIKE THIS...
THIS SEEMS...
TO BE A MOUNTAIN TEMPLE.
THIS AURA OF PURITY...
IS THIS THE CENTER OF THE SANCTUARY...?
!
WAFT...

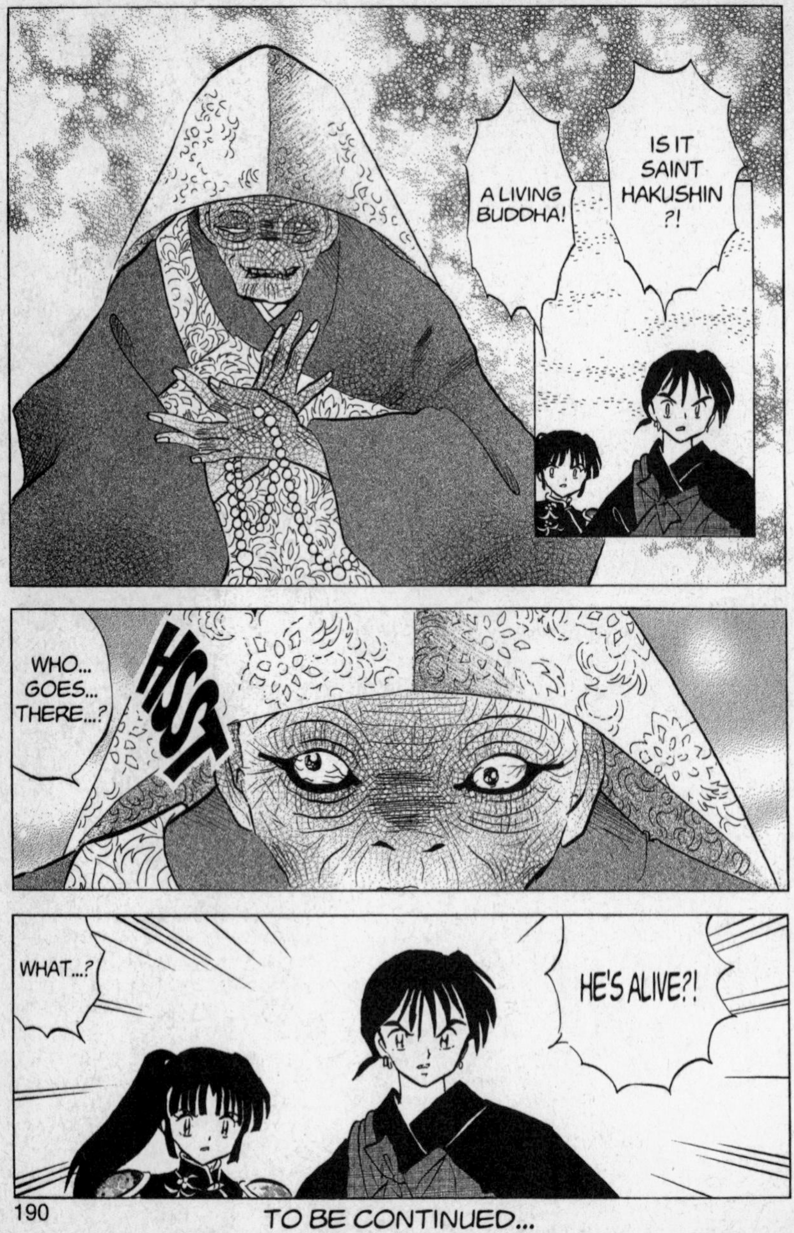
IS IT SAINT HAKUSHIN ?!
A LIVING BUDDHA!
HSST
WHO... GOES... THERE...?
HE'S ALIVE?!
WHAT...?

TO BE CONTINUED...

LOVE MANGA?
LET US KNOW WHAT YOU THINK!

HELP US MAKE THE MANGA
YOU LOVE BETTER!